DISNEYLAND™

&

SOUTHERN CALIFORNIA

with Kids

7th Edition

MICHAEL & TRISA KNIGHT

Published by Fodor's Travel Publications, a unit of Fodors LLC.

Fodor's is a registered trademark of Random House, Inc.

www.fodors.com

All products mentioned in this book are trademarks of their respective companies.

Every effort has been made to make this book complete and accurate as of the date of publication. In a time of rapid change, however, it is difficult to ensure that all information is entirely up-to-date. Although the publisher and authors cannot be liable for any inaccuracies or omissions in this book, they are always grateful for corrections and suggestions for improvement. Please feel free to send your comments and corrections to editors@fodors.com or Michael and Trisa Knight c/o Fodor's at 1745 Broadway, New York, NY 10019.

Previously published by Prima Publishing.

Seventh Edition

ISBN 0-7615-2829-6

PRINTED IN THE UNITED STATES OF AMERICA
10 9 8 7 6 5 4 3 2 1

To our children,
Beth, Sarah,
Connor, and Tanner.
Through their eyes,
the magic of the
world comes alive.

Contents

List of Maps and Quick Guide Reference Tables

Maps

Quick Guides

Helpful Phone Numbers and Web Sites

Airport Bus	714-938-8900
Alpine Motel	800-772-4422 or 714-535-2186
AMC Theatres (Downtown Disney)	714-781-4560
American Cinematheque at the Egyptian Theatre	323-466-3456 www.americancinematheque.com
Anaheim Carriage Inn	800-345-2131 or 714-740-1440 www.carriage-inn.com
Anaheim Desert Inn and Suites	800-433-5270 or 714-772-5050 www.anaheimdesertinn.com
Anaheim Desert Palm Hotel and Suites	800-635-5423 or 714-535-1133 www.anaheimdesertpalm.com
Anaheim–Orange County Visitors and Convention Bureau	888-598-3200 www.anaheimoc.org
Audiences Unlimited	818-753-3470 www.audiencesunlimited.com
Autry Museum of Western Heritage	323-667-2000 www.autry-musuem.org
Best Western Mission Bay Inn	800-457-8080 or 619-275-5700 www.bestwesternmissionbay.com
Best Western Raffles Inn and Suites	800-654-0196 or 714-750-6100 www.bestwesternrafflesinn.com
California Science Center	323-724-3623 www.casciencectr.org
Candy Cane Inn	800-345-7057 or 714-774-5284 www.candycaneinn.net
Carousel Inn and Suites	800-854-6767 or 714-758-0444

Casablanca Sightseeing Tours	323-461-0156
	www.casablancatours.com
Castle Inn and Suites	800-227-8530 or 714-774-8111
	www.castleinn.com
Catal and Uva Bar	714-774-4442 or 714-781-DINE
	www.patinagroup.com/catal.htm
CityPass	888-330-5008 or 208-787-4300
	www.citypass.net
Comfort Suites Mission Valley	800-997-2086 or 619-881-4000
	www.comfortsuitesmv.com
Del Sol Inn	888-686-1122 or 714-234-3411
	www.delsolinn.com
Disney Resort Map Requests	714-781-4560
Disney Resort Restaurant Reservations	714-781-DINE
Disney's Grand Californian	714-956-6425 or 714-635-2300
	www.disneyland.com
Disney's Paradise Pier Hotel	714-956-6425 or 714-999-0990
	www.disneyland.com
Disneyland Hotel	714-956-6425 or 714-778-6600
www.disneyland.com	
Disneyland Information	714-781-4565
	www.disneyland.com
Disneyland Merchandise Ordering	800-362-4533
Disneyland Resort Guest Relations	714-781-4773
Disneyland Tickets	714-781-4043
	www.disneyland.com
Disneyland Weather	714-550-4636
	www.disneyland.com
Doubletree Club Hotel	800-619-1541 or 619-881-6900
	www.doubletreesdzoo.com
The Dupre Hotel	714-971-5556
	www.thedupre.com
El Capitan Theatre	800-DISNEY6
	www.elcapitantickets.com
ESPN Zone Event Schedule	714-300-ESPN
ESPN Zone Reservations	714-300-ESPN

Getty Center	310-440-7300
	www.getty.edu
Griffith Observatory	323-664-1191 or 818-997-3624
and Planetarium	
(Laserium Shows)	
Guinness World of Records	
Museum	323-463-6433
Hilton Anaheim	800-774-1500 or 714-750-4321
	www.hilton.com
Holiday Inn Anaheim	800-545-7275 or 714-758-0900
at the Park	www.holiday-inn.com
Holiday Inn Sea World	800-405-9098 or 619-881-6100
	www.holidayinnseaworld.com
Hollywood Entertainment	323-465-7900
Museum	www.hollywoodmuseum.com
Hollywood Wax Museum	323-462-8860
House of Blues Reservations	714-778-2583 or 714-781-DINE
	www.hob.com/venues
	/clubvenues/anaheim
House of Blues Tickets	714-778-BLUE
Hyatt Regency Alicante	800-809-1956 or 714-750-1234
	www.hyatt.com
Jolly Roger Inn	800-682-9610 or 714-782-7500
	www.jollyrogerhotel.com
Knott's Berry Farm	714-220-5200
	www.knotts.com
La Brea Bakery	714-490-0233
La Brea Tar Pits	323-934-PAGE
	www.tarpits.org
LEGOLAND	760-918-LEGO
	www.legoland.com
Long Beach Aquarium	562-590-3100
of the Pacific	www.aquariumofpacific.org
Los Angeles Zoo	323-644-6400
	www.lazoo.org
Medieval Times	800-899-6600 or 714-521-4740
	www.medievaltimes.com
Movieland Wax Museum	714-522-1155
	www.movielandwaxmuseum.com

Museum of Television and Radio	310-786-1000
	www.mtr.org
Naples Ristorante e Pizzeria	714-776-6200 or 714-781-DINE
	www.patinagroup.com
	/naples.htm
Natural History Museum of Los Angeles County	213-763-3466
	www.nhm.org
NBC Studio Tours	818-840-3537
Park Inn Anaheim	800-670-7275 or 714-635-7275
	www.parkhtls.com
Park Vue Inn	800-334-7021 or 714-772-3691
	www.parkvueinn.com
Petersen Automotive Museum	323-930-CARS
	www.petersen.org
Pinocchio's Workshop	714-956-6755 (Child Care)
Portofino Inn and Suites	800-511-6907 or 714-782-7600
	www.portofinoinnanaheim.com
Queen Mary	562-435-3511
	www.queenmary.com
Radisson Resort Knott's Berry Farm	800-333-3333 or 714-995-1111
	www.radisson.com
	/buenaparkca.com
Rainforest Café	714-956-5260 or 714-781-DINE
	www.rainforestcafe.com
Ralph Brennan's Jazz Kitchen	714-776-5200 or 714-781-DINE
	www.rbjazzkitchen.com
Ramada Inn Maingate	800-854-6097 or 714-772-0440
	www.ramadamaingate.com
Ramada Limited Suites	800-526-9444 or 714-971-3553
	www.anaheim-ramadasuites.com
Ripley's Believe It or Not! Museum	714-522-7045
	www.movielandwaxmuseum.com
Six Flags Magic Mountain	661-255-4111 or 818-367-5965
	www.sixflags.com
Sony Pictures Studios Tours	323-520-TOUR
Starline Tours	800-959-3131
	www.starlinetours.com
Super Shuttle	800-258-3826
Tropicana Inn	800-828-4898 or 714-635-4082
	www.bei-hotels.com

Universal Amphitheater 818-622-4440
Universal CityWalk 818-622-4455
Universal Studios Hollywood 818-622-3801
www.universalstudios.com
Walt Disney Travel Company 800-225-2057 or 714-520-5050
www.disneyland.com
Warner Bros. Studio (VIP Tour) 818-972-8687
wbsf.warnerbros.com
Westcoast Anaheim Hotel 800-325-4000 or 714-750-1811
www.westcoasthotels.com
Wild Bill's Wild West
Dinner Extravaganza 800-883-1546 or 714-522-6414

Key to Icons

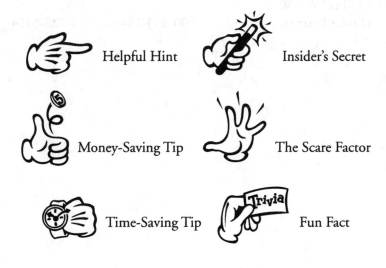

Helpful Hint

Insider's Secret

Money-Saving Tip

The Scare Factor

Time-Saving Tip

Fun Fact

Acknowledgments

We would like to thank Jamie Miller at Prima Publishing for making this book a reality in the first place. We also appreciate the help from the Maynes, the Hodgsons, the Swearingens, and the Pinders (with a combined total of 17 children between them), as well as the countless families at Disneyland and other Southern California attractions with whom we spoke for their personal tips, experiences, and observations. We would also like to acknowledge all of the cast members at the Disneyland Resort and the staff at other attractions for their inside information, as well as the public relations specialists for their help.

We also want to offer a big thanks to David Knight (Michael's brother) for his help in taking a trip with our family and for his expert ride testing and critiques. Steven Knight (Michael's other brother) also helped out a lot with the trivia, Hidden Mickeys, and other Disneyland information.

Introduction

Get Ready for a Great Family Vacation!

For nearly 50 years, families have been making pilgrimages to the most universally known and loved theme park in the world—Disneyland. Since the park first opened in July 1955, many things have changed both at Disneyland as well as throughout Southern California. In fact, this evolution in the family vacation continues to this very day and promises to evolve right on into the future!

In the past, many families just loaded up the station wagon and drove to Disneyland to spend a day at the park. If time allowed, they might also visit another attraction in the area. No real planning was needed: Just hop in the car and head to Disneyland for a day of fantasy and adventure.

Since those days, things have changed. Disneyland has become its own resort. Anaheim and the surrounding areas of Southern California have become the family playland of the West. To enjoy as much of it as possible, today's family must do a bit more planning and preparation for their vacation to Disneyland. No longer can you see Disneyland in just one day, and with the opening of Disney's California Adventure, you will want to take at least a couple of days, if not more, to experience it all.

Why This Book Is Special

This book has many important and unique features to make your family vacation a big success. We take you from the early stages of planning your vacation all the way to what to do just before you leave the park. In fact, this book offers just about everything you need to ensure a fun-filled family getaway.

Visiting Disneyland as an adult can be an exhilarating experience. And the joy and excitement increase as you see the wonders and magic through the eyes of your children. Therefore, we target much of the information in this book toward children as well as parents. To help keep kids happy and parents sane, this book contains information on the suitability of attractions for children of various ages, including height requirements as well as just how scary an attraction may be. We also include information about parent swaps and the FastPass system.

Not only did we write this book for families, but we also wrote it with the help of families. We have taken several vacations at Disneyland with our four children, at various ages from 4 months old and up. In addition, we have talked to dozens of other families to get their personal insights as well as tips from their experiences, such as the best place to sit for the parades or the best place to dine with the Disney characters.

Not every family wants the same type of vacation. Therefore, you can find information here not only to fit the time frame for your trip but also to fit your budget. It takes at least three to four days to fully see the Disneyland Resort, but your family can still have a great time in just a couple of days. Also, no matter how thrifty you may be, a vacation to the Disneyland Resort will cost you. However, with some planning, you can maximize your fun while minimizing the cost.

This book has three sections. The first section covers all the preparations you need to make a great vacation. It includes chapters on planning, hotels, and even packing. The second section covers the Disneyland Resort, with chapters on the Magic Kingdom, Disney's California Adventure, Downtown Disney, and Disney dining. The third section covers other attractions in Southern California. Here you can find chapters on Knott's Berry Farm, Universal Studios Hollywood, Six Flags Magic Mountain, LEGOLAND, and much, much more.

In addition to the usual travel guide information, this book contains hints, tips, and strategies for getting the most out of your vacation. Because there is so much to do, and often not enough time to do it in, every time-saving tip helps make your vacation that much better.

Disneyland & Southern California with Kids goes beyond planning, strategy, and hints. We wrote it for you to take along on your vacation and even into the parks and attractions. While you are waiting in the queue for a ride, read up on some interesting facts or trivia, as well as things to look for during the ride—such as Hidden Mickeys and other fun things. This enrichment can add a lot of new excitement for even the most veteran Disneyland visitors.

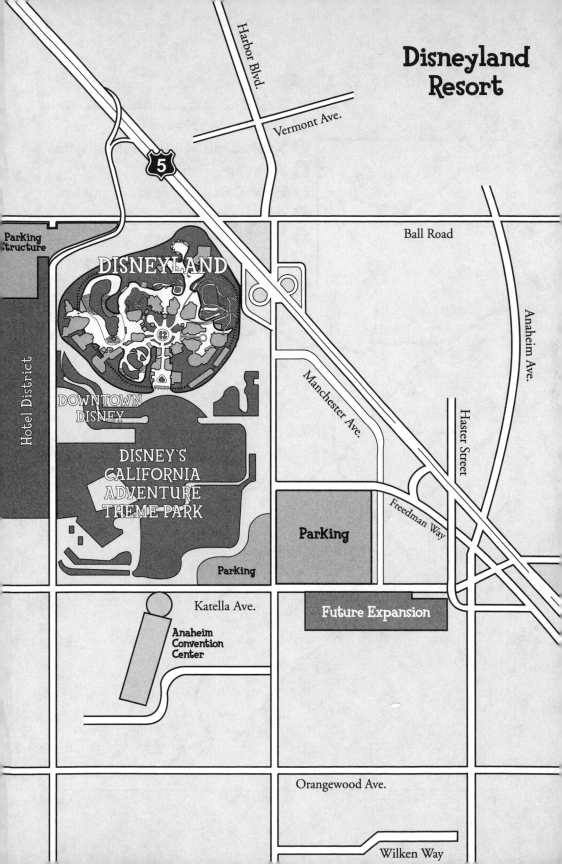

Southern California Attractions

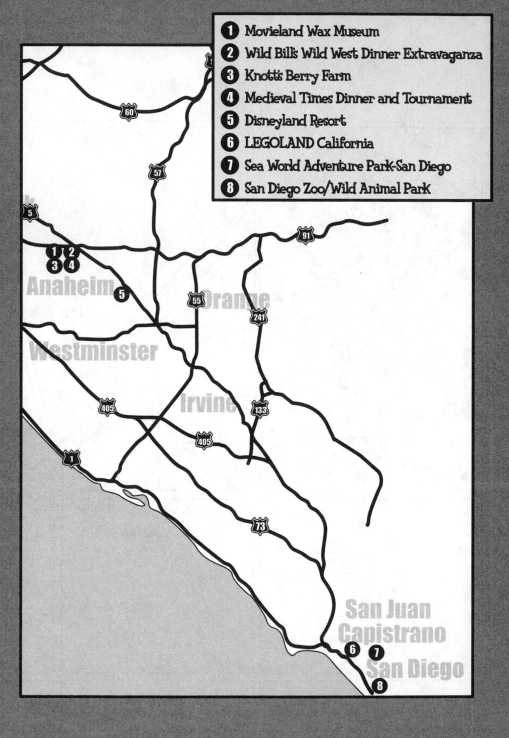

1. Movieland Wax Museum
2. Wild Bill's Wild West Dinner Extravaganza
3. Knott's Berry Farm
4. Medieval Times Dinner and Tournament
5. Disneyland Resort
6. LEGOLAND California
7. Sea World Adventure Park-San Diego
8. San Diego Zoo/Wild Animal Park

CHAPTER

1

Planning the Trip

Sunglasses ✓
Camera ✓
Tickets ✓
Flip-Flops
Swimsuits
Beach Bag
Sunscreen ✓
Guide Book ✓
Travel Games
Snacks ✓

When you are planning a family vacation to the Disneyland Resort, you should consider several things. Every family has different needs and expectations. Ask yourself three main questions with regards to your family: "When should we go?" "What do we want to do?" and "How long should we stay?" The answers to these questions will help you put together a plan for a family vacation that will be memorable and a whole lot of fun. The first part of this chapter deals with these three questions. The remainder of the chapter deals with putting your plan into action and booking your vacation. Now let's get started.

When Should You Go?

The first question you need to ask yourself is, "When should we go?" To answer it, look at three main factors: work schedules, school schedules, and how busy the resort will be at the time. Optimally, you would want to go when the park is least crowded. However, that is not always possible because of work and school.

The least crowded time to visit the Disneyland Resort is usually the first week of January to mid-February, the last week of April to Memorial Day week (in May), the end of Labor Day week (in early September) to mid-October, and after Thanksgiving week in November to a week before Christmas (in December). The busiest times are Presidents' Week (in February), the week before and the week after Easter, the second week of June to the last week of August (traditionally the time of summer vacation), Thanksgiving week, and Christmas Day through New Year's Day. In addition, Saturdays are always busy.

Although spring break and summer are probably the most convenient times for your family to vacation at the Disneyland Resort, everyone else will be there then, too! Try to avoid the busiest times if at all possible. However, if you must vacation then, we have included several tips to help make your stay more enjoyable and help you get the jump on the crowds.

In contrast, during the least crowded times, the resorts' hours are shorter and the parades and shows may only be running on the weekends, if at all.

The last two weeks of May and September are usually pretty good times to go. They offer a balance between small crowds, on the one hand, and shows and parades running,

Insider's Secret

The days of the week also matter. Saturday is always the busiest day throughout the year. Tuesdays, Wednesdays, and Thursdays are usually the slowest, though of course, relative to the time of year.

on the other. If you want to see all of the holiday decorations and activities, try the first two weeks of December.

Weather can also be a factor. Southern California tends to get most of its rainfall in the latter half of December through the first couple of weeks in March. However, even during these months there will be several dry days.

Should You Take the Kids out of School?

If your work allows you some flexibility in taking vacation time, then the limiting factor is school. Because many schools have the same or similar holidays, these are usually the times when the parks are at their busiest. So consider taking the kids out of school for a few days. The older the kids, the harder it is for them to miss school because there is usually a lot more schoolwork to make up. No matter what age your kids are, you should speak with their teachers beforehand. Ask if you can get, in advance, the assignments for the days they will miss. You might also ask if your children could do a special project or report while on the trip, to make up for work missed. Several educational places to visit in Southern California may even fit in with your children's course of study. (For more tips on making your vacation educational, see chapter 15.) Some school districts offer independent study programs for students who will be absent for a week or more. You need to check into this at least a week or even two before you leave. Talking to your children's teachers can also help you

Helpful Hint

Try to take advantage of school days off for in-service or teacher development and minimum or half school days. Your children will miss less instruction during those times.

avoid being gone during important tests and exams. If you finally decide to have them miss a few days of school, be sure to have them begin doing the makeup work before you leave. (They will want to do it even less when they return.)

What Do You Want to Do?

Once you have figured out a time frame for your vacation, you must decide what you want to do while you are in Southern California. In addition to the Disneyland Resort, which includes both Disneyland and Disney's California Adventure, a number of other attractions are in the area: Knott's Berry Farm, Universal Studios, Six Flags Magic Mountain, LEGO-LAND, Hollywood, the beaches, and much more. Unless your vacation will last a couple weeks, you will have to decide which things you want to do most.

To help you decide, take a look at the later chapters in this book, covering the various theme parks and attractions in Southern California. There truly is something for everyone.

How Long Should You Stay?

The third question goes hand in hand with the second. You need to know what you will be doing to determine how long to stay—at the same time, you need an idea of how long you will stay so that you can figure out how many things you can do.

For most families, the Disneyland Resort is their main reason for vacationing in the area. Although Disneyland can be seen in a single day, you will be very rushed and not get to do everything you may want to do. Two days is a bit better, but you are still going to be somewhat rushed to do everything. Three days is ideal, though some families could stay a fourth or fifth day as well. California Adventure can be covered in a single day. You may not get to do every single attraction there, but two days is probably too long. For the other theme parks in this area, plan on a day for each. Smaller attractions such as water parks or museums take about half a day each.

As a family, piece together the places you plan on going, as well as how long you will spend at each, to come up with a total number of days you will be in Southern California. Once you have this information, you are ready to start putting your plan into action.

Making Reservations and Travel Plans

While making reservations and travel plans, you must take care of three main things: choose and make reservations at a hotel, arrange for tickets, and book transportation. Chapter 2 covers finding a hotel and contains several important guidelines for choosing one that meets your family's needs. It also lists a few hotels in the Anaheim area that are good choices. Remember, when considering hotels, location is an extremely important factor—just as important as price. We recommend a hotel within easy walking distance of the Disneyland Resort, especially if you are not taking your own vehicle or renting one.

Package Deals

You can get several types of package deals through travel clubs such as AAA (Automobile Association of America), the Walt Disney Travel Company, travel agents, individual hotels, and even airlines. These packages include hotel accommodations and tickets for the Disney theme parks and possibly other Southern California attractions. Some packages may even include transportation.

Package deals are often great ways to get everything you need at once and even save money. However, be cautious. Some packages can be expensive or include things you don't really want to do. We suggest you look at several packages and then compare them to getting everything separately. Check with the Walt Disney Travel Company. You can get a quick quote for a package deal at its Web site at www.disneyland .com or by calling 714-520-5050. Also check with AAA (if you are a member) or with a travel agent. Finally, see what kinds of deals you can get on your own, especially if you will be flying, because you can sometimes get cheaper airfares separate from packages. Compare the various packages, and choose the one that best fits your price range and includes everything you want and nothing you don't.

For more information on package deals, see chapter 2.

Insider's Secret

Many packages include additional tours or attractions and may refer to them as "bonuses." Although they may seem to be included at no extra charge, their cost is already factored into the price of the package. If you don't want these add-ons, ask if you can remove them. Doing so usually lowers the price of the package. Although the agent usually does not tell you that you can delete options, always ask. Each bonus you delete can save you up to $40 per person.

Tickets

If you get a package deal, your tickets are usually included. However, if you are not using a package, you can get your tickets elsewhere. The key is to get your tickets in advance. You do not want to have to wait in line at the ticket booths. On some days, the wait for tickets can be over an hour long.

You can order tickets directly from Disneyland either through its Web site or by calling 714-781-4043. You can also purchase them at the Disney Stores, through AAA, and at some hotels. Prices as this book goes to print are listed next. Children under age 3 are free.

One-Day Ticket
Regular: $47
Child (ages 3–9): $37

Note: This ticket is valid either at the Disneyland Park or California Adventure. You cannot visit both on the same day with a single ticket. This ticket is not available for purchase online.

Two-Day Park Hopper Tickets
Regular: $99
Child (ages 3–9): $79

Note: Park Hopper tickets allow guests back and forth admittance to both Disneyland and Disney's California Adventure for the number of days purchased. This ticket is valid only 13 days after first use.

Three-Day Park Hopper Tickets
Regular: $119
Child (ages 3–9): $95

Insider's Secret
Guests staying at one of the Disneyland Resort hotels can purchase Park Hopper passes, which allow them to visit both parks in the same day.

Note: This ticket must be used within 13 days of first visit. You can visit both Disneyland or California Adventure as much as you like each day.

Five-Day Park Hopper Ticket
Regular: $175
Child (ages 3–9): $140

Note: This ticket must be used within 13 days of your first visit. Disney is currently running a special until January 2004 where you can get a Five-Day Park Hopper ticket for the price of a Three-Day ticket, saving a family $56 per adult and $45 per child. These cannot be purchased at the main gate. However, you can buy them online, at a Disney Store, at one of the Disneyland hotels, or even from AAA. Look for other special offers online after this promotion expires.

Money-Saving Tip
Specially priced Disneyland Resort tickets for U.S. military service personnel and Department of Defense employees and their families are available at MWR ticket offices throughout the United States.

Annual Passport

If you plan on visiting more than once in a year's time, we highly recommend getting Annual Passports. They are a lot less expensive than buying Two-Day Park Hopper tickets twice and allow you access to both parks. While you are at the resort, you can often cash in your tickets and apply their value toward an Annual Passport. For example, if you purchased the Three-Day Park Hopper ticket, you would only have to pay $46 per adult and $70 per child for an entire year of fun. You can even use them immediately if you want to stay a few more days. The nice thing about Annual Passports is that you do not feel rushed. If you arrive in Anaheim during the afternoon, you can hit one of the parks for a few hours and not feel like you are wasting one of your days on the ticket.

A few months before your passports expire, Disney will send out a renewal form for each person in your family. When you renew by mail, you can save $20 per person and usually get some special offers or discounts as well. However, if you will not be returning for a while after your passports expire, it is usually cheaper to let them lapse and buy tickets next time you go—then cash them in for Annual Passports later.

2-Park Deluxe Annual Passports
All ages: $165

This passport allows you to visit both parks as many times as you wish during 320 preselected admission dates. There are 45 blackout days (most Saturdays, Memorial Day weekend, Thanksgiving Thursday and Friday, and from Christmas Eve to New Year's Day). You can also get a 10 percent discount at some restaurants in the parks, special rates for Disneyland hotels, and discounts in Downtown Disney. For $40 more, you can add free unlimited parking (add this parking provision to one of the adult passes). You can still visit the parks on blackout days, but you'll pay a reduced rate, around $20 per person per day.

Premium Annual Passports
All ages: $225

This passport has no blackout days and includes free parking as well as 10 percent off merchandise throughout the resort, 15 percent discount at the Blue Bayou, 10 percent discount at several restaurants in the parks and some at the hotels, 10 percent discount on accommodations at the Disney hotels, and a free subscription to *Disney Magazine*. If you just want free parking and discounts but don't need the lack of blackout days, just have one adult get the Premium Passport while the rest of the family gets the Deluxe.

Southern California CityPass
Regular: $166
Child (ages 3–9): $127

If you are planning to visit other Southern California attractions in addition to Disneyland, consider purchasing the Southern California CityPass. For one low price, you get a Three-Day Park Hopper ticket for Disneyland and California Adventure (it is not upgraded to five days) and One-Day Tickets to Knott's Berry Farm, Sea-World in San Diego, and the San Diego Zoo. These can be purchased online at the Disneyland Web site or the CityPass Web site (www.citypass.net) as well as at the parks' ticket booths.

> **Insider's Secret**
> As this book goes to print, you can cash in your tickets while inside the Disneyland Park and get full credit for them to apply to an Annual Passport. The only requirement is that you must purchase the Annual Passports at the park while your tickets are still valid.

Transportation

There are two main ways to get to the Disneyland Resort: by plane or car. Depending on your budget and the distance you must travel to the resort, the choice is up to you. If you are more than 300 to 400 miles away, it is usually faster to fly. Remember to consider the extra time it takes to check in due to increased security restrictions. But taking your own automobile provides more flexibility and is often cheaper.

By Plane

If you will be flying into Southern California, you must first decide at which airport to arrive. Unfortunately, there is no Disneyland international airport, so you will have to choose from the ones in the area: LAX, John Wayne, and Long Beach.

Although LAX is the largest airport in the area, it is not the closest. Check the rates into each of these airports and see which has the best price. You will also need to arrange ground transportation from the airport to the resort. There are several options. You can rent a car, take the Airport Bus, or take the Super Shuttle. The Airport Bus is a motor coach that picks up guests at the airport and then makes several stops around the Anaheim area, including the main entrances of the Disney hotels. From LAX, the round-trip fare is $25 for adults and $16 for children 3 to 11. From John Wayne, the fares are $18 and $13, respectively. To find the Airport Bus, look for the red signs as you leave the baggage claim area at the airport. You will want the bus with Anaheim-Disneyland as its destination. For more information, call 714-938-8900.

The Super Shuttle is a van shuttle that carries your family from the airport directly to your hotel. The round-trip fare from LAX is $30 per person and $20 from Long Beach. Children under 3 are free. You will need to reserve a shuttle in advance. For more information and to make reservations, call 800-258-3826.

Helpful Hint

Some of the nicer hotels in the area (except for the Disney hotels) offer airport shuttles. Check with your hotel about this option.

The bus or van can be expensive, with a family of

Airport	Distance from Disneyland	Driving Time
Los Angeles International (LAX)	32 miles	45–60 minutes
John Wayne-Orange County Airport	14 miles	25 minutes
Long Beach Airport	19 miles	30 minutes

four paying up to $120. With that in mind, you may want to consider renting a car. If you can use discounts (such as AAA members or those with Entertainment discount books), renting a car can be cheaper than a bus or van ride and can give you flexibility in getting around the area. If you will be visiting other attractions in the area, especially those in Los Angeles or San Diego, then a rental car is a very good idea. Although you can often include transportation to these other attractions as part of a package, the costs add up and you must conform to a shuttle's schedule rather than your own. Some packages also either include a rental car or offer it at an additional price. Also, keep in mind that with a rental car you may have to pay for parking. At theme parks in the area, parking is usually $8. Although many hotels offer free parking, others charge. Be sure to ask about parking costs when you are making reservations.

By Car

If you will be driving to the Disneyland Resort, it is quite easy to find. You should get a map of Southern California as well as a city map of Anaheim and Orange County. Members of AAA can get free maps as well as TripTiks, which are custom-made routings for your trip that show you exactly how to get from your home to Disneyland. The main part of driving is getting to Interstate 5. Once there, the I-5 freeway will take you right to Disneyland.

For those traveling southbound on I-5, take the Disneyland Drive exit. If you want to go to the park, follow the signs to the parking structure. If you want to go to the Disney hotels, continue on Disneyland Drive. For the Disneyland Hotel, turn right on Magic Way and follow the signs. For the Paradise Pier Hotel and the Grand Californian Hotel, continue down Disneyland Drive past the Disneyland Hotel, and the entrances are on the right and left, respectively.

For those traveling northbound on I-5, exit on Katella Avenue and turn left. For the Disney parks, turn right on Harbor Boulevard and then left on Disney Way into the parking lot. For the hotels, continue on Katella Avenue and turn right on Disneyland Drive. The Paradise Pier and Grand Californian hotels are on your left and right, respectively. To get to the Disneyland Hotel, continue down Disneyland Drive and turn left on Magic Way. Follow the signs to the hotel entrance.

Insider's Secret
You can get directions from your house to the Disneyland Resort at the Disneyland Web site (www.disneyland.com).

California Traffic Laws
If you are traveling from out of state and will either be driving to the Disneyland Resort or renting a car, there are a few laws with which you should be familiar. All passengers, in both front and rear seats, must wear safety belts. Also, all children must be in a child safety seat or booster until they are either 6 years old or 60 pounds. If you do not obey these laws, you risk being pulled over and ticketed.

Budgeting Your Trip

Families with all types of budgets can enjoy a wonderful vacation at the Disneyland Resort and Southern California. The key is determining how best to spend your money. We have included some hints and tips next to help you fit into three different budgets. These budgets are only examples of what you can expect to spend during a vacation. *Note:* The budgets do not include travel expenses, transportation, rental car, or souvenirs and are estimated for a family of four with two adults and two children under age 17.

As Inexpensive as Possible

Even if you don't have a lot of money to spend, you can still have a great time. You just have to maximize the amount of fun for your dollar.

- If you can drive your own car, this is usually the cheapest way to get to the Disneyland Resort. However, if you must drive for more than a day and have to spend money for lodging on the way there and the way back, compare the cost of driving to flying.

- Look for all the discounts you can. If you don't belong to AAA, consider getting a membership. Not only does it include free roadside assistance and towing, but you can also get reduced rates on tickets, lodging, and airfare.

- Travel during the off-season, when rates are cheapest.

- Find the least expensive hotels you can that are within walking distance to the resort.

- Choose a hotel with a microwave and refrigerator, or even a kitchenette, so you can prepare some of your own meals.

- Choose a hotel that serves complimentary breakfast.

- Spend all of your vacation at the Disneyland parks. A Three-Day Park Hopper ticket is cheaper than one day at each of the two parks and a third day somewhere else.

- Only eat one meal per day at the resort.

  Here is a sample low-cost budget for a family of four:

- Lodging for two nights and Three-Day Park Hopper tickets in a package: $600

- Meals at $15 per day per person for meals at the park for three days (breakfast provided by hotel): $180

The total for three days at the resort is $780. You could cut it even further by eating dinner at a fast-food place outside the parks and by taking a sack lunch. (You can leave these lunches in lockers outside the parks at the picnic area.)

The Moderate Budget

This budget features a vacation with more amenities while saving money at the same time:

- If you want to stay on site, stay at the Paradise Pier Hotel during the off-season or with a special discounted rate from a travel club or the Disney Club.

- To save money at the parks, eat only two meals there. A late lunch and a light dinner are usually best, with a complimentary breakfast at the hotel or light breakfast. Or have a large, late breakfast and then an early dinner.

- Carry snacks with you at the park and take your own drinks (water bottles or juice boxes in backpacks).

@ Buy souvenirs that the entire family can share, such as videos or CDs, instead of souvenirs for each person. Mickey antenna balls for putting on your car's radio antenna are also a great idea.

Here is a sample moderate-cost budget for a family of four:

@ Three nights at the Paradise Pier Hotel, off-season, with discounts and Three-Day Park Hopper tickets: $800

@ Meals at $25 per day per person for four days: $400

@ Tickets to Knott's Berry Farm with coupon: $120

Adding an extra day, a nicer hotel, more money for food, and another attraction increases the cost to $1,320—a little less than double the previous budget.

The Luxury Budget

If money is not a limiting factor and you want to experience the Disneyland Resort to its fullest and even hit a few off-site attractions, here is what you can expect to pay:

@ Five nights at the Grand Californian, regular, but not peak season, concierge level with theme park view, with Five-Day Park Hopper tickets, plus tickets to Universal Studios Hollywood and Knott's Berry Farm as part of a package deal: $3,500

@ Meals at $40 per person per day: $800

This very nice package would cost a family of four $4,300 and would include every amenity available at the Disneyland Resort as well as three nice meals a day.

As you can see from looking at these three different budgets, families can spend as little or as much as they want

on their vacation. The more perks you want, the more it will
cost. When budgeting your vacation, separate the things you
really want from the things that would be nice to have. Once
you calculate how much the things you want will cost, then
start adding the things that would be nice, until you reach
your spending limit.

CHAPTER

2

Where to
Stay

Disneyland Hotels

Harbor Blvd.

Ball Road

Ramada Limited

Parking Structure

Holiday Inn Anaheim at the Park

Magic Way

Park Inn International
Carousel Inn and Suites

Disneyland Hotel

Disney's Paradise Pier Hotel

Anaheim Desert Inn and Suites

Disney's Grand Californian

Best Western Anaheim Inn

Candy Cane Inn

Alpine Motel   Desert Palm

Tropicana Inn
Park Vue Inn

Anaheim Best Inn Main Gate

Disney Way

Castle Inn and Suites

Katella Ave.

Ramada Main Gate Saga Inn

Jolly Roger Hotel

Portofino Inn and Suites

West Coast Anaheim Hotel

Hilton Anaheim

Disneyland Drive

Harbor Blvd.

Best Western Raffles Inn

Orangewood Ave.

The Dupre

Wilken Way

Anaheim Carriage Inn

Hyatt Regency Alicante

Chapman Ave.

A major part of planning your vacation involves determining where you will stay while you are in Southern California. There are hundreds of places near the Disneyland Resort, ranging from cheap motels to very luxurious hotels and everything in between. This chapter helps you decide what type of place to stay and then offers a few suggestions. You will also find several hints and tips to help you find the place that fits your budget and provides the amenities and services your family needs.

What Should You Look for in a Hotel?

A number of factors will determine where you stay during your vacation. Probably one of the biggest for most families is budget. How much can you spend on your lodging? On average, after adding hotel tax, plan on spending about $100 per night. During the off season, or with discounts, you can pay less.

The second factor is location. Some hotels are either in the Disneyland Resort or right across the street from it.

Others may be several miles away. You will usually want to be as close as possible, to save time traveling back and forth from the hotel to the parks.

Other things to consider include the amenities the hotel offers and whether there is an on-site or nearby restaurant. How these factors affect your decision depends on what you are looking for in a hotel.

Be Sure to Ask . . .

The best way to find out just what a hotel offers is to call and ask a lot of questions. Travel guides or advertisements can be vague and often do not include vital information you need to know. Once you have narrowed down your list of hotels to a few, begin calling them. We find it is good to have a list of the questions you want to ask in front of you, so you don't forget any. Also, be sure to write down the answers from each hotel so you can refer to them later. Here is a list of questions you should ask, as well as reasons why they are important:

- *What are the hotel's rates for when you will be there? Are there any discounts or specials? Do children stay free?*
  Hotels do not always offer you their cheapest rates to begin with. Because many customers just take what the hotels offer first, they might as well start high. Ask about seasonal discounts, Entertainment book discounts, or travel club rates, such as AAA rates, if you belong to such an organization. These often save you at least 10 percent.

- *How close is the hotel to the Disneyland Resort?*
  Although most hotels say they are close, ask just how close. Can you walk, or will you need to take a shuttle?

@ *Does the hotel offer shuttle service to the resort? If so, how often does it run?*
Although most hotels advertise shuttle service, the shuttles run at different intervals, and some run only twice a day.

@ *Does the hotel include a breakfast buffet or continental breakfast? If so, what types of items are served?*
Most hotels offer a continental breakfast. However, that is usually just sweet rolls, juice or coffee, and maybe some fruit. Others have buffets where you can get eggs, potatoes, toast, and even more. Also, be sure to ask the hours when breakfast is served. Make sure it starts before you plan to leave for the park, especially during the summer, when the park opens earlier.

@ *Is there a charge for parking?*
This may sound unnecessary to ask, but some hotels in the area add from $5 to $10 a day if you want to leave your car in their parking lot.

@ *Does the hotel have rooms with kitchenettes or at least a microwave and a refrigerator?*
You will usually need at least a refrigerator when traveling with children. A fridge lets you keep drinks cool and even store snacks from home or leftovers from meals. What the kids couldn't eat for dinner makes a good lunch the next day. And a microwave is very nice to have, too.

@ *Is there an on-site restaurant or one nearby? Do kids eat free? Does the hotel offer room service?*
Some hotels with an on-site restaurant offer free meals for kids when you buy an adult meal. Even if you eat only one meal a day at the restaurant, these savings can add up.

● *Is there airport pickup from the hotel? Does the hotel have shuttles to other attractions?*

If you will be flying into Southern California, having a hotel van pick you up can be nice and can save you money. Also, if you plan on going to other attractions, you will need either a shuttle or rental car.

● *What programs does the hotel offer for children? For what ages? When do the programs run? What are the activities? Are there any costs? Is there a swimming pool? Spa? Fitness center?*

Not many hotels in the area have children's programs. However, it doesn't hurt to ask. A swimming pool is about all most places offer for recreation.

● *Can arrangements be made for in-room baby-sitting? What are the qualifications of the sitters? What is the cost? How far in advance do you need to make reservations?*

If you would like an evening out for just the adults, be sure to see if child care is available and what reservations you need to make.

● *Does the hotel have rollaway beds or cribs? Is there a charge for them?*

Sometimes a rollaway can keep you from having to get a bigger room or suite and can save you money. If traveling with a baby, you may need a crib.

● *Is there a laundry at the hotel?*

Several hotels have coin-operated washing machines and dryers. These can come in handy if you get caught in the rain or just need to clean a few clothes.

● *Is there a car rental agency office on site?*

If you need to rent a car, this can be handy. Some agencies will even pick you up at the airport and drive you back to their office at the hotel.

@ *Does the hotel sell tickets to Disneyland and other attractions?*
You do not want to have to buy your tickets at the main gate. Therefore, if you don't get them before you leave on your vacation, then purchase them at your hotel.

@ *Does the hotel offer package deals?*
Several hotels offer packages that include the room along with tickets for Disneyland and possibly even other attractions. Some even include meals. Packages can often be cheaper than paying for lodging and the tickets separately.

Not all these questions will apply to your family's vacation. Just ask the ones that do, and customize them to fit your circumstances.

Vacation Packages

Unless you have an Annual Passport for Disneyland, it is usually a good idea to consider package deals. The basic packages include lodging and tickets; others may include meals and other bonuses. There are a variety of packages available. We have broken them down for you next.

Disney Packages

Some of the best packages are put together by the Walt Disney Travel Company. These include stays at any of the three Disneyland Resort hotels as well as at nearly 40 other hotels in the area. Although these packages change from year to year, here is a sampling of what is offered for 2003:

- Hotel accommodations

- Tickets

- A preissued FASTPASS ticket

- A breakfast in the park or tour

- A $10 ESPN Zone game card redeemable at Downtown Disney

You can also add a dining package that includes meals and snacks. Tickets to other attractions can be included as well.

To get a price quote for these packages, either call the Walt Disney Travel Company at 800-225-2057 or 714-520-5050 or visit the Disneyland Web site at www.disneyland.com. This lets you enter all your selections, gives you a price quote, and allows you to book your vacation. You can even arrange for plane reservations and other transportation needs.

Money-Saving Tip

AAA offers a number of Disneyland Resort packages that are very similar to those offered by the Walt Disney Travel Company. They usually include extras such as travel kits, free parking at the resort, coupon books, and discounts on the lodging part of the package during certain times of the year.

Off-Site Packages

If you plan on staying at an off-site hotel and the Disney packages don't fit your needs, look into packages offered by the individual hotels themselves. Several in the area offer deals that include lodging, tickets to the Disneyland Resort parks, and possibly even some meals and/or a rental car.

When you call about rates, just ask if the hotel offers any package deals.

Travel Agents

Many travel agencies offer packages to the Disneyland Resort. They are usually very similar to those offered by the Walt Disney Travel Company or AAA. You usually pay more for the package and do not get all the extras. However, a travel agent may be able to get you better prices on airline fares or be better at arranging other transportation to the resort and back home for your family. Just be sure you are getting a good hotel that meets your needs. If the hotel offered is not listed in this book, be sure to request a brochure and find out just how far away from Disneyland it really is. We know of families that were promised a nice hotel with great amenities and a shuttle to the resort. However, the hotel was 10 miles away, and the shuttle only ran once in the morning and once in the evening.

Insider's Secret

Also, be wary of tours to other places in Southern California. These include bus tours of the Los Angeles area, harbor cruises, and the shopping spree trips to Mexico. These can last all day, and there is usually no way to get back to the hotel during the middle of the trip. That usually makes them a bad idea for families with young children. Before you agree to these types of tours, ask how long they last and exactly what will happen during the tour, including contingencies for returning to the hotel early. Although they are usually part of a package, you are still paying for them. If you don't really want to go on these optional tours, then don't get them. Cutting them from the package often lowers the price of the package and saves you money.

They ended up having to drive back and forth between the hotel and the resort, paying for both parking and gas.

Discounts and Specials

Always try to take advantage of some type of discount when choosing a hotel. Almost all hotels offer reduced rates during the off season. Ask about discounts for travel club members such as AAA or military personnel or if you have an Entertainment discount book. Although the latter offers discounts of 50 percent, these are usually off the high-rack rates and only about 10 percent off the regular rate, so don't expect huge savings. You may also be able to get coupon books offering hotel discounts from your employer or credit union. When calling to check rates, be sure to mention you belong to a travel club or have a discount. Even if you don't have a discount of your own, ask if the hotel is running any specials or has lower rates. It never hurts to ask.

Money-Saving Tip

By making reservations early, such as several months in advance, you have a better chance of getting cheaper rates. Many hotels have a limited number of rooms they offer at lower prices as promotions. However, these fill up quickly. If you know when you will be on vacation, there is no reason not to make reservations early. You can always cancel them later if you have to change plans.

On Site Versus off Site

When deciding on whether to stay at one of the Disneyland hotels or an off-site hotel, there are a few factors you should consider.

Benefits of Staying on Site

1. Staying at the Disneyland hotels saves time. If you will be vacationing during the summer, holiday, or other busy season or if you only have a day or two, you can definitely see more of the resort by staying at one of the hotels.

2. It is easy to return to the hotel during the day. If you have small children who need naps or rest, a quick trip on the monorail will take you right back to the hotel in a matter of minutes. You can then return to the park the same way. This is also important if your family will be split up. Dad may want to take some of the younger kids back for a swim while Mom stays with the older kids at the park.

3. You don't need a car. If you won't be driving to the resort and plan on spending all of your time there, there is no need to rent a car. Everything is within walking distance, and you can also use the monorail.

4. You are guaranteed admission to the Disney theme parks. When the parks are extremely full, usually on days near holidays such as Thanksgiving, Christmas, or New Year's, they stop letting people in, even ones with valid tickets. However, guests of the Disney hotels are always admitted.

Benefits of Staying off Site

1. Off-site hotels are almost always less expensive. If you are trying to save money or would rather spend it on other parts of your vacation rather than lodging, stay off site.

2. Many off-site hotels offer complimentary breakfasts or have deals where kids eat free at their restaurant. Eating

at the Disneyland Resort can be expensive. Off-site hotels are often closer to fast-food and other inexpensive restaurants.

3. The Disney hotels can be booked months in advance during the busy season. If your vacation was arranged at the last minute, you may not be able to get reservations at a Disney hotel, especially for three or more nights.

4. If Disneyland is only a part of your vacation and you will be visiting several other attractions in the Southern California area, why pay a lot to stay by the Disneyland Resort when you will also be spending time elsewhere? In the past, we have stayed a couple of nights at one of the Disney hotels and then transferred to a less expensive hotel while we visited other attractions.

Getting More Information on Hotels in the Anaheim Area

The Anaheim–Orange County Visitors and Convention Bureau is a great way to get information about the Anaheim area. Check their Web site at anaheimoc.worldres.com (Note: There is no www in the Web address) for hotel availability, locations, prices, and descriptions. The Web site includes directories of hotels, restaurants, and much more. It also offers a hotel search: You list what you are looking for, and the site returns names of hotels in the area that match your needs. In fact, now reservations can even be made online through this Web site. You can print coupons right off your computer for a number of hotels, restaurants, and attractions, as well as request an official visitors' guide. The address for the site is www.anaheimoc.org. If you do not have Internet access, you can call the bureau at 888-598-3200 and request the guide over the phone. It takes about four to six weeks to get it via mail, so be sure to request it a couple of months or more before your vacation.

What the Star Ratings Mean

The following hotels are ranked using the star rating system:

★★★★ These hotels are top quality and offer superior amenities and guest services. In addition, they are located close to the resort.

★★★ These hotels offer not only good prices for what you get but also good amenities or are located very close to the resort.

★★ These hotels usually offer good value but may not be as close to the park as other hotels.

★ These hotels are basic and inexpensive but often are at some distance from the park.

The Disneyland Resort Hotels

When staying at one of the Disneyland Resort hotels, you will really feel that you are at a resort. All offer special amenities and guest services while providing a Disney atmosphere, so you never feel you have left the theme parks. You will usually find the staff at these hotels to be some of the friendliest and most outgoing of any hotels in the area. Guests at these hotels have special privileges unavailable to other tourists. Not only do they have access to the pool and fitness facilities, but they also have easy access to both parks by monorail or a short walk. One perk is that you can charge meals and merchandise you purchase anywhere in the resort to your hotel room. This

Quick Guide to

Hotel Name	Description	Price
Alpine Motel 715 W. Katella Avenue 800-772-4422 or 714-535-2186	Inexpensive; two-room units available	$
Anaheim Carriage Inn 2125 S. Harbor Boulevard 800-345-2131 or 714-740-1440 www.cariage-inn.com	Family suites and two-room suites available	$
Anaheim Desert Inn and Suites 1600 S. Harbor Boulevard 800-433-5270 or 714-772-5050 www.anaheimdesertinn.com	Family and two-room suites available; great value!	$
Anaheim Desert Palm Hotel and Suites 631 W. Katella Avenue 800-635-5423 or 714-535-1133 www.anaheimdesertpalm.com	Inexpensive rooms and suites; inexpensive for large families	$
Best Western Raffles Inn and Suites 2040 S. Harbor Boulevard 800-654-0196 or 714-750-6100 www.bestwesternrafflesinn.com	Disneyland theme rooms and suites available	$
Candy Cane Inn 1747 S. Harbor Boulevard 800-345-7057 or 714-774-5284 www.candycaneinn.net	Garden view rooms available	$
Carousel Inn and Suites 1530 S. Harbor Boulevard 800-854-6767 or 714-758-0444 www.carouselinnandsuites.com	Family suites available	$$

$$$$ $250 and up
$$$ $150–$250
$$ $100–$150
$ $ 50–$100

Resort Area Hotels

Distance from Resort	Rating	Amenities	Details On
Walking distance to Disneyland; tram available	★★	Heated pool; refrigerators available; free continental breakfast	Page 48
Two blocks from resort; shuttle available	★★	Heated pool and spa; microwaves and refrigerators available; free continental breakfast	Page 48
Across the street from main gate	★★★	Heated pool and spa; microwaves, refrigerators, and coffeemakers; free continental breakfast	Page 49
One block from Disneyland; located near the Anaheim Convention Center	★★★	Heated pool and spa; microwaves, refrigerators, and coffeemakers; free continental breakfast	Page 49
Two blocks from resort; shuttle available	★★	Heated pool; microwaves and refrigerators in some rooms; free continental breakfast	Page 50
One block from main gate; shuttle available	★★	Heated pool, spa, and children's wading pool; microwaves and refrigerators in some rooms; free continental breakfast	Page 50
Across the street from main gate	★★	Rooftop heated pool; microwaves, refrigerators, and coffeemakers in all rooms; free continental breakfast	Page 50

★★★★ **Top quality with superior amenities**
★★★ **Good prices with good amenities**
★★ **Good value with few amenities**
★ **Basic and inexpensive**

(continues)

Quick Guide to

Hotel Name	Description	Price
Castle Inn and Suites 1734 S. Harbor Boulevard 800-227-8530 or 714-774-8111 www.castleinn.com	Family suites available; with a medieval theme, the hotel looks like a castle	$
Del Sol Inn 1604 S. Harbor Boulevard 888-686-1122 or 714-234-3411 www.delsolinn.com	Inexpensive; two-room suites available	$
Disney's Grand Californian 1150 Disneyland Drive 714-956-6425 or 714-635-2300 www.disneyland.com	Normal hotel rooms, some with bunk beds for kids; on-site restaurants	$$$–$$$$
Disney's Paradise Pier Hotel 1717 Disneyland Drive 714-956-6425 or 714-999-0990 www.disneyland.com	Normal hotel rooms; suites available, but expensive; on-site restaurants	$$$
The Disneyland Hotel 1150 Magic Way 714-956-6425 or 714-778-6600 www.disneyland.com	Rooms for up to five people; suites available, but expensive; many on-site restaurants	$$$
The Dupre 2145 S. Harbor Boulevard 800-220-4820 or 714-971-5556 www.thedupre.com	Rooms and suites available, some with bunk beds; 100% nonsmoking	$–$$
Hilton Anaheim 777 Convention Way 800-774-1500 or 714-750-4321 www.hilton.com	Nice hotel with several restaurants and seasonal children's program	$$

$$$$ $250 and up
$$$ $150–$250
$$ $100–$150
$ $ 50–$100

Resort Area Hotels

Distance from Resort	Rating	Amenities	Details On
One block from main gate; shuttle available	★★	Heated pool; microwaves and coffee-makers in all rooms; microwaves in suites	Page 51
Across the street from main gate	★★	Microwaves, refrigerators, and coffee-makers; free continental breakfast	Page 51
On site	★★★★	Heated pool and spa; fitness center; stocked refrigerators; empty refrigerators available; children's care center for evenings; private entrance to California Adventure	Page 45
On site	★★★★	Heated pool and spa; fitness center; refrigerators in all rooms; private entrance to California Adventure	Page 43
On site	★★★★	Large pool area; fitness center; refrigerators in all rooms	Page 40
Shuttle available	★★	Pool and spa; microwaves and refrigerators; in-room Internet access; continental breakfast	Page 52
One block away; shuttle available	★★★	Great pool area; fitness center use for additional fee	Page 52

★★★★ **Top quality with superior amenities**
★★★ **Good prices with good amenities**
★★ **Good value with few amenities**
★ **Basic and inexpensive**

(continues)

Quick Guide to

Hotel Name	Description	Price
Holiday Inn Anaheim at the Park 1221 S. Harbor Boulevard 800-545-7275 or 714-758-0900 www.holiday-inn.com	Regular hotel rooms	$–$$
Hyatt Regency Alicante 100 Plaza Alicante, Garden Grove 800-809-1956 or 714-750-1234 www.hyatt.com	Regular rooms and a new tower with a variety of suites	$$
Jolly Roger Inn 640 W. Katella Avenue 800-682-9610 or 714-782-7500 www.jollyrogerhotel.com	Two-room units and regular hotel rooms; restaurant on site	$
Park Inn Anaheim 1520 S. Harbor Boulevard 800-670-7275 or 714-635-7275 www.parkhtls.com	Family suites available	$–$$
Park Vue Inn 1570 S. Harbor Boulevard 800-334-7021 or 714-772-3691 www.parkvueinn.com	Family suites available; 24-hour restaurant on site	$–$$
Portofino Inn & Suites 1831 S. Harbor Boulevard 800-511-6907 or 714-782-7600 www.portofinoinnanaheim.com	Family and kids' suites available	$–$$
Radisson Resort Knott's Berry Farm 7675 Crescent Avenue, Buena Park 800-333-3333 or 714-995-1111 www.radisson.com/buenaparkca	Family suites available; some rooms with Peanuts theme; restaurant on site	$–$$

$$$$ $250 and up
 $$$ $150–$250
  $$ $100–$150
   $ $ 50–$100

Resort Area Hotels

Distance from Resort	Rating	Amenities	Details On
Two blocks away; shuttle available	★★	Heated pool with play area; in-room video games; kids eat free restaurant	Page 52
Five blocks away; shuttle runs every 30 minutes	★★★	Heated pool; microwaves, refrigerators, and coffeemakers; package deals include breakfast buffet	Page 53
One block from Disneyland; shuttle available in rooms	★★	Heated pool and children's wading pool; coffeemakers	Page 53
Across the street from main gate	★★	Heated pool; refrigerators in all rooms, microwaves in suites; free continental breakfast	Page 54
Across the street from main gate	★★	Heated pool; refrigerators in all rooms; free continental breakfast	Page 54
Walking distance to main entrance; shuttle service available for a fee	★★★	Heated pool and spa; video arcade; refrigerators and microwaves in all rooms; free parking	Page 54
Several miles away; shuttle available; on site at Knott's Berry Farm	★★	Heated pool, spa, and children's pool; fitness center; tennis courts; packages include meals and tickets to Knott's Berry Farm	Page 55

★★★★ Top quality with superior amenities
★★★ Good prices with good amenities
★★ Good value with few amenities
★ Basic and inexpensive

(continues)

Quick Guide to

Hotel Name	Description	Price
Ramada Inn Maingate 1650 S. Harbor Boulevard 800-854-6097 or 714-772-0440 www.ramadamaingate.com	Suites with two or three beds available, some with kitchenettes; on-site restaurant	$–$$
Ramada Limited Suites 2141 S. Harbor Boulevard 800-526-9444 or 714-971-3553 www.anaheim-ramadasuites.com	All units are two-room suites with TV and phones in each room	$
Tropicana Inn 1540 S. Harbor Boulevard 800-828-4898 or 714-635-4082 www.bei-hotels.com	Two-room suites available	$$
Westcoast Anaheim Hotel 1855 S. Harbor Boulevard 800-325-4000 or 714-750-1811 www.westcoasthotels.com	Patios and balconies with some units; on-site restaurant and coffee shop	$–$$

$$$$ $250 and up
$$$ $150–$250
$$ $100–$150
$ $ 50–$100

Resort Area Hotels

Distance from Resort	Rating	Amenities	Details On
Across the street from main gate	★★★	Heated pool and spa; refrigerators available for fee; free continental breakfast	Page 55
Two blocks away; shuttle available	★★	Pool and spa; microwaves and refrigerators in all units; free continental breakfast	Page 56
Across the street from main gate	★★★	Heated pool and spa; refrigerators and microwaves in all rooms; free continental breakfast	Page 56
Near Anaheim Convention Center; one block from entrance; shuttle available	★★	Heated pool and spa; fitness center; in-room video games; refrigerators in some rooms; children eat free at restaurant	Page 56

★★★★ Top quality with superior amenities
★★★ Good prices with good amenities
★★ Good value with few amenities
★ Basic and inexpensive

saves you from having to carry around a lot of cash and provides an itemized statement of your spending. In addition, you can have purchases sent to the hotel so you do not have to carry them around with you. (The purchases will be at the hotel by 1 P.M. on the day after your purchase, so don't do this if you will be leaving that same day.) You can also have your packages sent to the park entrance to be picked up as you leave the park. All the hotels have quality on-site restaurants and are close to those in Downtown Disney. Guests can also have tickets waiting for them at the hotel when they check in. Although the Disney hotels are some of the most expensive in the area, they are worth the cost if you want the extras and perks they provide.

Note: Rates listed in the descriptions of the hotels are for the off season (dates depend on hotel) and may include a discount for travel club membership or for only a limited number of rooms. Be sure to ask for the hotel's best available rate.

The Disneyland Hotel	★★★★
1150 Magic Way	**714-956-6425 or**
www.disneyland.com	**714-778-6600**

The Disneyland Hotel is one of the best places to stay during a vacation to the Disneyland Resort. In addition to the amenities you would expect from a hotel of its caliber, several additional perks make a family vacation extra special. Because the Walt Disney Company owns and operates it, guests feel as if they are still at Disneyland even after leaving the park and coming back to their room. The rooms are decorated with Disney-inspired art, and even the soap and shampoo come in containers emblazoned with the famous mouse.

Staying at the Disneyland Hotel is very convenient. You can take the monorail right into Disneyland and then back to the hotel. You can walk through Downtown Disney to the main gate. These options make it very nice for families with young children to come back to the hotel in the afternoon for a nap or just a break. There are several different things to do at the hotel as well.

Located in the center of the hotel area is the Never Land Pool. This huge 5,000-square-foot swimming pool follows the Peter Pan theme, with Captain Hook's pirate ship and the crocodile as a centerpiece. Adults and older children can walk up a path and across a suspension bridge to Skull Rock, where they can then ride down a 100-foot water slide. For younger children, there is a smaller slide away from the larger one. There is also a spa and plenty of lounge chairs. The hotel provides towels poolside, as well as flotation vests for young children. The pool area is a great place to come during the afternoon to cool off and rest while the parks are at their busiest. There are also the Cove Pools, which are smaller shallow pools for young children. These have a beach theme, with a sandy area where you can relax and a jungle gym for kids to play on. There is even a net for beach volleyball. Or you can get a workout in the fitness center.

And as if that were not enough, the hotel includes an arcade as well as remote-control boats that guests can sail around a small pond. At night, the Fantasy Water Show features lights and water synchronized to familiar Disney tunes. Plus there are koi ponds and waterfalls, which further add to the fun. For families with both older and younger children, the older ones can find lots of things to do here while the younger siblings are taking a nap.

Insider's Secret

Although check-in time is 3 P.M., you can actually register earlier and be assigned a room. If your room is ready, you can go on up to it. Otherwise, you can have the bell captain hold your luggage, then you can head on over to one of the parks or Downtown Disney. When you return to the hotel, pick up your key and a bellhop will bring your luggage up to you. Registering early gives you a better chance of getting a good room. You can even ask for a room with a view, and if one is not reserved, you just might get it, even if you did not pay extra to reserve one in advance. However, don't plan on this happening, especially during the busy season.

There are several shops where you can purchase souvenirs as well as toiletries, and the hotel features a number of on-site restaurants. Granville's Steak House is an elegant restaurant serving seafood, steaks, and prime rib. Hook's Pointe specializes in mesquite-grilled seafood and meats along with other favorites. Goofy's Kitchen offers a buffet for breakfast, lunch, and dinner where Goofy and other characters visit with the guests while they dine. For a quick morning bite, try the Coffee House, where you can also get a cup of Java, hot chocolate, or tasty baked goods all day long. Croc's Bits 'n' Bites serves hamburgers and chicken sandwiches as well as ice cream, and the Captain's Galley is a poolside shop for sandwiches, salads, snacks, and even sushi. Or you can choose room service.

The Disneyland Hotel also offers a variety of guest services and maintains a list of baby-sitters licensed and bonded by the city of Anaheim. Bellhops will even carry your luggage up to your room and are full of information about not only the hotel but also the parks. Rooms are always clean, and each includes a refrigerator. A complimentary daily newspaper is even left by your door each morning.

The many bonuses of staying at the Disneyland Hotel do come with a price. A basic room starts at about $200 a night. You should make reservations early, especially if you plan on staying more than two nights. The hotel consists of three towers. The Marina Tower offers views of either the pool area or the parking area. The Sierra Tower looks out over the pool area or Downtown Disney. The Bonita Tower has views of the koi ponds and waterfalls or a parking area. We prefer the Bonita Tower with a room overlooking the waterfalls because it is a bit quieter and the sound of the waterfalls tends to drown out the noise from the pool area. There is an additional charge to reserve a room with a view.

Disney's Paradise Pier Hotel	★★★★
1717 Disneyland Drive	714-956-6425 or
www.disneyland.com	714-999-0990

Although not as glamorous as the Disneyland Hotel, the Paradise Pier is still a fine hotel and a bit more quiet. It offers most of the same amenities and guest services as the Disneyland Hotel, and guests can use the monorail for transportation into Disneyland. Guests also have their own private entrance into California Adventure. All rooms have refrigerators, and a newspaper will be left by your door each morning.

The hotel has a rooftop pool and spa as well as a workout center. However, guests are able to use the pool facility at the Disneyland Hotel as well. (This may change in the future, so be sure to ask at the front desk.) In addition to a few shops, the hotel has two on-site restaurants. The PCH Grill offers a variety of selections with a California and Pacific Rim theme. Yamabuki is an upscale Japanese restaurant serving teriyaki, tempura, fresh sushi, and other favorites. It also offers takeout if you want to eat in your room. Room service is provided from the PCH Grill's kitchen. In the morning, the PCH Grill features Disney's PCH Grill Breakfast. The all-you-care-to-eat breakfast buffet includes an omelet bar and other morning favorites as well as a traditional Japanese breakfast. While you are eating, Minnie and Daisy entertain with songs as well as visit each table to chat and take pictures with the guests. Minnie and Daisy may even ask you to dance. The hotel also offers Practically Perfect Tea hosted by none other than Mary Poppins. This traditional English tea serves a variety of teatime snacks and includes a children's menu.

Rooms at the Paradise Pier are a bit less expensive than the other Disney hotels, giving you the Disney experience with a bit of savings. Rooms range from $160 to $235. Because the rates are a bit cheaper, you may want to spend a bit extra and go for a room on the concierge level. It includes breakfast as well as snacks and drinks in the private lounge all day long. Each room on this level also has a VCR.

The rooms at the Paradise Pier Hotel overlook either California Adventure or the pool area and parking lot. The park view is a bit more expensive but worth it. Register early, before the normal check-in time, and ask for a corner room. Because of the way they are situated, corner rooms have a bit more space than the others, which is good if you need a crib or bring along a playpen.

Disney's Grand Californian ★★★★
1150 Disneyland Drive 714-956-6425 or
www.disneyland.com 714-635-2300

Disney's Grand Californian, which opened in 2001, is the most luxurious of the Disney hotels and one of the nicest in the area. You will also pay for what you get, with rooms starting at about $235 per night. During the busy season, expect to pay over $300 per night. It is designed after the Arts and Crafts movement such as that practiced by Frank Lloyd Wright. The hotel is filled with redwood and cedar and looks like a mountain chalet one would find in Yosemite rather than in Anaheim.

The hotel offers many of the same amenities as the other Disney hotels. A complimentary daily local newspaper is left by your door each morning. Each room features furniture crafted in the Arts and Crafts style, plus marble sinks in the bathroom area. The refrigerators in the rooms come filled with snacks and drinks. However, just picking up one of the items causes it to be charged to your room. Since that is not a good idea with children, who could have you buying the entire contents of the fridge, this can be locked electronically by the front desk. You can then request that housekeeping bring up an additional refrigerator in which to keep your own food and drinks cool. Each room also has an iron and ironing board, a hair dryer, a coffeemaker, a lighted wardrobe, and even robes for the adults (children's robes can be requested). Rooms also come with a portable crib, so if you are staying at the Grand Californian, you will not have to bring one of your own. Some rooms even have a bunk bed for the kids with a trundle bed under it so you can sleep three children in the room.

The main lobby of the hotel is fantastic and includes cut marble floors, lots of wood, a hearth made up of large river rocks, and a grand fireplace. Children can sit in kid-size rocking chairs and listen to cast members share stories from California's history by the fire at various times during the day. The hotel has two pools (one with a water slide) as well as a kiddie splash pool. The Eureka Springs Health Club (access is included with a stay at the hotel) offers a variety of workout equipment and weights, as well as dry and steam saunas. Massages are also available for an additional fee. For those interested in the artwork and architecture of the hotel, you can take an Art of the Craft tour.

The hotel features several restaurants and eateries. The Napa Rose is open for lunch and dinner and serves a variety of meals including seafood and much more. Storytellers Café features a character breakfast buffet in the morning in addition to a breakfast menu. A host of entrées are served for lunch and dinner. For a quick bite, stop by White Water Snacks, which carries sandwiches, salads, desserts, and snacks. The Hearthstone Lounge has coffees and pastries for breakfast, then mixed drinks, cocktails, and wine later in the day. Room service features the menu from the Storytellers Café.

One nice feature about this hotel is that it has its own private entrance into California Adventure. Guests of the hotel enter the theme park near the Grizzly River Run attraction. This lets you bypass the crowds at the main gate and also provides easy access if you need to come back during the day for a rest or even a swim. The hotel is also very close to Disneyland and attached to Downtown Disney. If the adults would like an evening out, Pinocchio's Workshop provides supervised activities for children ages 5 to 12. The cost starts at $9 per child per hour, and this fee includes a snack. Meals are also available for an additional fee. Hours are from 5 P.M. to midnight. Space is limited, so if you plan on using this service, make reservations in advance by calling 714-956-6755. Although there is self-parking available at the lots across from Disneyland Drive, it is usually best just to use the valet parking. The fee is $8 per night of your stay for hotel guests.

Helpful Hint

Most hotels offer one of three ways to get to the Disneyland Resort. Some are right across the street, within an easy walking distance. Other hotels, located farther away, offer shuttle service. Shuttle schedules vary according to the hotel. The third option is to drive your own vehicle and park in the Mickey and Friends parking structure.

Disney's Grand Californian is a great hotel for adults. However, families, especially those with young children, may be disappointed by the lack of Disney characters in the design. On the other hand, it is the closest hotel to both theme parks, making it handy for taking children back for naps during the day. For those who want to feel pampered and surrounded by luxury, we recommend staying here. If you want more of a Disney-type experience, stay at one of the other Disney hotels.

Off-Site Hotels

Anaheim and the surrounding area have literally hundreds of hotels. Some are right near the resort, whereas others are several miles away. We have listed just a few here and have included a variety of types and styles. If you have a large family,

Money-Saving Tip
Some of the following hotels are Disneyland Good
Neighbor Hotels. Special packages with these hotels can be booked through the Walt Disney Travel
Company, AAA, or a travel agent. They can reduce
rates for rooms, and the package usually includes
several amenities. You can also view these packages online at the Disneyland Resort Web site
(www.disneyland.com).

more than five people, consider one of the hotels that offers
suites.

Alpine Motel	★★
715 W. Katella Avenue	800-772-4422 or
	714-535-2186

This inexpensive motel is located across the street from the
Anaheim Convention Center and on the same block as
Disneyland. Rates can go as low as $50 during the off season,
and two-bedroom units are available. Stays include a free continental breakfast, and there is an adjacent restaurant as well.
Refrigerators are available in some units for an additional fee,
and there is a heated pool.

Anaheim Carriage Inn	★★
2125 S. Harbor Boulevard	800-345-2131 or
www.carriage-inn.com	714-740-1440

This nice inn is located two blocks away from Disneyland,
and it has a heated pool and spa. Continental breakfast is included, and each room has a microwave and a refrigerator.

There are single-room units, suites, and two-room suites. Prices start at $69 for a deluxe room and $80 for a suite. The inn offers a shuttle to the Disneyland Resort, and tickets are available for sale.

Anaheim Desert Inn and Suites ★★★	
1600 S. Harbor Boulevard	**800-433-5270 or**
www.anaheimdesertinn.com	**714-772-5050**

This hotel is located across the street from Disneyland's main gate, so guests can easily walk over to the Disneyland Resort. A stay here includes a complimentary continental breakfast, and each room has a microwave, a coffeemaker, and a refrigerator. Guests can use the heated indoor pool and spa year-round, no matter what the weather. This inn offers a variety of suites starting at $69 and single rooms at $45. Several families we talked to recommended this inn for its pricing, nice suites, and great location. Tickets are available here.

Anaheim Desert Palm Hotel and Suites ★★★	
631 W. Katella Avenue	**800-635-5423 or**
www.anaheimdesertpalm.com	**714-535-1133**

This inn offers good pricing and a variety of suites for larger families. It is located across the street from the Anaheim Convention Center and on the same block as Disneyland. Each room has a microwave, a coffeemaker, and a refrigerator. There is a heated pool. Single rooms start as low as $59 and suites at $89. Tickets are available.

Best Western Raffles Inn and Suites ★★
2040 S. Harbor Boulevard   800-654-0196 or
www.bestwesternrafflesinn.com   714-750-6100

Located two blocks from Disneyland, this inn offers shuttle service to the park. Microwaves and refrigerators are available in some rooms, and some suites feature a kitchenette. This hotel offers an exercise room, a heated pool and spa, and Internet access, and guests receive a complimentary continental breakfast. Rates start at $66 for regular rooms and $90 for suites. There are three suite floor plans to choose from. Tickets are available.

Candy Cane Inn ★★
1747 S. Harbor Boulevard   800-345-7057 or
www.candycaneinn.net   714-774-5284

This hotel has a nice atmosphere and is located across the street from the Disneyland Resort. Although it is a bit farther to walk from than some of the other hotels, it does offer a complimentary shuttle service. A continental breakfast is included, and each deluxe room has a microwave and refrigerator. There is a heated pool and spa as well as a children's wading pool. Rates for a basic room start at $82. Be sure to ask for a room with a garden view. Tickets are available. It is a Disneyland Good Neighbor hotel.

Carousel Inn and Suites ★★
1530 S. Harbor Boulevard   800-854-6767 or
www.carouselinnandsuites.com   714-758-0444

This inn is located across the street from the Disneyland Resort and within easy walking distance. All units have refrigerators, microwaves, and coffeemakers. There is a heated pool on the rooftop, which also allows a view of the fireworks at Disneyland. Basic rooms start at $79. It is a Disneyland Good Neighbor hotel.

Castle Inn and Suites	★★
1734 S. Harbor Boulevard	800-227-8530 or
www.castleinn.com	714-774-8111

The Castle Inn is hard to miss because it looks like a castle with turrets and towers. In addition to basic rooms, which start at $72, there are also suites for families of up to six people, starting at $98. Each unit has a refrigerator and a coffeemaker, whereas only the suites have microwaves. The inn is located a block away from the Disneyland Resort, and complimentary shuttle service is available. Guests can enjoy the heated pool and spa as well as a children's wading pool. Tickets are available.

Del Sol Inn	★★
1604 S. Harbor Boulevard	888-686-1122 or
www.delsolinn.com	714-234-3411

This inn is located just across the street from the Disneyland Resort and is a short walk to the main gate. Larger families can reserve two adjoining rooms as a suite. All rooms contain microwaves, refrigerators, and coffeemakers. A continental breakfast is included. Rates can be around $50 off season for single rooms and starting at $100 for two-room suites. Disneyland tickets are available for sale at the front desk. Vacation packages are also available. Coin-operated laundry is on site. The Del Sol also has a 24-hour on-site restaurant.

The Dupre ★★
2145 S. Harbor Boulevard   800-220-4820 or
www.thedupre.com   714-971-5556

The Dupre is a New Orleans–themed hotel. It is several blocks
from the main gate and offers shuttle service. Rooms are available starting at $45. Suites begin at $69. All rooms and suites
include a refrigerator, a microwave, Internet access, and cable
TV. This hotel is completely nonsmoking. Some of the suites
are available with bunk beds. A complimentary continental
breakfast is offered daily.

Hilton Anaheim ★★★
777 Convention Way   800-774-1500 or
www.hilton.com   714-750-4321

This hotel is one block from the Disneyland Resort and offers
complimentary shuttle service. The hotel offers a children's
program that runs from May 31 to September 1. Call for
more information. Rooms start as low as $99, and the hotel
features several restaurants ranging from a buffet to a sushi
bar, with a Ben & Jerry's ice cream shop and a Starbucks coffee shop as well. There is a heated pool. A fitness center can be
used by guests for an additional fee. This is a nice hotel, and
although it has a children's program, it seems designed more
for businesspeople and adults than for families.

Holiday Inn Anaheim at the Park ★★
1221 S. Harbor Boulevard   800-545-7275 or
www.holiday-inn.com   714-758-0900

Located two blocks from the Disneyland Resort, this hotel offers complimentary shuttle service not only to Disneyland but

also to Knott's Berry Farm and other local attractions. Kids will like this hotel because of the in-room video games; also, the pool area is open 24 hours a day and features a children's play fountain. The hotel has a restaurant on site, and kids eat free when adults buy meals here. Disneyland tickets are available, as are tickets for most other Southern California attractions. Rates start at $70, which makes this a good deal when you add the free children's meals. It is a Disneyland Good Neighbor hotel.

Hyatt Regency Alicante	★★★
100 Plaza Alicante, Garden Grove	**800-809-1956 or**
www.hyatt.com	**714-750-1234**

This hotel is located five blocks away from the Disneyland Resort. The complimentary shuttle service runs every 30 minutes. The new Suite Tower, which opened in the spring of 2001, features a variety of suites, including a kids' suite with a bunk bed in a separate room and a TV for the kids. It also offers microwaves, refrigerators, and coffeemakers. Package deals include breakfast buffet and kids' fun pack. The hotel has its own restaurant as well as two pools, a spa, and tennis courts. The concierge can even help arrange for in-room baby-sitting in the evenings. Rates start at $120 for a basic room and $150 for suites. It is a Disneyland Good Neighbor hotel.

Jolly Roger Inn	★★
640 W. Katella Avenue	**800-682-9610 or**
www.jollyrogerhotel.com	**714-782-7500**

The Jolly Roger is located near the Anaheim Convention Center; from it you can take the complimentary shuttle to the Disneyland Resort. The inn has a restaurant as well as a heated pool and children's wading pool. Rates start at $69 for a basic room. Four two-room units are available. You can also purchase packages that include tickets. It is a Disneyland Good Neighbor hotel.

Park Inn Anaheim	★★
1520 S. Harbor Boulevard	**800-670-7275 or**
www.parkhtls.com	**714-635-7275**

You can walk across the street to the Disneyland Resort from this inn. All rooms have refrigerators, while suites include microwaves. Continental breakfast is included, and guests can relax at the heated pool and spa. Basic rooms start at $89. Tickets are available. It is a Disneyland Good Neighbor hotel.

Park Vue Inn	★★
1570 S. Harbor Boulevard	**800-334-7021 or**
www.parkvueinn.com	**714-772-3691**

This inn is located right across the street from the Disneyland main gate and within easy walking distance. It features refrigerators in all units, a heated pool, and complimentary continental breakfast and has a 24-hour restaurant on site. Basic rooms start at $58 and family suites at $89. Tickets are available.

Portofino Inn & Suites	★★★
1831 S. Harbor Boulevard	**800-511-6907 or**
www.portofinoinnanaheim.com	**714-782-7600**

The Portofino Inn & Suites offers two floor plans. The Kids Suite has bunk beds, a sofa sleeper, and an activity table, as well as the standard amenities, including refrigerator and microwave. The kids' area can be closed off from the parents with French doors. The King Suite, on the other hand, offers a king-sized bed in one room and a sofa sleeper in the other. The hotel has a pool and spa, a sundeck, a video arcade, and a fitness center. This hotel is within walking distance of the parks. Shuttle service is offered for a small fee. Packages are available through the hotel. The Kids Suites start at $110, and the King Suites begin at $100.

Radisson Resort Knott's Berry Farm	★★
7675 Crescent Avenue, Buena Park	**800-333-3333 or**
www.radisson.com/buenaparkca	**714-995-1111**

Although this hotel is actually several miles away from Disneyland, it is right next to Knott's Berry Farm. Rooms start at $89, and the hotel offers package deals that include meals and admission to Knott's. There is a complimentary shuttle to the Disneyland Resort, and the hotel has a pool, a spa, a children's pool, a fitness center, and lighted tennis courts. There are even a limited number of Peanuts-themed rooms, which include a nightly Snoopy turndown service. Refrigerators are available in some rooms.

Ramada Inn Maingate	★★★
1650 S. Harbor Boulevard	**800-854-6097 or**
www.ramadamaingate.com	**714-772-0440**

This inn is directly across the street from the main gate of Disneyland, making it a short walk to the resort and back. In addition to basic rooms, which start at $70, the inn also offers two- and three-bed suites, some with a kitchenette. The suites start at around $120. There is also a shuttle to the park, and a continental breakfast is included. There is an on-site restaurant as well as a heated pool and spa. It is a Disneyland Good Neighbor hotel.

Ramada Limited Suites ★★
2141 S. Harbor Boulevard   800-526-9444 or
www.anaheim-ramadasuites.com   714-971-3553

Located two blocks from the Disneyland Resort, this hotel offers guests a complimentary shuttle to the parks. What is unique about this hotel is that all of the rooms are two-room suites. Each suite has a microwave, a refrigerator, two telephones, and two televisions. A complimentary continental breakfast is included, and a covered swimming pool and spa are available for guest use. The suites begin at $69, and the hotel offers Disneyland package deals as well as tickets.

Tropicana Inn ★★★
1540 S. Harbor Boulevard   800-828-4898 or
www.bei-hotels.com   714-635-4082

This inn is located across the street from the Disneyland Resort and is only a five-minute walk away from the main gate. Two-room suites are available for large families. Each room features a microwave and a refrigerator. A complimentary continental breakfast is included, and there is a heated pool and spa for the guests to enjoy. Basic rooms start at $78. Tickets are available. It is a Disneyland Good Neighbor hotel.

Westcoast Anaheim Hotel ★★
1855 S. Harbor Boulevard   800-325-4000 or
www.westcoasthotels.com   714-750-1811

This hotel is a block from Disneyland. Guests can take the complimentary shuttle. Many of the units have a patio and a balcony, and some rooms have a refrigerator. There is also a heated Olympic-size pool and spa, a fitness center, and an on-site restaurant and coffee shop. Children can eat lunch and dinner free with paid adult meals. Rooms start at $79. The hotel also offers Disneyland packages as well as tickets. It is a Disneyland Good Neighbor hotel.

San Diego Area Hotels

Best Western Mission Bay Inn ★★
2575 Clairemont Drive, San Diego   800-457-8080 or
www.bestwesternmissionbay.com   619-275-5700

The Mission Bay Inn is located just one mile from Sea World and is near Mission Bay beaches. A few minutes' drive and you will find yourself at the San Diego Zoo. Prices start at $69 for off season. A continental breakfast is offered every morning. The hotel has an outdoor pool and spa. Each room has a coffeemaker, a refrigerator, a microwave, and cable TV. You can walk to Mission Bay. Tickets for SeaWorld and the zoo are available at a discount through the hotel.

Comfort Suites ★★
631 Camino del Rio South, San Diego   800-997-2086 or
www.comfortsuitesmv.com   619-881-4000

Mission Valley Comfort Suites offers a standard suite or a kids' suite. The kids' suite has a room separated by French doors and houses bunk beds. This hotel has a heated pool and spa, a fitness center, a game room, and cable TV. A continental breakfast buffet is served daily. Passes for SeaWorld can be purchased at the hotel. Prices start at $100.

Quick Guide to

Hotel Name	Description	Price
Best Western Mission Bay Inn 2575 Clairemont Drive San Diego, CA 92117 800-457-8080 or 619-275-5700 www.bestwesternmissionbay.com	Standard rooms available	$
Comfort Suites 631 Camino del Rio South San Diego, CA 92108 800-997-2086 or 619-881-4000 www.comfortsuitesmv.com	Standard suites or kids suites available	$–$$
Doubletree Club Hotel 1515 Hotel Circle South San Diego, CA 92108 800-619-1541 or 619-881-6900 www.doubletreesdzoo.com	Family suites available; private balconies	$–$$
Holiday Inn 3737 Sports Arena Boulevard San Diego, CA 92110 800-383-5430 or 619-881-6100 www.holidayinnseaworld.com	Two-room suites and kids' suites available	$–$$

$$$$ $250 and up
$$$ $150–$250
$$ $100–$150
$ $ 50–$100

San Diego Area Hotels

Distance from Resort	Rating	Amenities	Details On
San Diego	★★	Pool and spa; microwaves and refrigerators; continental breakfast	Page 57
San Diego	★★	Pool and spa; fitness center and game room; microwaves and refrigerators; continental breakfast	Page 57
San Diego	★★★	Pool and spa; fitness center and game room; refrigerators and microwaves	Page 58
San Diego	★★	Pool and spa; health club and game room; refrigerators and microwaves	Page 58

★★★★ Top quality with superior amenities
★★★ Good prices with good amenities
★★ Good value with few amenities
★ Basic and inexpensive

Doubletree Club Hotel ★★★
1515 Hotel Circle South, San Diego   800-619-1541 or
www.doubletreesdzoo.com   619-881-6900

This upscale hotel offers regular rooms as well as family suites. The features include a heated pool and spa, an on-site restaurant, a video game center, and a gift shop. The hotel also offers a fitness center where you can work off the famous Doubletree fresh-baked cookies they give you upon arrival. Each room has a refrigerator, a microwave, cable TV, and a coffeemaker. Packages are available for SeaWorld and the San Diego Zoo, and discounted tickets are also available.

Holiday Inn ★★
3737 Sports Arena Boulevard,   800-383-5430 or
   San Diego   619-881-6100
www.holidayinnseaworld.com

Near SeaWorld and the beaches of Mission Bay, this hotel offers two different suites for families. The Kids Mini Suite has bunk beds and gives kids their own space. A standard two-room suite is also available. Rates begin at $80 for a standard room on up to $100 for a standard suite. The hotel has a heated pool and spa, a Bakers Square Restaurant & Pie Shop, a sports bar, and a video game room, and guests have free use of an adjacent health club. Tickets for SeaWorld are available to purchase at the hotel.

CHAPTER

3

Before You
Leave Home

tickets

directions

You already have your reservations for a hotel, made arrangements for tickets, and have your transportation arranged. This chapter covers some of the other things you should do before you leave home.

Getting the Latest Info

A week or two before your vacation, you may want to check on ride closures, special happenings, park operating hours, and even the weather. Even though you checked on these when first planning your trip, some may have changed. There are a couple of ways to check these things. You can access the Disneyland Web site at www.disneyland.com. There you can see the latest listing of rides and attractions scheduled to be closed for refurbishment. Knowing ahead of time which rides will not be up and running will keep you from being surrounded by disappointed faces while at the park. You can also look up show times and parade times at this site. The other route to this information is via telephone, by dialing 714-781-

4565. Local weather information in the Anaheim area is available by calling 714-550-4636.

What to Take with You

Whether you are an expert traveler or a novice, vacationing with children can be challenging. To help make things easier, we have provided some hints and tips on what you should take with you.

Clothing and Necessities

A well-planned packing list will make it much easier to gather each person's essential items. Make a list for each member of the family. If you are traveling with older children, let them help compile their own list. Each list should include clothing that is weather appropriate (remember, Southern California days can be hot, and evenings can be quite cool), shoes that fit comfortably (now is not the time to break in those new tennies), toiletries, a swimsuit, sunglasses, sunscreen, and so on. Remember to also list special needs items such as medications. If you are traveling during the rainy season, you might want to pack inexpensive ponchos for each family member. Don't try to include everything and the kitchen sink. Pack lightly; if something more is needed, it can most likely be found at the resort. Children can purchase T-shirt souvenirs that can double as either swim cover-ups or pajamas. If the weather changes drastically, sweatshirt souvenirs can also be purchased. (If you are on a very tight budget, be sure to prepare for weather changes so as not to break the budget.) Many of the hotels have laundry service or laundry facilities for your use. No matter what time of year you travel, be sure to include sunscreen. The Southern California sun can be deceiving in the fall and spring, and a nasty sunburn can result even when it is cloudy. Parents and older children should bring along fanny packs to carry money, room keys, snacks, and so forth. If you are traveling with children requiring a diaper bag, you may want to switch to a backpack for the trip. A backpack will free up your arms while also allowing you to tote all your baby care and family necessities. A basic first aid kit should also be included as a group item.

Helpful Hint

Put on your walking shoes weeks before your trip! The Disneyland Resort is a large place, so you can expect to walk several miles a day. Be sure to bring your most comfortable walking shoes as well as good socks. Several weeks before your trip you may want to begin a walking regimen with your family so that your body (mainly your feet) is prepared to traverse the Disneyland Resort in tip-top condition! Hi ho, hi ho, it's off to walk you go!

Helpful Hint

Take this opportunity to rotate out old toothbrushes. Instead of making the common mistake of forgetting to pack your toothbrush, buy new toothbrushes for everyone several days before and immediately pack them. Young children really enjoy getting a new toothbrush, especially if it is Disney themed. You can purchase different themed toothbrushes as well as toothpastes at most discount stores and drugstores.

Family First Aid Kit

Here is a list of first aid items that may prove useful while traveling. This list is a basic guideline. Customize your kit according to the needs of your family.

- Pain reliever
- Infants and/or children's acetaminophen (if needed)
- Teething medicine (if needed)
- Band-Aids
- First aid antibiotic
- Diarrhea medication
- Insect sting relief
- Sunscreen
- Sunburn relief
- Thermometer
- Allergy and/or cold medication

Instead of lugging a large first aid kit around all day with these items, leave it at the hotel and just take a few of the items, primarily Band-Aids, in a small container or even a Ziploc bag. All of the theme parks within this book have first aid centers. They are all equipped with basic first aid supplies. A few of the theme parks, including Disneyland, also carry pain relievers. The staff will administer them to you and document the time and the dose so that you may return later to receive a second dose if needed.

Communication

If you know your family will be splitting up for some of the time while at the Disneyland Resort, you may find it useful to invest in a pair of walkie-talkies. These are becoming popular with families that separate to different areas of the park. They let you stay in contact with each other even when at opposite ends of the park. Try to find walkie-talkies that have several different channels; chances are you will find your family using the same frequency as another family and have to change to another frequency. Since these are not secure forms of communication (other people may be listening in), avoid giving personal information over these walkie-talkies, such as your room number with the hotel, credit card numbers, and such.

Capture the Memories on Film

The one thing you are sure to see everyone toting along is a camera or video camera. Remember to bring along plenty of film and batteries for both your camera and video recorder. There are several spots throughout the park where professional pictures with the characters can be taken. The photographers will also be happy to take your family's picture with your camera, too, or if you choose not to be in the picture and just want a cute shot of the kids, you can take it yourself. Either way you'll be capturing the memories and saving a bundle. Film and batteries are available at the park; however, buying them here is more expensive than purchasing them in advance at home.

Video cameras are a great way to record your trip. However, after a while you can tire of carrying them around. We suggest you choose one day at the park as your video day and leave the camera at the hotel on other days at the same park. Shows and parades are great to record because children will love to watch them over and over again at home. Also, be sure to get shots of your family on various attractions. Filming in-

Helpful Hint

Not to worry if you left something behind! Located not far from Disneyland is Wal-Mart, a discount department store. Here you can buy almost anything you may have forgotten, without having to pay inflated prices within the resort. Wal-Mart is located right off the I-5 (Santa Ana) Freeway at the Euclid exit. If you are coming from the Disneyland Resort, take the freeway northbound to Wal-Mart and then southbound back to the resort.

side some attractions can be difficult because they are dark—although you are free to try. Using lights or flashes in these attractions is not allowed.

I'm Hungry!

During your stay at even the most expensive hotel, you may find you do not have all the comforts of home, especially if you are traveling with small children. While packing for your trip, you may want to include nonperishable snack foods and drinks such as juice boxes. You may find these useful when someone has a craving late in the evening. Small snacks can also be placed in fanny packs for midday munchies at the park. Remember to bring individual bottled water as well. It is important to stay hydrated, especially in the hot summer months. Bottled water is available within the park but at a premium price. It is also worthy to note that tap water always tastes different when you travel, so if you have a sensitive palate, you might want to bring some extra water along to refill your water bottles. Most hotels have in-room coffeemakers. These come in handy if you are on a tight budget. Use the coffeemaker to heat up some hot water to make instant oat-meal, noodle soups, hot cocoa, and so on. If a microwave is also included in your hotel room, be sure to pack a few bags of microwave popcorn for those late-night munchies.

Mom, I'm Bored!

You may find with small children that they become bored rather quickly in the hotel room—that is, if they haven't already collapsed from exhaustion. Most hotels around Disney-land offer the Disney Channel; however, bringing along a few activities may ward off boredom. For infants, be sure to take a few of their favorite toys. Preschool and young school-aged children will enjoy coloring or playing with a special toy as well as being read to or quietly looking at a picture book. A few containers of Play-Doh are often a welcome treat for small children. Have older children choose a book or two to bring along.

Helpful Hint

If your family is going to LEGOLAND, you might consider buying a small set of LEGOs to entertain your children at the hotel and as a souvenir. There is also a large LEGO store at Downtown Disney, which, among other things, sells sets featuring everyone's favorite mouse and his friends.

Should You Bring Play Yards, Cribs, and Strollers?

If you are traveling with an infant, you will have more needs than those traveling with older children. Disneyland and most hotels are able to meet those needs, but other options are available. Most hotels have portable cribs available for your use. If you are uncomfortable using someone else's crib, you can bring along a play yard. Most play yards today can double as a bassinet for newborns and a crib for older babies. During waking hours, the play yard can be used to keep your infant safe while in the nonchildproofed hotel room.

A stroller is a necessity when traveling with infants and small children. If you do not already have one or would rather not bring yours, strollers are available to rent for a minimal fee at the front entrance of Disneyland as well as at most area theme parks. The ones at Disneyland look much like a single-child jogging stroller. If you are staying for more than one day or visiting other attractions, you may be better off purchasing an inexpensive umbrella stroller. (Renting one every day can add up quickly.) Umbrella strollers can be found at a baby store or discount department store before your trip. These strollers are easily collapsible for travel and maneuverability. They also allow you to transport an exhausted child between the park and your hotel instead of having to carry the child because you had to leave the rented stroller at the park.

Preparing the Kids– Building up the Excitement

As exciting as it is just knowing you will soon be visiting the Disneyland Resort, the excitement can be multiplied by learning more about the park and its attractions. Bring the family together and explore the Disneyland Web site at www.disneyland.com. Also, discuss and plan the trip together using this book as your guide. Talk about or even watch the movies that inspired some of the rides, such as *Dumbo* or

Helpful Hint

Make a "countdown to Disneyland" chain to en-
hance the anticipation of the trip. To make a chain,
cut 1-inch by 8-inch strips of colored paper (8-inch
by 10-inch sheets of construction paper work great)
and loop them around each other, securing with
tape or staples. At the top of the chain, attach a
cutout of a castle or a Mickey Mouse silhouette to
represent the day of arrival at Disneyland. You can
make it as far ahead of time as you like; however,
two weeks to a month is usually sufficient.

Snow White. You can even make a "countdown to Disneyland" chain or calendar.

Height Checks

Some of the rides at the Disneyland Resort and other places
have height requirements. About a week before your trip, line
up the kids and measure their height with the shoes they will
be wearing at the parks. If a child is just barely under the
height requirement for some rides, you might consider shoes
with a higher heel or sole to get the child above the height
limitation. The height restrictions at Disneyland and other
parks are strictly enforced, and your child may be measured
more than once for the same ride. However, the parks have
begun using a new system called Goofy's Magic Measure. At
one location in each park, children can be measured once
using an ultrasonic device and receive a color-coded wristband
that lets you and your children know exactly which rides they
can go on and which they can't. For more information on this
program, see chapter 4. See the Quick Guides to rides and attractions in chapters 5 and 6 for all height requirements.

Planning the Fun

A successful and memorable trip takes some amount of planning. Gather together for a family night of planning. Grab a pad of paper, anything you may have received from your hotel or travel agent, this book, and anything you may have printed out from the Disneyland Web site, and have a planning session. List the number one priority for each family member to accomplish while at the park, and put those at the top of your "to do" list. Continue making the list of things to do, ride, see, or eat in order of how important they are for the family to do while at Disneyland. Use the map provided in this book to arrange a logical and timely plan. If your children do not know what they would like to do, you can read them the ride descriptions located in chapters 5 and 6. With younger children, remember to keep in mind height requirements and scare factors.

Special Needs

Illness

No matter how much planning anyone does, an illness cannot be predicted. Disneyland is a popular place, attracting people from all over the world. Everyone comes to Disneyland with enthusiasm and excitement as well as germs! As unpleasant as it may sound, people do come down with stomach ailments or the commom cold there as well. Be prepared for someone to possibly come down with something while at Disneyland. Bring along medications just in case. The best prevention is to wash your hands often. Throw a few antibacterial wet wipes into each person's fanny pack to use when hand washing is inconvenient. Remember, an ounce of prevention is worth a pound of cure. There are times when medical care is needed, be it to treat an illness, a deep wound, and so on. While most hotels can give you directions to local hospitals, we have listed a few nearby ones.

Anaheim Area Hospitals

Anaheim General Hospital
3350 W. Ball Road, Anaheim, CA 92804
714-827-6700

Anaheim Memorial Hospital
1111 W. La Palma Avenue, Anaheim, CA 92801
714-774-1450

Kaiser Foundation Hospital
441 N. Lakeview Avenue, Anaheim, CA 92807
714-978-4000

Martin Luther Hospital
1830 W. Romneya Drive, Anaheim, CA 92801
714-491-5200

Disabilities

Disneyland and other theme parks offer special services and/or ride accommodations for guests with disabilities. To request *The Guidebook for Guests with Disabilities* for the Disneyland Resort, you can call or write to

Disneyland Resort Guest Relations
Box 3232, Anaheim, CA 92803
714-781-4773

Allow two to three weeks for delivery. You can also download the guidebook by going to www.disneyland.com and doing a search for "disabilities." This guidebook tells where to locate wheelchair entrances and describes wheelchair accessibility to rides, restaurants, and shopping. Disneyland also has programs for blind and hearing-impaired guests. Portable tape players are available for those with visual impairments. There are also volume-controlled telephones available for the hearing impaired. Visit City Hall at Disneyland and Guest Relations at California Adventure to find out further information on disability assistance. You can also call Guest Relations for further information. Wheelchairs are available to rent at the stroller rental stand near the front entrance. Electric convenience vehicles are also available for about $30 a day. Remember, Disneyland is frequented by guests with illnesses and disabilities, and Disneyland cast members will assist you in any way they can to make your visit enjoyable; however, cast members are unable to help transfer guests to or from their wheelchair onto an attraction.

Pregnancy

If you are traveling while pregnant, remember that you have special needs. It is important to drink plenty of water and take care not to overheat. There are many shady areas where you can take a load off your feet and cool down. Another place to take a break is in the Baby Care Centers located on Main Street at Disneyland and behind the Mission Tortilla Factory at California Adventure. Note that many of the more turbulent rides at Disneyland as well as other parks do not allow pregnant women to ride.

Babies and Young Children

When traveling with babies and young children, you will always have extras to worry about. Remember that your little one has special dietary needs, so don't forget the baby food. If your infant is on formula, be sure to bring bottled water with which to prepare it. Little tummies can be sensitive to water from a different source. Diapers may be bulky to pack, but be sure to bring along plenty of them—they are rather expensive at the park. Young children can be very messy, so don't forget extra clothing for them as well. If you are traveling with a potty-training youngster, remember to bring extra undergarments. Within Disneyland, there are a few locations that have toddler toilets: the Baby Care Centers and Mickey's Toontown. Forewarn your little ones that some of these toilets are "magical" and flush automatically when the child stands up. A pacifier, binki, nukki, plug—whatever you might call it—can be vitally important on your trip, both to you as well as your little one. Pack extras, along with a pacifier holder. Many a lost pacifier has been seen lonesome and abandoned on one side of the park while an inconsolable infant is screaming on the other.

Helpful Hint

Never fear, your loyal Baby Care Center is here! Baby Care Centers are located on Main Street next to the Plaza Inn at Disneyland and behind the Mission Tortilla Factory at California Adventure. If you happen to run out of diapers or wipes or are in need of a pacifier, formula, or baby food, the Baby Care Center is ready to help. All these items can be purchased there, as well as teething gel and diaper cream.

CHAPTER

4

Touring the Disneyland Resort

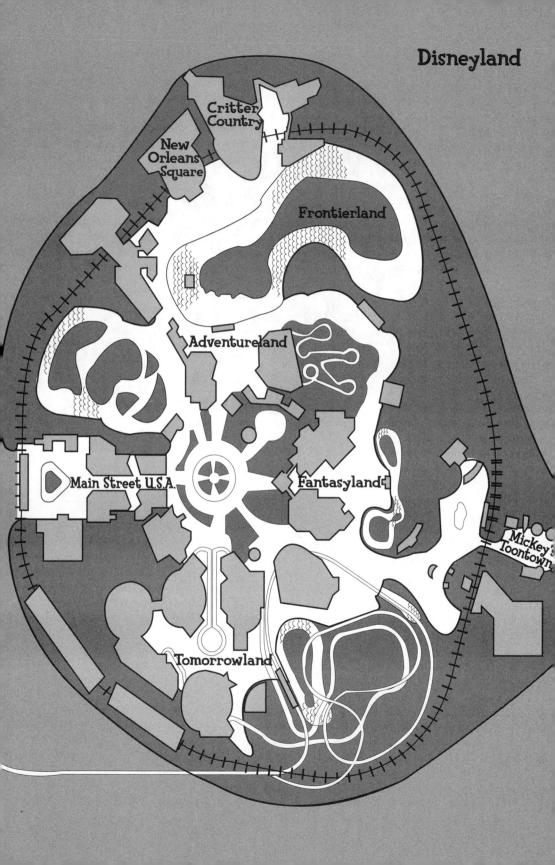

From talking to many different families, as well as from our own family's experiences at the Disneyland Resort, we have come up with several hints, tips, and suggestions that will help make your family's vacation and visit to the Happiest Place on Earth as happy as it can be.

Plan Your Day

Although most people are good at planning their daily schedule at work or at home, they often fall short during vacations. They plan where they will go and find a place to stay, but they often leave the rest to chance. We have found that a little bit of additional planning can go a long way. Disneyland is a large place with lots of exciting things to do and see. While talking to different families, we were surprised that some didn't see everything they wanted to even after spending two or three days at the park. In each case, the family didn't take the time to plan or even find out what Disneyland had to offer.

Although it is unnecessary to plan each and every hour at Disneyland, there are a few basic things you should consider before stepping through the gates at the main entrance or at least during your first hour there.

Before Entering the Parks

One of the first things you need to find out is when the parks open. You can find this on the Disneyland Web site or by asking at the front desk of your hotel. The Disneyland hotels have the schedule, as do most of the nearby hotels. Plan on getting to the front gates an hour before opening. Disneyland will usually begin letting guests in onto Main Street half an hour before the park opens.

If you need to board a pet in the kennel for the day, you should get to the kennel 15 to 20 minutes before it opens, to avoid the lines. The kennel opens 30 minutes before the park officially opens.

If you want to watch the *Fantasmic!* show from the balcony of the Disney Gallery above Pirates of the Caribbean, you will have to make reservations in advance at Guest Relations, located to the right of the front gates. You can also phone in your reservations up to 30 days in advance by calling 714-781-4400. Because the balcony only seats 15 to 17 people, you need to make your reservations early. Since advance reservations are allowed now instead of only same-day

Helpful Hint

To ensure the safety of their guests, Disneyland and Disney's California Adventure now search the backpacks and bags of their guests as they enter the park. Therefore, to save time in line, get your bags opened and ready for inspection prior to reaching the cast member.

reservations, we suggest calling exactly 30 days in advance to secure these reservations. In fact, call first thing in the morning, since others may have the same idea. The charge is a steep $45 per adult and $35 per child, but it includes a dessert sampler in a keepsake box or a child's dessert in a Mickey Mouse souvenir cup and a beverage. When there is more than one show per night, try to book the early show. This will give you a longer stay on the balcony, since you can arrive early. For the late show, you have to wait at least until after the first show. If you can afford it, try watching the show from the balcony at least once.

What to Eat

Everyone has to eat sometime. If children get hungry, they will not have a good time—and neither will you. The first step to planning is to determine what types of meals your family will have for the day. Will you eat breakfast at the hotel, at a fast-food restaurant, or in the park? What about lunch and dinner? Will you have a big lunch with a light dinner or a light lunch with a big dinner? If you wait until you are hungry, then it's too late.

Time-Saving Tip

As we have mentioned before, remember that it is important to purchase your tickets in advance. Most packages include tickets. They can also be purchased at some hotels, at Disney stores, from AAA, and through some employee organizations. The last thing you want to do is stand in line at the ticket booths in front of Disneyland. Sometimes your wait in line can be over an hour long on busy days! And then you still have to get into the park.

Planning your meals in advance saves time and money. That way, your family is not spending time trying to figure out where to eat after they have already become hungry, and it is easier to budget the cost if you know what to expect.

We recommend eating a fairly good breakfast. You want to hit a lot of popular rides in the morning before they get too busy, so don't spend time eating then. As for lunch, you should try to eat this meal in the early part of the afternoon, between 1 and 3 P.M. This is when the attractions are usually at their busiest and the restaurants and eateries have shorter lines. Then have a light dinner later in the evening. The meals on the lunch menus are often less expensive than the same items on the dinner menus. You may also decide to eat some meals outside of the park, either during the middle of the day or after the park closes. Although you can choose specific places to eat in advance, you can also decide later while waiting in line for attractions. Just knowing the types of meals and when you will eat them saves a lot of time and lets you schedule snacks and breaks throughout the remainder of the day.

If you are spending several days at Disneyland, you may want to determine when you would like to eat at certain places. For example, you may decide to try the Blue Bayou restaurant for lunch on your second day. That means you will need to make reservations early that same day or call and

Money-Saving Tip

Because snack foods and drinks can be expensive inside the park, it is a good idea to take some water bottles and snacks with you. Some that are ideal are granola bars or individual packages of nuts or other snacks that will easily fit in a pocket, fanny pack, or backpack and that won't melt.

make reservations up to two months in advance. The same goes for a number of restaurants at California Adventure that offer reservations, such as Ariel's Grotto. For a guide to what is available at the Disneyland Resort, please see chapter 8, "Disney Dining." Use this guide before you even leave on your vacation to decide on some of the special places where you would like to eat.

What to Do First

Even before you pass through the main gate at either of the parks, you should have an idea of which attractions you want to do first. Then, once inside the park, you can walk quickly to that attraction before the queues begin to get long. Since you can quickly get on many attractions first thing in the morning, don't waste your time deciding what to do next. As a general rule, prior to entering the park you should plan the first three or four attractions you want to visit. Chapters 5 and 6 provide suggestions for each park based on the ages of your children.

When to Get There—Early!

Disneyland begins allowing guests to enter the park about 30 minutes before it officially opens. These guests are held on Main Street until opening time. However, they can shop and visit the eateries here for a quick breakfast. At the official opening time, guests are then allowed to enter the rest of Disneyland. If you want to hit Main Street early so you can line up near the Central Plaza prior to opening, get to the main gate about an hour before the official opening time.

California Adventure does not allow guests in early, so you need to arrive at the main gate only 30 minutes in advance.

Many visitors don't arrive until the parks open or even later, making the lines to get into the parks grow longer throughout the morning—especially during the busy season. Therefore, be sure to get in line early.

Time-Saving Tip

Remember to purchase your tickets in advance. If for some reason you cannot, then get in line at the ticket booths an hour before the parks open or even earlier. The ticket lines can get quite long, and after you purchase your tickets, you still have another line to get into the park.

The FASTPASS System

Beginning in 1999 and 2000, Disneyland began testing the FASTPASS system on just a few attractions. It worked so well that most of the popular attractions now offer this system. The FASTPASS system was designed so that guests at Disneyland would not feel they were spending most of their day waiting in long lines. For those willing to wait for an assigned time to do an attraction, there is a much shorter line with a wait time of usually no longer than 10 to 15 minutes. Sound good? Here's how it works.

At a ride that has the FASTPASS system, near the entrance will be a number of small machines that look like they might make change. Instead, these issue FASTPASS tickets. Insert your ticket as directed by the instructions on the machine, and it will issue you a FASTPASS for the attraction. On the ticket will be two times, one hour apart. This is your window of time when you can return to the attraction and enter it using the much faster FASTPASS entrance or queue.

At the entrance to the FASTPASS machines is a sign that lists current FASTPASS windows the machines are issuing tickets for, as well as the length of the stand-by wait for those without a FASTPASS. The return window of time can vary from half an hour later to three or more hours later, depending on how many guests are using the system. Although your FASTPASS is reserving you a place in line, you can go visit other attractions, shop, or even have a meal.

Before you run around and get a FASTPASS for every attraction that offers it, know that there are some rules. First, you can have only one FASTPASS at a time. Also, every person in your party must have his or her own FASTPASS as long as the person is old enough to need a ticket for entrance into the park. As this book goes to print, Disneyland is currently offering the FASTPASS system on the following attractions:

- Autopia
- Big Thunder Mountain Railroad
- Haunted Mansion
- Indiana Jones Adventure
- Pirates of the Caribbean
- Roger Rabbit's Car Toon Spin
- Splash Mountain
- Star Tours
- The Many Adventures of Winnie the Pooh

Disneyland may later add the system to the Matterhorn Bobsleds or other attractions. During November and December, the holiday version of "It's a Small World" gets a temporary FASTPASS system.

California Adventure also uses the FASTPASS system. Because this park has fewer attractions, guests tend to group more at the few popular attractions. Therefore, using the FASTPASS system becomes even more important in saving time. The following California Adventure attractions currently use the FASTPASS system:

- California Screamin'

- Soarin' Over California

- It's Tough to Be a Bug

- Grizzly River Run

- Mulholland Madness

- Jim Henson's *Muppet*Vision 3D*

- *Who Wants to Be a Millionaire—Play It!*

Strategies for Using the FASTPASS System

From talking to other families and Disneyland cast members and from personal experience, we have found how to best use the FASTPASS system to save time during your vacation.

- Although everyone in your party needs a FASTPASS to board an attraction, not everyone has to wait in line to get his or her own FASTPASS. Instead, one person can take everyone's tickets and get FASTPASSes for them all while they are waiting in line for another attraction, meeting characters, or listening to a storytime.

- Most of the FASTPASS attractions are rides for older children and adults. Because the FASTPASS tickets are not assigned to a specific person, families with children unable to go on these attractions can still use the children's tickets to get FASTPASSes for adults or older children. Therefore, you could get two FASTPASSes for the same attraction or different attractions at the same time.

@ Although you can have only one FASTPASS at a time, the way the system works, you can actually have two. Once you get a FASTPASS, you cannot get another until after the first time of the window has passed. You then have an hour to use that FASTPASS. However, during that window, you can get a second FASTPASS. That way, while you are on the first attraction, you are also waiting for the window of the second. For example, you have a FASTPASS for Space Mountain with a window of 1 to 2 P.M. After 1 P.M., you could first get a FASTPASS for Autopia, then go on Space Mountain.

@ As a general rule, always get another FASTPASS before using the one you have.

@ For attractions where the window is more than two hours away, you can get a second FASTPASS two hours after you have received your first one. If you can't remember when you picked it up, the time is located on the bottom right corner of your FASTPASS.

@ There is no penalty for not using a FASTPASS. If you miss your window or decide to skip an attraction, you can get another FASTPASS following these guidelines. Therefore, you should always try to have a FASTPASS in your possession, even if you are unsure whether you will be able to use it.

@ Except for Main Street and Fantasyland, every land has at least one attraction using the FASTPASS system. If you pass by one and think you might want to ride it, get a FASTPASS.

@ Some attractions, especially Splash Mountain, can have very long waits for a return window. Unless you have to ride that attraction during that time window instead of later on, don't get a FASTPASS. Instead, get FAST-PASSes for attractions with shorter return waits. Often you can do two or even three FASTPASS attractions instead of waiting for only one. For the busy attractions, get your FASTPASS early.

@ If you are going to eat a meal, get a FASTPASS first so you can be waiting while you are eating.

Although the FASTPASS system is the best way to do the most popular attractions, it may not always fit your schedule, and at times the stand-by wait may be quite short. Even if you don't use the FASTPASS system on an attraction, the fact that it is there often reduces the wait in the stand-by line because many guests are willing to come back later.

Helpful Hint
When you have two lines from which to choose, whether for an attraction, a shop, or a dining venue, choose the line on the left. Studies show that people tend to choose the line on the right, so the left line is often shorter.

Height Requirements

Some of the rides at Disneyland and Disney's California Adventure require riders to be at least a certain height. (To view height requirements for each attraction, please see chapters 5 and 6.) While there are measuring sticks or signs to judge height at every attraction, each park now offers Goofy's Magic

Measure. This ultrasonic device allows a child's height to be checked one time rather than at every ride. Not only does this help avoid discrepancies and disappointments at the entrances to rides, but it also allows families to plan effectively which rides their children can go on. Each child is then given a colored wristband with a Disney character on it. For example, children under 35 inches tall receive a white wristband with Mickey Mouse on it. This allows them to ride all attractions that have no height requirements. Children over 35 inches but under 40 inches receive an orange Minnie Mouse wristband, which allows them to go on these attractions as well as the Matterhorn Bobsleds and Gadget's Go Coaster. Children at least 40 inches but under 46 inches receive a blue Donald Duck wristband, which allows them to ride these attractions plus Space Mountain, Big Thunder Mountain, Star Tours, and Splash Mountain. Finally, children 46 inches and above receive a green Goofy wristband, which allows them to ride all attractions, including Indiana Jones Adventure. These colors and characters on the wristbands are subject to change. California Adventure has its own color wristband system, since it has different height divisions.

Parent Swap

To accommodate families with small children who are unable to go on attractions that have height requirements or that might be too scary for them, Disneyland and California Adventure offer rider swaps. This allows part of a family to go on a ride while a parent or another adult waits with the younger children. Let the cast member at the entrance to the attraction know you want to do a parent swap, and he or she will give the waiting adult or group a pass. After the first group has waited in line and done the attraction, the waiting group can then go in through the exit or other designated area and give a cast member the pass. The group will then be allowed to board with little or no wait. Some attractions let you do a parent swap together with a FASTPASS. Ask the cast member at the entrance of the attraction for more information about parent swaps.

The Baby Care Centers

If you have infants or young children, the Baby Care Centers may become some of your favorite spots in the theme parks. That may seem a bit of an exaggeration, but, really, these places are great for changing diapers and taking care of other needs.

The Baby Care Center in Disneyland is located at the end of Main Street, by the photo shop and near the Plaza Inn. Disney's California Adventure also features a Baby Care Center. It is located near the Mission Tortilla Factory in the Pacific Wharf District. When you first enter, a cast member will welcome and direct you where to go based on your need. The Changing Room is very nice and contains four padded changing tables. Each has high sides and even Velcro belts to help keep your child safe. In addition, there is a dunking toilet for rinsing out cloth diapers and a sink for washing up. Al-

Insider's Secret

If any of your little ones are potty training, be sure to bring them to the Changing Room, where there are two small toilets that are just their size. There is even a short sink where they can wash up.

though most restrooms around the park have small changing stations, it is worth the walk to visit the Baby Care Center unless you are in a hurry. Both moms and dads can take a child into the Changing Room.

The Baby Care Center also has a Feeding Area with several high chairs. A cast member can warm up baby food or a bottle for you if needed. Some children have trouble eating in loud areas with lots of action going on, such as are found at most of Disneyland's restaurants. However, the Feeding Room is nice and quiet, giving both the child and the parent a chance to rest and relax for a bit. The Nursing Area has several comfortable chairs for mothers to nurse a child. You can use this area for bottle feeding as well. Unlike the other areas, fathers are not allowed in here.

The cast members are quite helpful. However, the Baby Care Center has some rules that must be followed. Each adult can take only one child in at a time, and only one adult can go in per child. This can be difficult for families with more than two small children or single parents with more than one small child. However, if it is a slow day and the Baby Care Center is not busy, these rules may be relaxed a bit.

Helpful Hint

Two words about Disneyland Resort bathrooms: magic toilets. Many of the restrooms at Disneyland have an automatic flush feature. Although this is convenient and sanitary, some children may be frightened when the toilet flushes by itself. These toilets can be identified by their little red sensor. Warn your children in advance that these toilets flush on their own, so they will think the toilets are cool rather than scary.

The Baby Care Center also sells a number of commonly needed items. These include diapers, baby wipes, powder, diaper rash ointment, formula, bottles, baby food, pacifiers, and even children's acetaminophen (Tylenol). You will pay more for these things here than at a regular store, but if you need them, they are available.

First Aid

Each park has its own first aid station. In Disneyland, it is located by the Plaza Inn. California Adventure's first aid station is next to the Mission Tortilla Factory. In addition to taking care of minor injuries, each first aid station also has a variety of medicines for allergies, coughs, diarrhea, and pain. These are provided one dose at a time. The first aid station will even record when you took the dose and let you know when you can come back for another dose if necessary.

Helpful Hint

It is always a good idea to carry basic first aid supplies (such as Band-Aids and cleansing wipes) around in your backpack. This allows you to take care of small cuts or scratches without having to go to the first aid station.

Expectant Mothers

Disneyland and California Adventure each have several attractions that could be dangerous for expectant mothers. Each is noted in the guides for the parks as well as at the entrances to the rides themselves. Heed these warnings! They are not there just for legal reasons. Even if you have been on the ride before and don't think it is too rough, still refrain. These rides may have sudden stops or jolts during the course of operation, possibly causing injury or complications.

Although most people would not think this ride rough, there are warning signs even on the Autopia at Disneyland. The ride may seem tame, but the driver behind you may not stop in time and may hit your car, causing a sudden bump. Also, the drops in Pirates of the Caribbean can be uncomfortable for some expectant mothers. Check with your doctor before going on vacation, and ask what types of attractions you should avoid.

Although there are some things expectant mothers cannot do at the Disney Resort, there are even more things they can do. Most rides are fine, and of course there are the shows and other nonride attractions.

Stroller Rentals

You can rent strollers at a number of places within the Disney parks. At Disneyland, the rental place is on the right, just inside the main gate, as well as at Star Traders in Tomorrowland. At California Adventure, you can rent strollers to the right of the main gate. During the busy season, they may also be available at the Fly 'n' Buy in Condor Flats and Souvenir 66 in Paradise Pier. Strollers are $7 for the day. Be sure to keep your receipt. If your stroller is lost, or if you leave the park and come back later, you can just take the receipt to a stroller rental location, and the attendant will be happy to provide another for you.

We suggest bringing your own stroller if at all possible. Not only does this save you money each day, but you also have the stroller for transporting tired children back to the car or hotel after a long day at the park. It is also a good idea if you plan on visiting Downtown Disney or the hotel shops and restaurants.

It is important to mark your stroller in some way. No matter where you got your stroller, chances are, there is at least one just like it at the park. We have found that brightly colored luggage tags work quite well. Attach the tag to the handle, or right next to it, so other people will see right away that the stroller is not theirs. Be sure you have your name printed on the tag. Balloons also work well for distinguishing your stroller from someone else's. During the day, you will have to park and leave your stroller several times while going on attractions. Try to park the stroller close to the attraction's exit so you can quickly load up and head on to the next attraction. Also, be sure to take any valuables with you. If your stroller is missing when you come back, don't panic. At times, cast members move strollers to a parking area to clear an area for a parade or another event. Just look around or ask a cast member for help.

When riding the monorail or a tram, you will have to fold up your stroller to take it aboard. A cast member is usually around to help out if needed.

Insider's Secret

At the Tomorrowland monorail station, there is an elevator for handicapped guests. However, cast members also let families with sleeping children in a stroller use the elevator. You still have to take them out before boarding the monorail, but you can hold off until the train actually arrives. The Downtown Disney station's elevator has no restrictions.

Lockers

Both parks offer lockers for storing items while visiting. These are great for holding coats or sweatshirts during the day so you don't have to carry them around. Then get them when it gets cold. At Disneyland, they are located on Main Street near the cone shop as well as by the Fantasyland Theatre. The lockers in California Adventure are inside and to the west of the main gate.

If you will be doing several attractions close to one another, such as in Fantasyland, park your stroller in a central location and leave it while you do all the attractions. This saves the time of loading, moving the stroller to the next stop, and then unloading again.

Rain and Bad Weather

During your vacation at the Disneyland Resort, it may rain on you. This is less likely during the summer, but it can happen at any time of the year. Often short showers drop a bit of rain and then move on, leaving the remainder of the day nice and sunny. However, at times you may have nonstop rain all day long. Although many of the attractions are actually indoors, a few are not. However, even the outdoor attractions still operate in the rain. If the rain continues, parades, character greetings, and outdoor shows will probably be canceled.

If you expect rain, it is advisable to bring a raincoat or poncho. You can also purchase ponchos inside the parks: children's are $5, and adults' are $6. Not only do they keep you dry, but they also make great souvenirs. An adult poncho easily covers most strollers and keeps the occupants dry.

Although rainy days may seem like a bad time for Disneyland or California Adventure, attendance then is usually down and the queues are quite short. When we visited the parks on rainy days, we could walk onto just about every attraction without a wait. The Jungle Cruise was a lot of fun, and the rain made the attraction all the more realistic.

Child Safety

Disneyland is a large place with lots of people, especially small children. A child can easily slip away from your group, causing instant panic for Mom and Dad. Here are a few tips to keep your child safe and easily identifiable.

- For each day you are at the resort, pick a bright color, such as yellow, orange, or light blue, for all family members to wear. This will help you easily spot your children in a crowd and also make it easier for your children to see you.

- Carry a photo ID card or a photo with vital information on the back for each child touring with you. Then if they get separated, you have a photo to show to cast members and you can tell them he or she is wearing the same color as you are.

- In your child's pocket or shoe, place a card with your child's name, your name, your cell phone number or other number where you can be reached, the name of your hotel, and at least one emergency contact.

- Do not dress your child in Christmas colors if you are traveling during the holiday season. Just about every small child will be wearing red or green during this time.

- If you have a child that is always running away or wandering off, try using a child safety leash. These are available at most children's stores and can prevent a lot of parental stress, in that you won't have to chase your child down Main Street. Some children even feel more secure while wearing a safety leash. If your child does not want to wear it, try explaining that you're using it so Mommy or Daddy will not get lost.

CHAPTER

5

Disneyland®–
The Magic
Kingdom®

Disneyland Attractions

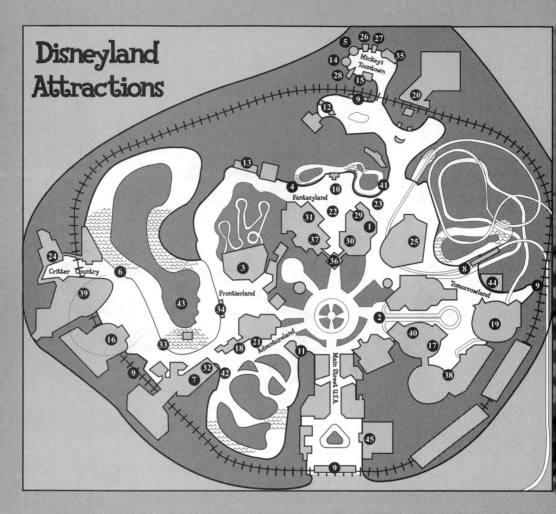

1. Alice in Wonderland
2. Astro Orbitor
3. Big Thunder Mountain Railroad
4. Casey Jr. Circus Train
5. Chip 'n' Dale Treehouse
6. Davy Crockett's Explorer Canoes
7. Disney Gallery
8. Disneyland Monorail
9. Disneyland Railroad
10. Dumbo the Flying Elephant
11. Enchanted Tiki Room
12. Fantasyland Theatre
13. Festival of Fools
14. Gadget's Go Coaster
15. Goofy's Bounce House
16. Haunted Mansion
17. Honey, I Shrunk the Audience
18. Indiana Jones Adventure
19. Innoventions
20. It's a Small World
21. Jungle Cruise
22. King Arthur Carrousel
23. Mad Tea Party

24. The Many Adventures of Winnie the Pooh
25. Matterhorn Bobsleds
26. Mickey's House
27. Minnie's House
28. Miss Daisy
29. Mr. Toad's Wild Ride
30. Peter Pan's Flight
31. Pinocchio's Daring Journey
32. Pirates of the Caribbean
33. Rafts to Tom Sawyer's Island
34. Riverboat and Sailing Ship
35. Roger Rabbit's Car Toon Spin
36. Sleeping Beauty Castle
37. Snow White's Scary Adventure
38. Space Mountain
39. Splash Mountain
40. Star Tours
41. Storybook Land Canal Boats
42. Tarzan's Treehouse
43. Tom Sawyer's Island
44. Tomorrowland Autopia
45. The Walt Disney Story

Disneyland first opened on July 17, 1955. Since that time, millions of families have enjoyed this happy place and created memories that will last a lifetime. We have written this chapter to help you create some great memories with your family.

Plan Your Day

Chapter 4 emphasized the importance of planning your day at the Disneyland Resort. In addition to getting your tickets in advance and deciding on the types of meals you want to eat in the park, you should also have an idea of what attractions are available, where they are located, and when you want to do them. Following are some hints and suggestions to help you see and do as much as possible during your visit.

What to Do First?

By the time you walk through the front gates of Disneyland, you should know what attraction you are going to hit first.

When the park first opens, and for about the first hour or two, the queues, or lines, for most attractions are quite short. Therefore, you want to hit the most popular rides first. If you have young children, this is simple—go to Fantasyland. This land gets really busy and congested by midmorning and will usually remain that way until evening. If you want to ride the Tomorrowland Autopia afterward, make a detour and pick up some FASTPASSes for it on your way to Fantasyland.

For families with older children, head toward Splash Mountain, the Indiana Jones Adventure, and Big Thunder Mountain. Or you can do the Matterhorn and Autopia. You want to spend most of your time riding during the first hour or two, so try to keep walking to a minimum. If you will be visiting Disneyland for two or more days, choose one side of the park to start on one morning and then hit the other side the next morning. With Space Mountain closed until 2005, there is really no rush to get to Tomorrowland. In fact, older children will probably want to stay on the opposite side of the park for most of the day, only venturing to Tomorrowland to

Time-Saving Tip

If you need a stroller, you can rent one just inside the front gate on the right side. However, if there is a long line there, head over to Star Traders in Tomorrowland. Most people don't realize that strollers are also available there, and the lines are much shorter. However, to save both time and money, it is often advisable to just bring along your own stroller. If size and weight are a concern, the small umbrella strollers are light and fold up quite nicely.

take in Star Tours and Autopia during the afternoon when the other rides are busy.

Although the morning may seem a rush, you don't have to keep up this pace all day long. In fact, once the queues start to get long, you can take a break and begin seeing the shows or more restful attractions.

Shows and Parades

Along with meals, you should also plan which shows and parades your family would like to see. These take place only at certain times, and only on certain days off season. At the Disneyland Web site, you can see the days the major shows and the parades are showing as well as the show times. They are listed in the *Disneyland Today* guide, which you can pick up at the entrance. During times waiting in queues, you can decide which shows you want to see and when. As a general rule, the early showings are usually less crowded.

Disneyland's newest fireworks shows are incredible. The current show as this book goes to print, "Believe . . . There's Magic in the Stars," is fantastic and features a choreographed display of fireworks and music with a special appearance by Tinkerbell, who flies down from the Matterhorn and over Sleeping Beauty's Castle. When the fireworks show starts, you want to be in a good position to watch it. A lot of guests line up in front of Sleeping Beauty's Castle, which is lit up during the show, and some fireworks actually launch from the castle itself. However, you have a better view in Fantasyland by the King Arthur Carrousel or near "It's a Small World." Disneyland usually has a parade that runs throughout the year. During the off-season, it may run only on weekends. Check the

Disneyland Today guide for the days and times it runs. As a general rule, you want to find a seat close to where the parade begins. If there is only one parade during the day, it will begin by "It's a Small World" and end at Main Street. This is the same route the parade takes for the first showing when it runs twice a day as well. For the first showing, you want to find a place to sit near "It's a Small World." That way, once the parade has passed, you can get back to the attractions. The second showing of the parade takes the same route but in reverse, beginning on Main Street. Therefore, try to find a seat near the Central Plaza. Main Street is often very crowded, so try to avoid it.

Time-Saving Tip

Even if you don't plan on watching a parade or a big show like *Fantasmic!* check out when these start. During the parade, it can be very difficult, if not impossible, to get from Tomorrowland to the rest of the park. Also, these events attract a lot of guests, meaning shorter lines at the popular rides. Take advantage of this.

Character Greetings and Locations

This section applies primarily to families with younger children. When you receive a copy of the *Disneyland Today* guide, check it for the times and locations of character greetings. You can also find the times for the character storytelling, which is great for the little ones. Because the characters are usually around for most of the day, you don't have to rush around to catch them. However, if you will be in an area near them, you might as well stop by and see them. Most characters head back to their homes later in the afternoon or early in the evening, so don't put off meeting them until late or you may miss them.

Before You Leave the Park

If you plan on leaving the park during the day and then return later, be sure to have your hand stamped and hold on to your tickets. You will need both to get back in. Also, if you rented a stroller, return it and hold on to the receipt and you can get another stroller when you return to the park later that day. The same goes for your parking ticket. Save it and you will not have to pay a parking fee again for the day.

No matter what time the park closes, there is always a mad rush to the front gate around closing time. Rather than wait in another line, stay and enjoy Disneyland some more. Although the attractions will stop operating, most shops and restaurants will stay open for a bit, and everything on Main Street remains open for an hour after the park closes. So take some time to do a little shopping or get a bite to eat.

If the park closes early and the wait isn't too long, take the monorail to Downtown Disney and spend time at these shops and restaurants, some of which stay open as late as 2 A.M. when Disneyland stays open until midnight. Check the Disneyland Web site for show times if you plan to see a movie or take in some of the live entertainment at one of the restaurants. This is a very good idea when the park closes at 6 P.M. and you have to drive. Not only do you want to avoid the rush out of the parking lots or garage, but you also want to miss the traffic on the freeways as Southern California heads home for the evening. You might even consider catching a movie.

Touring Plans

It is always a good idea to have a plan of how you want to tour Disneyland. That way you do not waste time deciding every little thing while you are at the park and you are sure to not forget anything. In this section, we have put together some tips for making your own touring plan and have provided some sample plans of our own. Because every family is different, each should have its own plan. Use our samples as an outline, and then customize one to fit your family.

The key to a good plan is to be prepared. A week or two before you leave on your vacation, you should get a map of the park to acquaint yourself with where everything is located. You can find a map on the Disneyland Web site or request one by calling 714-781-4560. You can also use the map included in this book. Second, read about each attraction in the following section of this chapter. Depending on the makeup of your family, not all attractions will appeal to you. Third, once you are familiar with the attractions available, have a family meeting where everyone gets to provide input as to what they want to do at Disneyland.

Fourth, divide each day into three main sections: morning, afternoon, and evening. In the morning, you will want to hit the popular attractions, which get busy later in the day. The afternoon is good for meals and restful attractions. If you are staying for several days and the park is open late, you might even consider returning to the hotel with younger children so they can take a nap before returning in the evening. Then in the evening, you can watch the parade, the fireworks, and *Fantasmic!* and also hit some more attractions.

While organizing all the attractions into your schedule, use the map so you are not running back and forth from one side of the park to the next. Not only would that waste time, but it would also wear out your family. We are not recommending you see everything in one area before moving to the next; that would be just as bad. Instead, think of your plan as making laps around the park. During the morning you make one lap, hitting the popular rides. In the afternoon you make a second lap, covering shows and attractions with shorter queues as well as the popular rides with FASTPASSes. Then in the evening, the final lap lets you hit the attractions you missed earlier or want to do again.

The following lists divide the attractions according to the best times to do them. Throughout this book, we refer to younger and older children. Where the cutoff is depends on your child. Younger children are the ones who will not care for the roller coaster and fast rides or are not tall enough to meet the minimum height requirements. These children are usually 5 or 6 years of age or younger. Older children love the fast and wild rides and want to avoid the kiddie rides. They are 7 years or older. If you have children in both categories, then you will have to make compromises to keep everyone happy. Now let's take a look at what to do when.

Popular Attractions for the Morning Lap

Here's a touring plan for first thing in the morning:

@ Younger Children (6 and Under)

The Fantasyland rides (Dumbo and the dark rides: Peter Pan, Mr. Toad, Snow White, Pinocchio, and Alice)

Toontown—best seen in the morning because it gets busy in the afternoon and closes early

Autopia

Astro Orbitor

ℰ Older Children (7 and Up)

Indiana Jones Adventure

Splash Mountain

Big Thunder Mountain Railroad

The Matterhorn Bobsleds

Popular Attractions for the Afternoon Lap

Now that you've been in the park all morning, here's a plan for the afternoon:

ℰ Younger Children (6 and Under)

Mickey's Detective School

"It's a Small World"

Enchanted Tiki Room

Jungle Cruise

Tarzan's Treehouse

Pirates of the Caribbean

The Many Adventures of Winnie the Pooh

Canoes and riverboats

Tom Sawyer Island

Disneyland Railroad

Innoventions

Character Storytimes and Greetings

Afternoon Parade

Main Street Cinema

@ Older Children (7 and Up)

Pirates of the Caribbean

Haunted Mansion

Jungle Cruise

Tom Sawyer Island

Canoes and riverboats

Innoventions

Star Tours

Mad Tea Party

Popular rides with FASTPASSes

Popular Attractions for the Evening Lap

To finish up your day at Disneyland, here is a touring plan to please all ages:

Honey, I Shrunk the Audience

Fantasmic!

Fireworks

Anything you missed earlier or want to do again

These are just basic lists to give you a good idea of when to do the various types of attractions. You may have noticed that we did not list every attraction. However, you can get the general idea from those included.

Next we have put together some sample plans. The first two are for those families with only a single day at the park, with separate plans for younger and older children. The final two are two-day plans for younger and older children, respectively. For all plans, arrive at Disney an hour before opening so that you can enter Main Street early and be near the end of Main Street when they drop the rope and begin allowing guests to enter. (*Note:* You may not have time to do everything on these sample plans. They are designed for a typical day. However, on days when it is very busy, you will have to cut some of the attractions.)

Sample One-Day Touring Plan (Children 6 and Under)

Morning

Right at the start, head straight to Sleeping Beauty's Castle. Pass through the castle and ride the Dumbos.

Ride all the dark rides you care to (Peter Pan's Flight, Mr. Toad's Wild Ride, and so on), as well as the Casey Jr. Circus Train. Walk toward the Matterhorn and then turn left and continue past "It's a Small World" to Mickey's Toontown. Ride Roger Rabbit's Car Toon Spin and Gadget's Go Coaster. Have a snack while you wait in line for Mickey's House.

Go to Minnie's House.

Afternoon

Have a late lunch somewhere other than Toontown or Fantasyland. If you eat in Tomorrowland, get a FAST-PASS for the Autopia first. Elsewhere, get a FASTPASS for Splash Mountain or The Many Adventures of Winnie the Pooh first.

In Tomorrowland, ride the Autopia, see *Calling All Space Scouts . . . A Buzz Lightyear Adventure,* and then go to Splash Mountain for a FASTPASS; otherwise, take in the following attractions after lunch until your FASTPASS time for Splash Mountain or The Many Adventures of Winnie the Pooh.

Ride Pirates of the Caribbean.

Ride the Jungle Cruise.

Visit Tarzan's Treehouse.

See *Mickey's Detective School.*

Evening

If the park is open late, have dinner. (If it closes early, eat afterward.)

Ride "It's a Small World."

Watch the parade.

Ride anything you missed earlier or want to do again.

See *Fantasmic!*

Sample One-Day Touring Plan (Children 7 and Up)

Morning

Right at the start, head left to Adventureland and ride the Indiana Jones Adventure.

Take a left at the exit and head toward Splash Mountain. Ride it.

Backtrack to Frontierland and pick up a FASTPASS for Big Thunder Mountain Railroad.

Ride the Matterhorn Bobsleds.

Get a FASTPASS for Pirates of the Caribbean.

Ride Big Thunder Mountain Railroad.

Ride Pirates of the Caribbean.

Afternoon

Go to New Orleans Square and get a FASTPASS for the Haunted Mansion.

Eat lunch in Frontierland or New Orleans Square.

Ride the Jungle Cruise.

Pick up a FASTPASS for Indiana Jones Adventure or Splash Mountain (whichever you would like to do again).

Ride the Haunted Mansion.

Visit the Enchanted Tiki Room or The Many Adventures of Winnie the Pooh.

Use the FASTPASS you picked up earlier.

Evening

Get a FASTPASS for the Autopia.

If the park is open late, have dinner. (If it closes early, eat afterward.)

Ride Star Tours.

Ride the Autopia.

Watch the parade.

Ride anything you missed earlier or want to do again.

See *Fantasmic!*

Sample Two-Day Touring Plan (Children 6 and Under)

With a couple days, you can see more attractions and slow down the pace a bit.

Day 1—Morning

Right at the start, head to Fantasyland. Ride the Dumbos.

Ride the other rides in Fantasyland.

See a Princess Storytelling.

Day 1—Afternoon

Have lunch away from Fantasyland and then head back to the hotel. Or head back to the hotel and eat nearby. (*Note:* If the park closes at 6 P.M., stay at the park and skip ahead to the evening activities.)

Rest by the pool or take a nap.

Return to the park and see *Calling All Space Scouts . . . A Buzz Lightyear Adventure.*

Day 1—Evening

Get a FASTPASS for the Autopia.

See Innoventions or have dinner.

Ride the Autopia.

Ride "It's a Small World."

Watch the parade.

Ride the Astro Orbitor.

As the children get tired, the adults can choose some rides, using the parent swap if necessary.

Watch the fireworks.

Head back to the hotel and rest up for day 2.

Day 2—Morning

Eat at one of the character breakfasts before the park opens.

On entering the park, walk past the Matterhorn and on to Mickey's Toontown.

Ride Roger Rabbit's Car Toon Spin.

Ride Gadget's Go Coaster.

Line up at Mickey's House and get a family picture.

Visit Minnie's House.

Day 2—Afternoon

Pick up a FASTPASS for The Many Adventures of Winnie the Pooh.

Eat lunch in Frontierland or Critter Country.

Ride the canoes and/or riverboats.

Ride The Many Adventures of Winnie the Pooh.

If the children are old enough, take the rafts over to Tom Sawyer Island.

Ride the Jungle Cruise.

Day 2—Evening

Have dinner in New Orleans Square.

Ride Pirates of the Caribbean.

Ride any other rides you missed or want to ride again.

See *Fantasmic!*

Sample Two-Day Touring Plan (Children 7 and Up)

Day 1—Morning

At the start, head to the Indiana Jones Adventure and pick up a FASTPASS.

Then go to the Blue Bayou restaurant and make reservations for around 2 P.M. if you did not call ahead of time for reservations.

Continue on to ride Splash Mountain.

If it is time for the Indiana Jones Adventure, pick up a FASTPASS for Big Thunder Mountain Railroad and then return to Adventureland.

Ride the Indiana Jones Adventure.

Pick up a FASTPASS for either Haunted Mansion or Pirates of the Caribbean—whichever has the longest line (Haunted Mansion during holidays).

Ride the attraction above with the shorter line.

Ride Big Thunder Mountain Railroad.

Ride either the Haunted Mansion or Pirates of the Caribbean, for which you picked up a FASTPASS.

Day 1—*Afternoon*

Have lunch in Tomorrowland.

Pick up a FASTPASS for the Autopia.

Ride Star Tours.

See *Honey, I Shrunk the Audience.*

See Innoventions.

Ride the Autopia.

Ride the Disneyland Railroad through the diorama to New Orleans Square.

Day 1—*Evening*

Pick up a FASTPASS for Big Thunder Mountain Railroad.

Have dinner in Frontierland.

Ride Big Thunder Mountain Railroad.

Watch the parade.

Watch the fireworks.

Hit some of the popular rides or even Fantasyland as people begin to leave.

Day 2—Morning

Head for the Matterhorn and ride the bobsleds.

Continue on to Toontown and ride Roger Rabbit's Cartoon Spin.

Make your way to Critter Country and pick up a FASTPASS for Splash Mountain.

Ride The Many Adventures of Winnie the Pooh.

Ride Splash Mountain.

Ride any of the popular rides you may have missed on day 1.

Get FASTPASSes for the busiest attractions and ride those that aren't so busy while waiting.

Day 2—Afternoon

Pick up a FASTPASS for the Indiana Jones Adventure.

Have lunch at the Blue Bayou restaurant.

Ride the Jungle Cruise.

Ride the Indiana Jones Adventure.

Ride canoes or riverboats.

Take rafts to Tom Sawyer Island.

Day 2—Evening

See attractions you missed earlier or want to do again.

Have a light dinner.

See *Fantasmic!*

Ride the Matterhorn and other popular rides before the park closes.

Depending on how busy Disneyland is when you visit, you may have to either delete some of the attractions from the plan or even add more to fill in time.

Three Days or More at Disneyland

If you have time for three or more days at Disneyland, use the two-day touring plan and then fill it in with more attractions. From talking to different families, as well as from personal experience, we have found that spending three days or even more at Disneyland lets you take a more leisurely pace and makes your family's vacation less stressful. You have time to go back to the hotel and take a nap or go for a swim without feeling as if you will miss something. Also, you have more time to spend at Disneyland for shows or storytelling times as well as the attractions that you can see at your leisure, such as Innoventions or Tom Sawyer Island.

During the mornings, still try to hit as many of the popular attractions as possible, then relax during the afternoon, picking up the pace a bit in the evening. Families that purchase a five-day Flex Passport might even spend a day at other attractions in Southern California and then come back to Disneyland in the evening. No matter how you choose to spend your time, we suggest spending the last day of your vacation at Disneyland as "favorites" day, going back to the attractions you liked best for one last time.

Because you have more time at Disneyland, you can also spend some of it shopping as well as experiencing the number of great restaurants. With the opening of Downtown Disney, there are now a number of great shops and dining establishments just outside the park in addition to those inside.

Disneyland FASTPASS Rides

As this book goes to print, Disneyland is currently offering the FASTPASS system on the following attractions:

- Autopia
- Big Thunder Mountain Railroad
- Haunted Mansion
- Indiana Jones Adventure
- The Many Adventures of Winnie the Pooh
- Pirates of the Caribbean
- Roger Rabbit's Car Toon Spin
- Splash Mountain
- Star Tours

The FASTPASS system may later be added to the Matterhorn Bobsleds or other attractions. During November and December, a temporary FASTPASS system is added to the holiday version of "It's a Small World."

As a general rule, you should always try to have a FAST-PASS for some attraction in your possession. You might as well be waiting for a FASTPASS time while waiting in line for another attraction, watching a show, or even enjoying a meal.

For more information on using the FASTPASS system, see chapter 4.

Time-Saving Tip

Don't forget to use the parent swap if you have small children who are unable to go on a ride. This allows part of a group to go on a ride while the rest stay with the younger children. When the first group is through, the waiting group can then go on without having to wait in the line again. This works great for all of the rides with height or age restrictions and even some of the others if you have a baby sleeping in the stroller or for other such reasons. See chapter 4 for more information on this service.

The Lands of the Magic Kingdom

Disneyland is divided into eight different lands—Main Street, Fantasyland, Tomorrowland, Mickey's Toontown, Frontierland, Adventureland, New Orleans Square, and Critter Country. Each has its own unique theme, and you will notice that the cast members dress differently depending on where they are working. The remainder of the chapter is organized by land. Each section contains information on the attractions in that land, shows you can see there, where to meet characters, basic tips for saving time in the land, and brief descriptions of the dining and shopping in the land.

The Scare Factor

In the following Quick Guide, as well as others covering attractions and rides, there is a column listing the scare factor

Hidden Mickeys

You may be asking yourself, "What is a Hidden Mickey?" Although Hidden Mickeys have been around for a long time, the general public is just beginning to become more aware of them. Just about everything built by or for Disney has an image of Mickey hidden somewhere. This includes every attraction at Disney theme parks, the Disney hotels, restaurants, and even the Disney Store in malls throughout the world. In all the excitement over finding these Hidden Mickeys, people are finding them everywhere—even where there are none. Therefore, there must be a standard. The following list gives the most commonly agreed-on standards we have been able to find.

1. The Mickey must consist of three circles—two smaller circles of the same approximate size attached to a larger circle to make the famous head and ears.

2. The Mickey must be intentionally placed, not an accidental arrangement.

3. The Mickey must be hidden. A Mickey pattern in carpet or wallpaper or other repeated use of the image does not count as a Hidden Mickey.

Now that the basic rules are in place, you are ready to begin your hunt. There are more than enough Hidden Mickeys at Disneyland to write a complete book about. We mention a few in the descriptions of the rides and attractions; however, this only represents a small fraction of those out there. While visiting Disneyland, politely ask cast members about Hidden Mickeys on the various attractions. Although most will not tell you specifically where one is, some may offer hints on where to look. Looking for Hidden Mickeys can add a new excitement to Disneyland for those on their first visit as well as veterans. Have fun and good luck on your hunt.

for attractions. This provides a general guide for how frightening the ride may be for young children. The causes for this range from a ride in the dark to a wild, breathtaking roller coaster or even an attraction where things pop out at you. To find out just what makes a ride scary, read the description of the ride within the chapter. Here is a key for the scare factor for this and other chapters in this book:

0 Not scary at all.
! Might be somewhat frightening for some children.
  Usually either dark or a mild roller coaster.
!! Most young children will find this scary.
!!! This attraction may frighten some adults. This is usually reserved for high-speed roller coasters and other thrill rides.

Main Street, USA

After entering the Magic Kingdom at the main gates and passing through one of the two tunnels under the railroad, you will find yourself on Main Street, USA. It is designed to represent a typical American town around the turn of the century (1900, not 2000, that is). Although Main Street consists mostly of shops, there are a few attractions here as well. As you stroll down the street, you may hear ragtime music, a barbershop quartet, or other types of entertainment from this era. The streets are lined with gaslights that originally lit the city of Baltimore, and the two cannons in the Town Square are French-made guns from the Franco-Prussian War. Although most guests rush down Main Street to get to the rest of the Magic Kingdom, there is a lot to see here. If you have the time, check out the buildings that line the streets. Whereas the ground level has real shops, read the names of the shops on

Quick Guide to

Attraction	Location	Height or Age Requirement
Aladdin and Jasmine Storytale Adventures	Adventureland	None
Alice in Wonderland	Fantasyland	None
Astro Orbitor	Tomorrowland	None
Autopia	Tomorrowland	1 year
Big Thunder Mountain Railroad	Frontierland	40 inches
Calling All Space Scouts . . . A Buzz Lightyear Adventure	Tomorrowland	None
Casey Jr. Circus Train	Fantasyland	None
Davy Crockett's Explorer Canoes	Critter Country	None
Disneyland Monorail	Tomorrowland	None
Disneyland Railroad	Main Street	None
Dumbo the Flying Elephant	Fantasyland	None
Enchanted Tiki Room	Adventureland	None
Fantasmic!	Frontierland	None
Frontierland Shootin' Exposition	Frontierland	None
Gadget's Go Coaster	Toontown	3 years
Golden Horseshoe Stage	Frontierland	None

0 Not scary at all.
! Might be somewhat frightening for some children. Usually either dark or a mild roller coaster.
!! Most young children will find this scary.
!!! This attraction may frighten some adults. This is usually reserved for high-speed roller coasters and other thrill rides.

Disneyland Attractions

Duration	Scare Factor	Age Range
15 minutes	0	All
4 minutes	0	All
1.5 minutes	0	3 and up
Approx. 4 minutes	0	All
3 minutes	!	4 and up
15 minutes	0	All
3 minutes	0	All
Approx. 10 minutes	0	5 and up
N/A	0	All
N/A	0	All
2 minutes	0	All
Approx. 15 minutes	0	All
Approx. 25 minutes	!	All
N/A	0	7 and up
1 minutes	0	3 and up
Approx. 15 minutes	0	All

(continues)

Quick Guide to

Attraction	Location	Height or Age Requirement
Goofy's Bounce House	Toontown	3 years and under 52 inches
Haunted Mansion	New Orleans Square	None
Honey, I Shrunk the Audience	Tomorrowland	None
Indiana Jones Adventure	Adventureland	46 inches
Innoventions	Tomorrowland	None
"It's a Small World"	Fantasyland	None
Jungle Cruise	Adventureland	None
King Arthur Carrousel	Fantasyland	None
Mad Tea Party	Fantasyland	None
The Many Adventures of Winnie the Pooh	Critter Country	None
Mark Twain Riverboat	Frontierland	None
Matterhorn Bobsleds	Fantasyland	3 years
Mickey's Detective School	Fantasyland	None
Mickey's House	Toontown	None
Minnie's House	Toontown	None
Mr. Toad's Wild Ride	Fantasyland	None
Peter Pan's Flight	Fantasyland	None
Pinocchio's Daring Journey	Fantasyland	None

0 Not scary at all.
! Might be somewhat frightening for some children. Usually either dark or a mild roller coaster.
!! Most young children will find this scary.
!!! This attraction may frighten some adults. This is usually reserved for high-speed roller coasters and other thrill rides.

Disneyland Attractions

Duration	Scare Factor	Age Range
NA	0	3 to 8
Approx. 7 minutes	!!	5 and up
Approx. 25 minutes	!	4 and up
3 minutes	!!!	7 and up
N/A	0	All
Approx. 12 minutes	0	All
8 minutes	0	All
2 minutes	0	All
1.5 minutes	0	3 and up
2½ minutes	0	All
14 minutes	0	All
Approx. 2 minutes	!	4 and up
Approx. 20 minutes	0	All
N/A	0	All
N/A	0	All
2 minutes	!	4 and up
2 minutes	0	All
3 minutes	!	4 and up

(continues)

Quick Guide to

Attraction	Location	Height or Age Requirement
Pirates of the Caribbean	New Orleans Sq.	None
Princess Storytelling	Fantasyland	None
Roger Rabbit's Car Toon Spin	Toontown	None
Sailing Ship Columbia	Frontierland	None
Snow White's Scary Adventures	Fantasyland	None
Space Mountain (closed until 2005)	Tomorrowland	40 inches
Splash Mountain	Critter Country	40 inches
Star Tours	Tomorrowland	40 inches
Storybook Land Canal Boats	Fantasyland	None
Tarzan's Treehouse	Adventureland	None
Tom Sawyer Island	Frontierland	None
The Walt Disney Story, featuring "Great Moments with Mr. Lincoln"	Main Street, USA	None

0 Not scary at all.
! Might be somewhat frightening for some children. Usually either dark or a mild roller coaster.
!! Most young children will find this scary.
!!! This attraction may frighten some adults. This is usually reserved for high-speed roller coasters and other thrill rides.

Disneyland Attractions

Duration	Scare Factor	Age Range
Approx. 14 minutes	!	4 and up
Approx. 15 minutes	0	All
3 minutes	0	5 and up
14 minutes	0	All
2 minutes	!	4 and up
Approx. 3 minutes	!!!	7 and up
Approx. 10 minutes	!	5 and up
7 minutes	!!	5 and up
10 minutes	0	All
Approx. 10 minutes	0	All
N/A	0	5 and up
Approx. 25 minutes	0	All

the second and third floors. The names of the proprietors are actual people who had a part in building Disneyland or were corporate executives. You may notice that the ground level seems a bit shorter than usual. This is especially apparent at the porch with a bench on it. The ground level is really $\frac{7}{8}$ scale, whereas the second floor is $\frac{5}{8}$ scale, and the third floor is $\frac{1}{2}$ scale. The buildings were designed this way to give the impression that they are actually taller than in reality, using the technique of forced perspective.

Main Street, USA, is also the business part of the Magic Kingdom. City Hall is the information center, where you can inquire about shows and guides for guests with disabilities, as well as pick up lost children.

Insider's Secret

If you are at Disneyland on the birthday of one of your family members, be sure to tell a cast member at City Hall. He or she will give you a personalized sticker to wear. People wearing these stickers will be wished happy birthday by cast members throughout the day, and characters will give them special attention.

You can purchase Disney Dollars as well as exchange foreign currency at the Bank of Main Street. There is also an ATM here. AAA has a Touring and Travel Services Center, where all guests can purchase travelers checks or AAA memberships. AAA members can pick up maps and tour guides and take advantage of several other services, such as hotel reservations and complimentary towing. The Baby Care Center has facilities for preparing formula and baby food, nursing, and changing diapers and sells various baby sundries.

Helpful Hint

If you need some cash, ATMs are located at the main entrance, at the Bank of Main Street, and in Frontierland, Fantasyland, and Tomorrowland.

Disneyland Railroad

The main station for the Disneyland Railroad is located at the south end of Main Street and the first thing guests see as they enter the park. Here you can board one of five steam-powered trains that circumnavigate the Magic Kingdom. (The number of trains running depends on the day and the expected crowd.) The train also makes stops at New Orleans Square, Mickey's Toontown, and Tomorrowland. In between the Tomorrowland and Main Street stations, the train passes through a large diorama depicting the Grand Canyon. After passing by the various wildlife of this area, the train continues into the Primeval World, featuring 46 animated dinosaurs. Although most young children love this part and want to see it again, it may be scary for some. You can either get off at Tomorrowland before the diorama or just tell them to close their eyes. Usually the dark tunnel preceding the

Fun Fact

Walt Disney used to stay in an apartment located over the Fire Station. As a memorial to Disneyland's founder, a light in the window remains lit at all times. During the holidays, the light is replaced by a small Christmas tree.

diorama is scarier than the animatronic dinosaurs. The train takes around 20 minutes to circle the park.

Fun Fact

The Main Street Station contains a display of a model train that was hand built by Walt Disney himself.

Insider's Secret

If it is a slow day and the railroad is not very busy, ask one of the conductors if you can ride in the steam engine. Each has either one or two jump-seats, which are for adults only. The conductor will ask the engineer if it is all right. Main Street Station is the only place where you can board and disembark from the engine. Be warned that the engineer's compartment is oily.

Helpful Hint

You can fold up your stroller and take it on the train with you. Otherwise, you will have to go back to the station where you boarded to pick up your stroller instead of getting off at a different station during your ride.

The Walt Disney Story, featuring "Great Moments with Mr. Lincoln"

Housed in the Disneyland Opera House, this attraction has two parts. First, there is a 15-minute film about Walt Disney and a display of his offices from the Burbank studio. On his desk are models of his two personal airplanes, the *Mickey I* and the *Mickey II,* and beside the desk is his briefcase. The second part of the attraction features a short slide show on the Civil War. When it is over, a seated audio-animatronic Abraham Lincoln rises and begins speaking. His discourse is taken from various speeches the president made.

Older children will usually enjoy learning about Walt Disney and how he created his animated characters and films. Mr. Lincoln's speech is very stirring and patriotic, and children who have studied the president will be impressed. Younger children will not care for this as much.

Insider's Secret
This attraction is a good place to visit in the afternoon. It is rarely crowded and offers a chance to sit down and rest for a while. Unlike other attractions, you can stay as long as you want, and on hot days, the air conditioning makes it nice for cooling down.

Main Street Cinema
This small theater continuously plays old Mickey Mouse cartoons. Since the theater is air-conditioned, it makes a good place to take a break. Children also usually like to see the older cartoons, which are rarely shown outside this theater. If your family is waiting on Main Street for a parade, part of your group can go watch some of the cartoons while the rest hold the spot. Then you all can swap so everyone has a chance to enjoy the entertainment.

Main Street Vehicles
Main Street is traveled by four different vehicles that carry passengers from Town Square to Central Plaza. You can

choose to ride a horse-drawn streetcar, a fire engine, a horse-less carriage, or an omnibus. Each has its own stop at either end of Main Street, and the ride is one way only. They stop operating in the afternoon or an hour or more before the parades begin. Although young children may enjoy the ride, older children will want to get on to the rides in other areas of the park.

Central Plaza

Located at the opposite end of Main Street from the train station, Central Plaza is the hub of the Magic Kingdom. The Partners statue, featuring Walt and Mickey, stands in the middle and makes a great place for a family photo. If you look at the ring on Walt's finger, you will see a Hidden Mickey.

Helpful Hint

In the Central Plaza, near the entrance to Adventureland, is an Information Center. The cast member here can provide information on show times and most other types of questions. In addition, there is an information board here showing which attractions are closed for the day and approximate wait times for the more popular attractions. Because this is located in the center of Disneyland, pass by here after you leave one area to help plan where you should go next.

Shows

Although Main Street does not have any shows per se, you can find live performers here throughout the day. There is usually a pianist at the Refreshment Corner. Watch out for the Dapper Dans. This quartet sings as they pedal down Main Street on their four-person bicycle. Just after the park officially opens, the Disneyland Marching Band parades from Town Square, down Main Street, through Sleeping Beauty's Castle, and into Fantasyland. At times they will board the King Arthur Carrousel and treat guests to a rousing performance, which may include the "William Tell Overture." (This was the theme for *The Lone Ranger.*) At sunset each day, you can view the patriotic flag retreat as the flag at Town Square is lowered.

Character Greetings

Children can meet several different characters near Town Square and by the Fire Station. These characters are usually here from park opening until later in the afternoon.

Main Street Tips

Although Main Street is the first area you enter at Disneyland, just walk right down to the end and head to one of the other areas containing popular rides. It is better to come back to Main Street later and use the attractions here as a break or rest for the children.

Main Street opens 30 minutes before the rest of the park. If you arrive that early, while you are waiting you might want to pick up a cinnamon roll and some orange juice or a hot drink, or browse through the many shops.

People begin lining up along Main Street 30 minutes to an hour before a parade. If you want to view the parade here, get your place early. Otherwise, make sure you stay clear of the area until after the parade has passed. The crowds can be difficult to get through, especially with a stroller.

Dining on Main Street

Main Street is a great place to have a snack or lunch because most guests are in other parts of the park and eating at places in those areas. The Plaza Inn offers a character breakfast buffet in the morning and buffeteria-style dining for lunch and dinner.

Carnation Café is the only table service restaurant on Main Street and serves salads, sandwiches, and other meals. At Refreshment Corner you can find foot-long hot dogs and Mickey Mouse pretzels. The Blue Ribbon Bakery serves great cinnamon rolls and other baked goodies. For ice cream or frozen yogurt, try the Gibson Girl Ice Cream Parlor or the Main Street Cone Shop for just ice cream. Seasonally, there are two carts near the Plaza Inn. One sells corn dogs—the only ones in the park—and the other sells tamales and chimichangas. There is also a fruit stand that sells a variety of seasonal fruit. For more details on these restaurants, including pricing and sample menus, see chapter 8.

Main Street Shopping

You can do almost all of your shopping on Main Street. The Emporium stocks just about every Disneyland souvenir imaginable. There are also several other specialty shops that line Main Street. Disneyana offers Disney collectibles including figurines and animation cels, along with other types of limited-edition art. At the 20th Century Music Company you can find all types of Disney music, including sheet music to play yourself. You can also create your own souvenir CD of your favorite music from Disneyland. There are over 150 selections from which to choose for your 10-track CD. The Candy Palace sells yummy treats, some of which are made in a kitchen with a large window facing Main Street. From Main Street, you can watch through this window to see the cooks making all types of treats. During the Christmas season, be sure to ask one of the cast members in the shop when they will be making candy canes. It is fun to watch; and if you want to buy some, stay close because they sell as fast as they're packaged. Adjacent to this shop is the Penny Arcade, where you can find penny-type candy as well as old-time arcade games to play. The China

Closet carries snowglobes and figurines, and Crystal Arts sells glass and crystal creations. Be careful taking small children into these two shops. Disney Clothiers sells fashionable clothing (not souvenir-type T-shirts) and accessories that feature Disney characters in some way. The Disney Showcase is the place for sports-related items, featuring the Anaheim Angels and the Mighty Ducks of Anaheim. You can also purchase tickets for these two teams during their respective seasons. The Main Street Magic Shop stocks not only magic tricks but also gags and books on the subject. Need some mouse ears? The Mad Hatter Shop can help cover you with a variety of headwear. The Main Street Photo Supply Company sells cameras and film and will even help you with your camera if it develops problems. In addition, if you have souvenir photos taken by a cast member somewhere in the park, this is where you go to view and purchase them. You can also find some nice frames for displaying your family's photo. The Market House has gourmet food, kitchen accessories, and treats. New Century Jewelry offers Disney-inspired pieces, and New Century Time Pieces is the place for watches and clocks. Finally, at the

Helpful Hint

No matter what your budget, you can find something on Main Street to remind you of your visit to Disneyland. The inexpensive Mickey and Minnie antenna balls are very popular. Videos and CDs are also great ways to relive your vacation long after you have returned home. Note that most of the merchandise you find at Disneyland is available nowhere else—not even the Disney Stores in many shopping malls. However, if you forget something you just have to have, you can call the Disneyland order line: 800-362-4533.

Silhouette Studio, you can find a souvenir, watching the creation of which is not only interesting but also half the fun.

Fantasyland

Fantasyland is the place where many of Disney's animated features come to life. The area has a medieval European village theme, with Sleeping Beauty's Castle as the focal point. There are several attractions here, and because this is where many of the kiddie rides are located, Fantasyland can become quite congested, even on a day with a moderate number of guests. For families with younger children, you will spend quite a bit of time here, probably going on some of the rides a number of times.

Time-Saving Tip

If your family is using a stroller, park it in one location while in Fantasyland. All of the attractions are fairly close to one another, so it is easier to just carry a small child from one ride to the next rather than loading and unloading the stroller at each place.

Sleeping Beauty's Castle

Though currently closed with an indefinite reopening date, Sleeping Beauty's Castle is also an attraction in itself. Inside are dioramas that tell the story of Princess Aurora, a.k.a. Sleeping Beauty. The pathway through the castle is narrow and involves climbing and descending stairs, making it difficult to see with toddlers. If you read all the text at each diorama, the walkthrough of the castle takes approximately 10 minutes. Look for a Hidden Mickey in one of the storybooks! However, while the interior attraction with the dioramas is closed, guests can still walk through the drawbridge connecting Main

Street to Fantasyland and visit the shops. Rumor has it that the castle interior may be refurbished for Disneyland's 50th anniversary in 2005. If this is the case, there may be something completely new inside.

Fun Fact

Sleeping Beauty's Castle is adorned by a number of 22-karat gold-plated spires. However, you may notice that one spire is not gold plated. Walt Disney did this as a reminder of his quote that Disneyland would never be completed as long as there was imagination left in the world. The shield over the drawbridge displays the Disney family crest.

Fun Fact

Some of the dolls in the diorama were donated by Shirley Temple, who did the voice of Snow White for Disney's animated feature.

King Arthur's Carrousel

It was during weekend visits to ride the carousel at Griffith Park with his young daughters that Walt Disney first began thinking of creating Disneyland. Therefore, it is no surprise that he wanted his carousel as the center of Fantasyland. The ride contains 72 horses that were carved over 100 years ago in Germany. Each horse is unique. This ride is a favorite for children of all ages, and there is rarely a long line because it can accommodate so many guests at a time. The carousel plays Disney music as it goes around and is a sight at night when all lit up.

Helpful Hint

For a great place to watch the fireworks display, sit on the planters that surround the carousel, on the side toward Mr. Toad's Wild Ride. Not only can you sit down, but also you are in perfect position to view Tinkerbell as she flies right over you.

Peter Pan's Flight

One of the five dark rides in Fantasyland, Peter Pan's Flight carries guests in hanging pirate ships out through the nursery window, over London, and on a journey to Never Land. The ride does an excellent job following the story line of the movie, and children of all ages will enjoy it. Some children may not like the darkness of the ride. However, we have found that if you point out different things to look at, they will soon forget that the ride is dark and want to go on it again. There are several Hidden Mickeys in this ride. Look for the one on the moon while flying over London.

Fun Fact

As you go through the nursery, notice the picture of Mickey Mouse and the blocks on the floor that spell *Peter, Pan,* and *Disney.* (The s in *Disney* is an upside-down 5.)

Mr. Toad's Wild Ride

This tends to be one of the more popular rides in Fantasyland and usually has the longest lines of the five dark rides. Mr. Toad's Wild Ride takes guests on little motor cars through various scenes from the movie *The Adventures of Ichabod and Mr. Toad.* After crashing through a fireplace, the cars take you through a number of close calls, reminiscent of Toad's crazy driving, before ending in a fiery inferno with heat added for realism. Although small children often want to ride this attraction because they can turn the steering wheel on the car and pretend they are really driving, many get scared during the ride, especially during the inferno at the end.

Scare Factor
Some small children may get scared during Mr. Toad's Wild Ride, especially during the inferno at the end.

Fun Fact

Trivia

Above the entrance to the attraction, a shield bears the motto *"Toadi Acceleratio Semper Absurda."* Translated from the Latin, this means "Speeding with Toad is always absurd."

Snow White's Scary Adventures

Just as its name suggests, this ride can be scary for little children. Guests board mine cars and ride along through scenes from the movie, including the house of the Seven Dwarfs, the mine where they work, a dungeon, and a scary forest. The evil queen even offers you a poisoned apple (it is a hologram). Some children may be scared, but others really like it. Use their reactions to scary parts of the movie as a way to judge what their reactions might be. Even during the scary parts, you can point out things that aren't so scary to divert their attention. In the room where Snow White is going up the stairs, look at the shell of the turtle to find a Hidden Mickey.

Scare Factor

Some children may be scared by Snow White's Scary Adventures, but others really like it. Use their reactions to scary parts of the movie as a way to judge what their reactions might be.

Insider's Secret

Watch the windows above the entrance to this ride. Every so often, the evil queen looks out from behind a curtain. Also, when you are at the entrance to the ride, be sure to touch the golden apple. It will cause thunder to sound and the evil queen to give a wicked laugh.

Pinocchio's Daring Journey

Similar to the other dark rides, this one takes guests through various scenes from the movie. It tends to be a bit scary in several places, such as when Monstro the Whale jumps up at you, Stromboli tries to cage you, or the bad guys on Pleasure Island try to crate you up and ship you off to the salt mines. The scary parts pass quickly; the darkness of the ride is usually what frightens young children the most. See how they do on Peter Pan's Flight first, and if the darkness is no problem, they

Scare Factor

The darkness of Pinocchio's Daring Journey is usually what frightens young children the most. They will probably be fine as long as a parent or older sibling is sitting next to them.

will probably be fine on this one as long as a parent or older sibling is sitting next to them.

Insider's Secret

At the end of the ride, be sure to point out the Blue Fairy to kids. She appears only for a moment, and if you are looking somewhere else, you will miss her. It is a neat effect. Also, look for Jiminy Cricket with his new badge.

Alice in Wonderland

On this ride, guests travel in caterpillars following the White Rabbit through Wonderland. Although this is listed as a dark ride, Alice in Wonderland is actually quite bright. There are several special effects and lots of things to look at. In fact, be sure to look in all directions, even behind you, as some characters are difficult to see

Insider's Secret

If you look down at the pathway outside this attraction, you will see the footprints of the White Rabbit.

until you pass them by. After meeting the Queen of Hearts and then escaping from her deck of card retainers, the ride

Fun Fact

While going through the five dark rides, you may notice that the main character in each rarely appears. For example, Alice and Snow White appear only once in their respective rides. The reason for this is because in the ride the guests are supposed to be experiencing the story as the main character.

continues on to the Mad Tea Party, with an exploding un-birthday cake as the finale. Young children should have no trouble on this ride because there is so much to look at and none of it is scary.

Dumbo the Flying Elephant

This has to be one of the most popular rides for younger children. There is almost always a long wait here, even on slow to moderate days. On busy days, waits can be up to an hour long! Part of the attraction is the guest's ability to make the little elephants go up and down as they fly around in a circle. All the while, a circus-type organ belts out Disney tunes. Usually the busiest time on this ride is late morning through the afternoon. Therefore, get to this ride early and do it a few times before the queue lengthens. In the evening, the queue shortens as families with young children begin to leave the park.

Insider's Secret

You can do a parent swap on this ride if you have a baby that is asleep or you just don't want to take your baby on the Dumbos. Just have the parent in the queue tell one of the cast members that you want to do a parent swap and explain why. They will then let the other parent in after the first parent and child are finished. If you have only one child in addition to the baby, that child can go on the ride twice in a row without having to wait!

Casey Jr. Circus Train

Based on the train that carried Dumbo and his circus around the country, this attraction takes guests on a ride around Storybook Land. You can ride in one of two gondola cars or the caboose. However, most children want to ride in either the Wild Animal or Monkey Cage cars. Although these are a bit cramped for adults, children love to look out through the bars. This ride is fun for all ages, and the queue can move pretty quickly because they often run two trains at a time. On slower days, they run only one train, making the wait a bit longer. However, the line is usually shorter to begin with.

Fun Fact
The Casey Jr. Circus Train was originally planned as Disneyland's first roller coaster ride.

Mad Tea Party

For this ride, guests sit in oversized teacups, reminiscent of the tea party in Disney's animated classic *Alice in Wonderland,* and spin them by turning a wheel in the center. Because the riders control the speed of rotation, you can make it as mild or as wild as you want. The queue for the Mad Tea Party can vary

Insider's Secret
It is reported that the plain lavender cup is the fastest. Although it seems faster than the other cups, there are a few things you can do to make any of the cups go fast. First, spread out the weight as evenly as possible. Adults should sit across from each other rather than together. Second, take turns spinning the wheel. If more than two people are turning the wheel, their hands will usually get in each other's way. Even two people need to synchronize their moves. Finally, all riders should lean toward the center as much as possible without getting in the way of the person who is turning the wheel. Sometimes when it is slow, the cast member operating the ride may serve as a judge and announce which teacup is spinning the fastest.

without regard to time of day. One moment you can walk right on; 10 minutes later you may have to wait. This is one ride where you check the queue as you walk by. If it's not busy, go for it. Otherwise, just check it again later.

Storybook Land Canal Boats

The canal boats take guests into the mouth of Monstro the Whale and then on through miniature villages and buildings based on classic Disney movies. All the plants here are real. The towering 12-inch pines and other trees are really bonsai trees shaped to look like larger trees. There is no animation on this ride, and often boys do not care for it much. Girls seem to like it better because the small buildings are a lot like dollhouses. The canal boats travel past Cinderella's Castle, the houses of the Three Little Pigs, the castle of Agrabah from *Aladdin,* the home of the Seven Dwarfs, Prince Eric's castle and ship from *The Little Mermaid,* and much more. This ride closes before and during parades. Right after the parade passes, it will start up again, so if you are close by, get in line and the wait will be short.

Helpful Hint

To make the ride more enjoyable for the whole family, make a game out of seeing who can find unique details throughout Storybook Land. Can you find the White Rabbit's mailbox, Cinderella's coach, or the mine of the Seven Dwarfs?

"It's a Small World"

This ride will fascinate young children, and even older children will like going through it once. Don't be surprised if your little ones begin singing along or even dancing to the music. The tune is infectious and will stay in your mind for the rest of the day. The queue for this ride is usually not too long, and even if it is, it moves quickly. This ride is a great way to take a 12-minute break, and during the summer the air conditioning inside can be quite welcome. It also provides an opportunity for mothers to nurse babies while keeping the other children entertained at the same time. Outside on the quarter hour, the clock chimes and numerous wooden children parade around the clock. Throughout the fireworks show, this attraction may be closed. During the winter holiday season, beginning in mid-November and lasting through December, the ride is transformed into "It's a Small World" holiday. The song "Jingle Bells" is interspersed with the standard tune. The mermaids have their own version of the holiday classic—"Jingle Shells."

> ### Insider's Secret
> The best place to sit in these boats is the front row. If you are assigned a different row, just ask the cast member if you can wait for the next boat and sit up front. Not only do you have a better view because no one is in front blocking your children, but also this row has more space for stowing backpacks and other carry-on items.

Matterhorn Bobsleds

Disneyland's first roller coaster, the Matterhorn Bobsleds, was actually the first tubular steel roller coaster in the world—designed to give a smooth ride similar to an actual bobsled. Riders board sleds that can seat up to eight people (two per seat) and are then pulled up a dark climb. At the top of the climb, the sleds begin their downward journey to the bottom, passing through tunnels inside the mountain as well as around the outside. You pass by the growling abominable snowman a few times during your descent. The ride ends with a splashdown in an alpine lake. Unlike the other thrill rides in the park, the Matterhorn does not have a height requirement. Instead, riders need only be at least 3 years of age. The ride is a bit wilder than Big Thunder Mountain, mainly because the cars are smaller and whip around tighter turns. Although a few 3-year-olds are fine on the ride, most children should wait until they are 5 or 6 years old. The dark climb and the abominable snowman seem to be the scariest part of the ride for young children rather than the motion of the sleds. Our daughter Beth rode it when she was 3. She just closed her eyes during the climb and when the snowman went by. The snowman is rather small and your bobsled rushes by him quickly.

Insider's Secret

There are two different tracks on the Matterhorn, and each gives a bit of a different ride. The right queue, next to Alice in Wonderland, is the slower side. The turns are a bit wider, and there are no sudden drops. This side also has a more scenic ride because it is on the outside track. The left queue, toward Tomorrowland, is the faster track. The turns are tighter, and there is one quick drop as your sled dives beneath the other track. The ride on the right, slower track is about 30 seconds longer than the one on the left, faster track. No matter which track you ride, to maximize your thrills ask the cast member seating guests the best place to sit. The cast member is usually happy to strategically place your party. The main key is to put the heavier people in back.

Triton Gardens

Located near the walkway from Main Street to the Matterhorn, this water garden is fun for children as they watch the jets of water shoot out over the walkway and then try to dodge them so as not to get wet. At night, the gardens are lit and quite beautiful.

Snow White's Grotto

This quiet little spot is located just to the east of the moat around Sleeping Beauty's Castle. There are statues of Snow White and the Seven Dwarfs here next to a waterfall fountain. You can hear Snow White singing "I'm Wishing" here. Although the Snow White statue appears larger than those of the dwarfs, it is actually about the same size. Disneyland again used forced perspective to make her look larger by putting her up higher.

Shows

Mickey's Detective School is a musical Toondunnit show currently playing several times daily in the Fantasyland Theatre, to the west of "It's a Small World." Targeted for younger children, this can still be a fun show for the entire family, as Mickey tries to solve the mystery of Pluto's dognapping. Minnie, Goofy, and other characters, as well as the audience, also take part in the show. Older children may want to skip the show. However, whether your children are young or old, this is a good

Insider's Secret

Although most people flock to sit in the middle rows of the theater, one of the best places is the front row on the far right side. Characters from the musical come down to shake the hands of children sitting here.

place to take a break and have a snack.

The Sword in the Stone ceremony takes place near the King Arthur Carrousel, daily during the summer and on weekends the rest of the time. Merlin chooses a child to pull Excalibur from the stone. If you have little children, be sure to see this.

Character Greetings

One of the best activities for small children, and one that few people know about, is the Princess Storytelling, which takes place several times a day at the Tinker Bell Toy Shoppe. Either Aurora (Sleeping Beauty), Belle, Cinderella, or Snow White tells her story. A male assistant supplies the voices of other characters as well as sound effects. A different princess tells her story once per day, so try to see them all if you have the time. After the story, the children get to meet the princess. Because the queue forms on the left side near the wall of stuffed animals, seat your children here so that at the end of the story they are near the front of the line.

Ariel, the little mermaid, can be visited at Ariel's Grotto, located near Triton Gardens. A photographer is there to take a professional photo for you to purchase, or one of the cast members will be happy to take a shot with your own camera.

Various Disney princesses can be found near Sleeping Beauty's Castle throughout the day.

Fantasyland Tips

If you plan on visiting Fantasyland, do it first thing in the day. As the morning progresses, this area just gets busier. Even if you want to hit some of the more popular rides throughout the park, take your young children on the Dumbos and a few of the dark rides before heading for the Indiana Jones Adventure or another popular ride. After the park has been open for a couple of hours, Fantasyland is usually quite busy. Things die down in the evening hours as families with young children begin to leave. So come back after 7 P.M. and try the rides you missed earlier, or do them all again.

If you want to go from Tomorrowland or Toontown to Frontierland, don't think you can save time by cutting through Fantasyland. The area is usually congested, and it is faster just to go through the Central Plaza.

Fantasyland offers some great places to take a family picture. The main spot is in front of Sleeping Beauty's Castle. However, you can also get some great shots elsewhere, such as at the Mad Tea Party or on the stationary Dumbo next to the ride, or even a shot of the children peering through the bars of the Wild Animal Cage on the Casey Jr. Circus Train.

When you first enter the park, check the *Disneyland Today* schedule for the times of *Mickey's Detective School* and the Princess Storytelling. Try to see the earliest shows if possible because subsequent showings are usually busier.

Dining in Fantasyland

Fantasyland has only two places for meals. The Village Haus Restaurant is located across from the Casey Jr. Circus Train along the pathway to Frontierland. Here you can find individual-sized pizzas and hamburgers, as well as a limited selection of sandwiches and salads. Troubadour Treats is near the entrance to the Fantasyland Theatre and is usually open only on the days *Mickey's Detective School* is showing. You can get a hot dog, nachos, pretzels, and other snacks here. For more details on these restaurants, including pricing and sample menus, see chapter 8.

Insider's Secret

Fantasyland restaurants do not offer anything exclusive or special. Because this area is often busy, especially during lunchtime and most of the afternoon, it is usually a good idea to eat elsewhere to avoid the crowds.

Fantasyland Shopping

Fantasyland has several quaint little shops where you can purchase souvenirs as well as gifts. The Mad Hatter Shop sells mouse ears and other types of Disney headwear. Even if you don't want to buy anything here, take the children in to see the mirror hung up near the ceiling. Every so often, the Cheshire Cat appears within the mirror and then disappears. The Heraldry Shoppe, located in Sleeping Beauty's Castle, sells histories of family names as well as a number of items emblazoned with your family crest. Right next door, the Princess Boutique offers dress-up clothes and costumes for girls as well as jewelry and other items fit for a princess. The Tinker Bell Toy Shoppe carries all types of Disney toys, including dolls and plush characters. At Geppetto's Toys and Gifts, you will find a variety of specialty and collectible dolls and accessories. If you are looking for items featuring the bad guys and girls of Disney films, check out the Villains' Lair. After riding "It's a Small World," you exit through "It's a Small World" Toy Shop, which sells many types of Mattel toys as well as other popular items. If you are just looking for some quick souvenirs, you can find these at Fantasy Faire Gifts, Le Petit Chalet Gifts, or Stromboli's Wagon.

Tomorrowland

When Tomorrowland first opened in 1955, it was designed to show how the future might be in far-off 1987. When Tomorrowland was redone and rededicated in 1998, it had a completely new look. Now it appears like the future as envisioned by Jules Verne and H. G. Wells. In addition to the favorite attractions, Tomorrowland has added some new ones in the past few years. The planters are all filled with fruit trees and edible plants. Many children, and even adults, are amazed at what their favorite fruits and vegetables look like on the tree or in the ground. Currently Tomorrowland is going through a lot of changes in preparation for Disneyland's 50th anniversary in 2005. Space Mountain will undergo refurbishment until 2005. During this time, there is not as much to do here as there was in the past or as there will be in the future. Although Tomorrowland may not be the land you'll want to hit first on arrival, there are still some quality shows and attractions here that your family will enjoy.

Rumors have been circulating as this book goes to print that the Submarine Voyage may be returning as early as late 2003, though 2004 is more likely. Closed since 1998, this was one of Tomorrowland's more popular attractions, and Disney fans have been hoping for its return. Be sure to check the Disneyland Web site for more information on the return and redesign of this attraction.

Astro Orbitor

Located at the entrance to Tomorrowland, this ride is the centerpiece of the newly redesigned area. Guests ride in two- or three-passenger rockets as they fly around a constellation of spinning planets. Riders use a control stick to make the rockets go up and down. Basically, this is a Dumbo-type ride that appeals to older children and adults because it goes higher and faster. Although there are no height restrictions, children must be at least 1 year of age and small children must ride

Fun Fact
When you look at the tail fins of the 12 rockets, notice that each has a different sign of the zodiac.

with an adult. The queue for this ride is usually shorter than the one for Dumbo, and the Astro Orbitor is fun to ride at night when Tomorrowland is all lit up. If you watch the planets rotating, one large and two small will come together to form a Hidden Mickey once or twice a minute.

Star Tours
A FASTPASS ATTRACTION

Did you ever want to enter one of the *Star Wars* movies and take a ride through hyperspace? Star Tours gives you that chance. Guests board Starspeeders for a flight to Endor (home of the Ewoks). These aircraft are really the same type of flight simulators used to train military and commercial pilots. Your Starspeeder is piloted by a robot named Rex. If his voice sounds

Fun Fact
There are lots of inside jokes and secrets throughout Star Tours and especially in the queue area. Be sure to look at everything. Listen to the announcements and pages, too! You may hear an Egroeg Sacul paged to the booth. That is George Lucas spelled backward. Also, for you *Star Wars* diehards—notice that after the destruction of the Death Star as the X-Wings go into hyperspace, they do not retract their S-foils but leave them extended in the X configuration.

familiar, that's because it's the voice of Paul Reubens, who played Pee Wee Herman. Rex makes one mistake after another. Although you never make it to Endor, you do get to go crashing through a comet, get caught in a tractor beam, and then follow a flight of Rebellion X-Wings during a bombing run on the Death Star. During this flight, you are bumped and jostled around, making you feel as if you are really flying in outer space. Star Tours has a

> **Insider's Secret**
> The intensity of the ride depends on where you sit. If it is slow, you can usually pick your seat. When it is busier, you can usually ask the cast member giving seating assignments if you could wait for the next speeder and choose your row. The mildest ride is toward the front and center of the speeder. Try sitting in the back row in one of the corners for the most motion.

40-inch height requirement. The combination of motion in synchronization with the movie makes your brain think you are doing a lot more moving. If it gets to be too much for you or your children, just shut your eyes and you will notice the ride tones down. It is probably a bit rough for children under 5. Although this attraction has been around for nearly 16 years, Star Tours is still impressive to both children and adults alike.

Honey, I Shrunk the Audience
This 3-D film carries on the continuing story that began in the Disney movie *Honey, I Shrunk the Kids*. Reprising his role, Rick Moranis plays the inventor of a shrinking ray and accidentally shrinks the audience. This film combines 3-D illusions with special effects, including a shaking floor and several things that jump out at you, such as a snake and a cat—both

giant size because you are shrunk down. Because most of the effects that could be scary are visual, young children can close their eyes to avoid them. Although it is fine for children 4 and up, you will be the best judge for your younger children.

Space Mountain
A FASTPASS ATTRACTION

What would it be like to ride a roller coaster in the dark so that you could not see the track ahead? If you have ever asked yourself that question, you will find your answer on Space Mountain. Although the ride is pretty mild in terms of roller coasters, consisting primarily of fast turns and a few quick drops, the fact that it is difficult to anticipate the next turn multiplies the thrill. During the Tomorrowland refurbishment, a soundtrack was added to the ride, which is supplied through speakers located on coaster cars. The minimum height requirement for this ride is 40 inches. Even though a young child may like Thunder Mountain, if the child doesn't like the dark, Space Mountain will be just too much. Most children between 7 and 8 years of age and older seem to handle it fine.

Fun Fact

Space Mountain is actually sunk into the ground nearly 20 feet so that it does not dwarf Sleeping Beauty's Castle.

Insider's Secret

Although a lot of people like to ride roller coasters with their hands up in the air, follow the directions to keep your hands in the car. The clearances are quite low, and you could seriously injure your fingers or hands if they are up.

Space Mountain is currently closed and not scheduled to reopen until 2005. This appears not to be a refurbishment but a redesign, with the ride being modernized and made even more thrilling. A rumor speculates that the new ride may even include an inversion such as a loop, but Disney has been silent about any such plans.

Innoventions

The latest attraction housed in the building that was home to Carousel of Progress and America Sings, Innoventions allows guests to learn about and explore how innovation and invention will affect their lives in the near future. The robot Tom Morrow hosts the attraction. The bottom floor contains five different pods covering different aspects of our lives: entertainment, sports, transportation, work, and, of course, the home. At each pod, a cast member gives a brief presentation illustrating new types of products that will make our lives easier. In the hub of the first floor are a number of computer terminals and exhibits displaying a variety of software, from the educational to the purely entertaining. All these games are free to play, so you won't need any quarters. Up the stairs are a number of exhibits and demonstrations sponsored by various companies. Here you can take a virtual test drive of GM's latest vehicles, see how Pixar creates movies like *A Bug's Life*, learn

Helpful Hint

All the exits are located on the second floor. Therefore, to get out you must go up. An elevator is located in the center hub. There is a small emergency bathroom upstairs; however, don't rely on using this. Instead, use the one outside behind the Hatmosphere shop.

about your heart and other health topics, and much more. Innoventions is a great place to take a break during the day, and the air conditioning makes it good for cooling down on hot days. All ages will find something to do here.

Fun Fact

You may recognize the voice of Tom Morrow. It is the actor Nathan Lane, who did the voice for Timon in *The Lion King.* Also, if you can't read the note in his pocket, it says "Buy 10 W 30." If you have the time, watch the robot after he gives his spiel and the other guests have moved on. He will move and act like a person who is bored and waiting for his next group of guests.

Tomorrowland Autopia
A FASTPASS ATTRACTION

In 2000 the completely new and redone Tomorrowland Autopia opened. Combining both the old Fantasyland and old Tomorrowland Autopias, the new attraction features four lanes of traffic and travels through an entertaining course with lots of things for you to look at. Part of the course even goes "off road." This attraction is very popular, so you may often have a long wait in the queue. Children of all ages love this ride because they get to drive a car. Children must be at least 52 inches tall to drive alone, and passengers must be at least 1 year old. Guests are given a

Fun Fact

The Tomorrowland Autopia features three types of cars. Suzy is a little coupe. Dusty is the off-road vehicle. Spark is the classy sports car.

complimentary driver's license and can purchase a photo to put on the license at the gift shop located near the exit.

Insider's Secret
There are a lot of cool things to watch for during your drive. There is a stand selling hot nuts (the nut-and-bolt type) and a mouse crossing complete with mouse holes in the curb. Also, water shoots up as you drive through a puddle off road.

Disneyland Monorail

One of Disneyland's hallmark attractions, the monorail first opened in 1959 and carries passengers from Tomorrowland to Downtown Disney and back. (It used to stop at the Disneyland Hotel.) The track is 2½ miles long and leads across the front of Disneyland, then circles around Tomorrowland. After stopping at the station, the monorail continues outside Disneyland and toward Disney's California Adventure, where it crosses the Golden Gate Bridge over the entrance to this theme park and on through the Grand Californian Hotel. Although the monorail is a great way to get from the hotels and Downtown Disney to the Magic Kingdom and back, many guests just take the round-trip ride to see the sights.

Cosmic Waves

Located near the center of Tomorrowland, this fountain invites guests to come and play. A large granite ball in the middle is supported by a powerful jet of water and can be spun around by the guests. Surrounding it are many water jets that spurt up in patterns, making it fun to watch as well as get wet. The ground around the water is spongy, so it is not slippery, and the fountain is lit up at night.

Fun Fact

The water jet that supports the granite ball would shoot up 150 feet into the air if the ball were removed. Also, the ball can be rotated at speeds approaching 60 mph. See how fast you can get it spinning.

Starcade

Starcade is a two-story video game arcade containing all types of games. Prices range from a quarter to $4 per game. Because many children lose track of time in an arcade, it is best to avoid this area altogether, especially if you are on a tight schedule or a short vacation. Otherwise, give the kids either a time limit or a budget, and use this as a break for yourself and younger children in the afternoon.

Radio Disney Booth

Guests can watch Mark and Zippy broadcast live from their booth located directly beneath the Observatron. They are there weekdays from 1 to 6 P.M. and occasionally invite guests to participate in the show.

Helpful Hint

Tune in to Radio Disney during your vacation in Southern California on AM 710.

Shows

Tomorrowland features a great live-action show—*Calling All Space Scouts . . . A Buzz Lightyear Adventure*. Showing on the stage at Club Buzz, formerly Tomorrowland Terrace, this musical production features everybody's favorite space ranger, Buzz Lightyear. Other characters include the evil Emperor Zurg, the Little Green Men (a.k.a. LGMs), and your host, Space Cadet Starla. This show is very interactive and aimed at children 8 and younger, but adults will have a good time as well. Since it is located at Club Buzz, you can easily pick up lunch or a snack to enjoy either before or during the show, allowing you to eat a meal or take a break and catch a show at the same time.

On most weekend evenings, you can listen to various types of live music at Club Buzz. Check the *Disneyland Today* schedule for show times.

Character Greetings

Although there are no scheduled character greetings, you can sometimes find Mickey Mouse or one of his friends in Tomorrowland, usually in between Innoventions and Redd Rockett's.

Tomorrowland Tips

Tomorrowland contains some popular rides. Luckily, most of them have FASTPASS systems. For younger children, the Autopia can get quite busy in the morning and stay that way for most of the day. So get there early, or get FASTPASSes for the ride and then hit other attractions while you are waiting.

Star Tours, even though it has a FASTPASS system, usually does not have a long wait except on very busy days. So get a FASTPASS for another ride and then hit Star Tours while you wait. *Honey, I Shrunk the Audience,* the Astro Orbitor, and Innoventions are other great things to do while waiting for FASTPASS times.

It's best to hit Tomorrowland in the afternoon or evening. At night, it is all lit up.

For younger children, the Autopia is the main attraction in this area. Other than Fantasyland attractions, this may be an attraction you want to head for first. In fact, get a FAST-PASS before getting in line, and when you get off the Autopia, it will almost be time to go on it again.

Dining in Tomorrowland

Tomorrowland has two restaurants as well as a drink stand. Redd Rockett's Pizza Port offers pizza (whole or by the slice), pasta, and salads. Club Buzz—Lightyear's Above the Rest features breakfast meals in the morning, then burgers, chicken sandwiches, wraps, fried chicken, and Caesar salads. At the Spirit of Refreshment, underneath the Moonliner rocket, you can order soft drinks, which are launched into the hands of the cast member serving you.

For more details on these restaurants, including pricing and sample menus, see chapter 8.

Fun Fact

The burger conveyor-belt grill was first used at the Tomorrowland Terrace, which is now Club Buzz. You can see this type of grill at a number of fast-food restaurants.

Tomorrowland Shopping

Star Traders carries a large selection of Disneyland souvenirs, from T-shirts to plush characters, with mugs and key chains as well. In addition, one part of the shop is dedicated to *Star Wars,* with all types of toys, clothing, and other items based on the movie series. Star Tours exits through this shop as well. The Premiere shop stocks Tomorrowland items and has stations where you can create your own CD of your favorite Disneyland music and attractions. Located near the exit to the Autopia, the Autopia Winner's Circle is where you can purchase a photo for your driver's license or pick up other Chevron and Autopia items. Finally, at the Hatmosphere, you can find all types of Disney headwear, including mouse ears.

Mickey's Toontown

Disneyland's newest land, Mickey's Toontown, which opened in 1993, allows guests to see how their favorite cartoon stars live and work. Although there are several attractions in Toontown, there are also lots of other things to see and do. The curvy architecture almost begs you to find a straight line. In the downtown area, there are all types of interactive gags. Take your children around and have them lift lids, push buttons, pull on door knobs, listen to phones, and so on. Just about everything does something. For example, pushing the plunger located by the Fireworks Factory sets off a series of explosions. These interactive gags not only are a lot of fun but also make great photo opportunities. Although Toontown is designed for children, with all the jokes and gags it is still a lot of fun for adults.

Roger Rabbit's Car Toon Spin
A FASTPASS ATTRACTION

In this attraction, Benny the Cab takes guests for a ride. As you drive around trying to find and save Jessica Rabbit, the weasels try to get you with the Dip. If the car begins to spin, turn the wheel to straighten it out. Or you can spin it to better see things along the ride. The cabs are similar to the Mad Tea Party in that riders can spin them around as much or as little as they like. The ride contains many sight gags as well as cartoon clichés. Even though the ride is in Toontown, it is dark inside and contains a lot of loud sounds and strobing lights, making it scary for young children. We recommend children under 5 skip this one.

Scare Factor

Even though Roger Rabbit's Car Toon Spin is in Toontown, it is dark inside and contains a lot of loud sounds and strobing lights, making it scary for young children. We recommend children under 5 skip this one.

Jolly Trolley

Toontown's own public transit, the Jolly Trolley rocks back and forth as it makes its way from one side of Toontown to the other. Rides are one way, with stops in front of Roger Rabbit's Car Toon Spin and Mickey's House. The trolley itself is a visual gag, with the wind-up key turning around on its roof as it putts down the street.

Gadget's Go Coaster

The inventing mouse from *Chip-n-Dale's Rescue Rangers* has created a kiddie coaster from things she found lying around. Gadget's Go Coaster seats riders in a train of acorn shells, carries them up one climb, and takes them twisting and turning back down to the loading platform. Riders must be at least 3 years of age. Most children will like the ride. Because the entire ride is visible before entering the queue, let children make their own decision on whether they want to ride or not.

Mickey's House

Mickey's House is a fun walkthrough attraction. There are a lot of fun things to look at and great photo opportunities. Guests walk through the house, out into the backyard, and on to the Movie Barn. Here you find a queue for getting your picture taken with Mickey. While you are waiting, Goofy and Donald will show you scenes from some of Mickey's movies.

You will then be escorted in small groups for photos with Mickey on one of four sets from his movies *Steamboat Willie, Through the Mirror, The Band Concert,* and *The Sorcerer's Apprentice.* On busier days, all four sets will be used. Although the cast members will not admit there is more than one Mickey, if you request a certain set, he or she may tell you to wait for the next group. The photographer will take a photo for you to purchase on Main Street if you wish. The cast member in the studio will also be happy to take a shot with your own camera.

Fun Fact

Trivia

When you enter Mickey's House, the first room contains a passport with stamps from everywhere a Disneyland is located.

Minnie's House

Like Mickey's House, Minnie's House is full of things to look at and do. Press buttons on her oven and dishwasher to see them work. In her dressing room, children can design new fashions for Minnie on her computer. Minnie can be found at her house during most hours of the day for photos.

Chip-n-Dale Treehouse

This attraction is pretty simple. It is essentially a tree with stairs inside that children can climb to the top and look around. Although you might take some photos here, usually it is best just to skip this one.

Donald's Boat

Docked on Toon Lake, the *Miss Daisy* is Donald's houseboat. Children climb a spiral staircase or a rope ladder to get to the top. From there they can steer the wheel and toot the horn.

Goofy's Bounce House

In this house, children can jump on all the furniture and even bounce off the walls. To enter, children must be at least 3 years old and no taller than 52 inches. Parents can watch through the windows and admire all the strange plants in Goofy's garden.

Character Greetings

Mickey and Minnie can be found at their houses during most of the hours Toontown is open. Goofy, Donald, Pluto, and other characters are also around at various times throughout the day for autographs and photos.

Mickey's Toontown Tips

Toontown can get quite busy, so you should try to hit it early— usually right after you do the popular rides at Fantasyland.

If there is a long line for Roger Rabbit's Car Toon Spin, get a FASTPASS and then browse around Toontown looking at the gags, get a snack, or see "It's a Small World."

Don't wait in a long line for Gadget's Go Coaster. The ride is only 45 seconds long. Instead, come back later.

Toontown closes earlier than the park because the fireworks are launched right over it. Be sure to find out when it closes, and try to get there about an hour before, when the queues are shorter and the area is less crowded.

Dining in Mickey's Toontown

Mickey's Toontown only has fast food and snacks available. Daisy's Diner serves individual-size pizzas and garden salads. Pluto's Dog House is where you can find a hot dog. Goofy's Free-Z Time sells slushy drinks. Clarabelle's Frozen Yogurt is where you can find frozen yogurt and other treats. There aren't a lot of places to sit down for a meal in Toontown, so we recommend eating elsewhere or just getting snacks while in

Toontown rather than meals. For more details on these restaurants, including pricing and sample menus, see chapter 8.

Mickey's Toontown Shopping

The only shop is the Gag Factory, where you can find all types of Toontown souvenirs with some of the town's most famous residents emblazoned on them.

Frontierland

As you walk through the doors of the wooden fort, you are instantly carried back to the days of the Old West. Welcome to Frontierland!

Big Thunder Mountain Railroad
A FASTPASS ATTRACTION

This is the only big attraction in Frontierland. Big Thunder is a roller coaster with a runaway mine train theme. Guests ride in ore cars pulled along by a small engine that takes them up and down hills, in a cave of bats, past assorted wildlife, and even through a cave-in. As far as roller coasters go, this one is fairly tame and has only short drops and several fast turns. The hard bench seats can be a bit shaky, and children sitting together or an adult alone may find themselves sliding right and left in the seat as they go around the turns. The height requirement is 40 inches. Although some 4-year-olds really like the ride, some of the dark parts in the caves are a bit scary. Therefore, we recommend it for those 5 years and older.

Scare Factor

Although some 4-year-olds really like Big Thunder Mountain Railroad, some of the dark parts in the caves are a bit scary. We recommend it for those 5 years and older.

Insider's Secret

For the best ride on Big Thunder Mountain Railroad, ask the cast member giving seat assignments if you can sit in the very back. Because the drops are not all that high and the train is quite long, those in the front are almost to the bottom before the last car is over the hump and the train begins to pick up speed.

Tom Sawyer Island

Located in the middle of the Rivers of America, Tom Sawyer Island is only accessible by raft. Once across the river, children will have a great time as they explore the island's many features. There is a treehouse complete with spyglasses, several rock formations that create castles to climb around in, as well as a teeter-tottering rock and one that spins around. The pontoon bridge is fun to cross, as is the suspension bridge. For those who don't mind the dark, there is Injun Joe's Cave to explore. Finally, Fort Wilderness has towers where youngsters can defend the fort from attack. There is a lot to do and see here, and this gives

Fun Fact

Tom Sawyer Island was officially annexed and recognized by the Missouri state legislature.

children a chance to run around and burn off some excess energy. Plan on spending at least an hour here, and come late in the morning or early in the afternoon. The island closes as dusk, so be sure to note when the last rafts will be leaving.

Mark Twain *Riverboat*

This steam-powered riverboat was one of the original attractions when Disneyland first opened in 1955. The steamboat sails around Tom Sawyer Island, and Mark Twain gives a spiel over the speakers. The ride is fairly slow and takes about 15 minutes. You can wait for 10 minutes just for passengers to board before you even get moving. If you are on a tight schedule, you should usually skip this attraction. However, it is a good break during the middle of the day and gives you a chance to rest. Although there are only a few seats, many guests just sit on the deck, and we have seen several small children fall asleep for a quick nap.

Fun Fact

Walt Disney used to love to pilot the *Mark Twain* around the river. On one of his first times, he would blow the whistle over and over again. A cast member told him to lay off or the boat would run out of steam. Sure enough, the steam pressure got too low and the boat was stuck until the pressure could build up again.

Insider's Secret

If you would like to ride in the pilot house on top of the boat, ask one of the cast members as you are boarding. This is limited to adults and possibly older children. The cast member will let you know if you can on that day and will give you instructions on what to do. Once up there, the captain will let you turn the wheel (don't worry, the boat is really on a track) and tell you when to ring the bell and blow the whistle.

Sailing Ship Columbia

The other ship that sails around the Rivers of America is the *Columbia.* This is a full-scale replica of the original ship built in 1787, which was the first American ship to circumnavigate the globe. It runs only occasionally, and guests can board it at the same dock as the *Mark Twain*. Below deck is a small maritime museum that shows how sailors of the time lived. It is amazing how men could live on such a small boat for such a long time. The around-the-world cruise took three years.

Frontierland Shootin' Exposition

This shooting gallery uses infrared rifles that cause targets to react when a hit is registered. This is fun for children and a good break. Unlike most attractions, this one is not included with your admission. It costs 50 cents for 20 shots.

Shows

Frontierland offers some of the best shows in Disneyland. The Golden Horseshoe Stage hosts a couple of different shows at a time. The *Variety Show* combines humor, magic, and music from the time period, and the original was a favorite of Walt Disney's, who had a private box in the upper level to the left of the stage. Also check out *Billy Hill and the Hillbillies,* a funny show with great music and comedy. Billy and his brothers, all also named Billy, perform a variety of music and songs from Elvis to classic bluegrass. As you are walking through Frontierland, you may witness a show by the Golden Horseshoe, featuring a sheriff trying to apprehend an outlaw or two. There are no stunts, just good laughs.

One of the biggest shows ever at Disneyland is *Fantasmic!* Showing twice nightly during the summer and on weekends and holidays throughout the remainder of the year, this show combines lasers, animation, pyrotechnics, and live action. The 22-minute show is incredible, and if you haven't seen it before, you must. People begin to pick seating and wait over an hour before it starts. Because the show is on Tom

Sawyer Island in the Rivers of America, it can be seen from just about anywhere along the Frontierland and New Orleans Square riverfront. Although the show does have some scary parts, there are also a lot of parts that younger children will like. Those 6 and older will like the whole show, whereas younger ones may need to hide their eyes or hold on to a parent at times.

Helpful Hint

You should find a spot about an hour before the show starts and camp out. However, not everyone has to stay at the spot. One or two can hold it for the rest, using jackets, backpacks, or even a stroller to reserve the area. Meanwhile, the rest of the family can go on some of the nearby rides and other attractions. Or you can get a meal or snack and eat while you are waiting.

Insider's Secret

For the ultimate *Fantasmic!* experience, you can watch from the balcony of the Disney Gallery. It holds only 15 to 17 guests, and you must make reservations by calling 714-781-4400 up to 30 days in advance or by trying to find an opening first thing the morning of the performance at the Guest Relations window at the park entrance. The cost is $45 for adults and $35 for children and includes a dessert, drinks, and more. These spots sell out quickly, so you must get there early if you want to do this.

Character Greetings

The characters from the *Toy Story* movies often stroll around Frontierland. Check your *Disneyland Today* schedule for times and locations.

Frontierland Tips

Big Thunder Mountain Railroad is the only major attraction in this area. Although you can get there early, you will usually want to spend the morning hours elsewhere. Instead, do Big Thunder later or even in the evening. It is fun to ride at night.

While waiting for a FASTPASS time for Big Thunder, go over to Tom Sawyer Island or hit nearby attractions in New Orleans Square or Adventureland.

If you are going to see a show at the Golden Horseshoe, pick up a FASTPASS for Big Thunder or other nearby attractions so you can do your waiting while being entertained. Get to the Golden Horseshoe at least 10 to 15 minutes early. That way you can get a good seat and still have time to pick up something to eat or drink at the eatery inside.

Tom Sawyer Island and the boats on the river all stop operating at dusk. If you plan on doing them, be sure to fit them in while the sun is still shining. The Mark Twain may run on evenings that *Fantasmic!* is not showing.

Dining in Frontierland

Frontierland offers some great places to eat. Rancho del Zocalo features both Mexican cuisine as well as barbecue fare. This is a great place for dinner because it offers a variety of items; just about everyone in a family can find something he or she likes. The River Belle Terrace serves breakfast in the morning and sandwiches and meals including chicken and fish for lunch and dinner. The Stage Door Café serves hot dogs, hamburgers, and salads both to the guests inside the Golden Horseshoe and to those outside. Finally, if you just have to have some McDonald's french fries, pick some up at Conestoga Fries.

For more details on these restaurants, including pricing and sample menus, see chapter 8.

Frontierland Shopping

There are several nice shops in Frontierland. Bonanza Outfitters carries Western-style clothing and gift items. Pioneer Mercantile is a great place to find Western-inspired toys, books, videos, and even children's costumes. To help calm a sweet tooth, the Westward Ho Trading Company sells a variety of goodies.

Adventureland

As you leave Central Plaza and pass through the bamboo gateway, you are taken back in time as well as transported across the world to a land of adventure. This area has the look and feel of a jungle outpost in the 1930s. Although Adventureland has only four attractions, they are ones you don't want to miss.

Enchanted Tiki Room

This attraction was the first at Disneyland to incorporate audio-animatronics. Guests sit in a Polynesian-style building around a central fountain. When the doors close, the birds come to life, as do the plants and wooden tikis. The air fills with music as the various characters sing a number of songs. The effects are dated, but the Enchanted Tiki room is a good place for a rest in the afternoon. Small children usually enjoy the show and sing along with the birds. The only part that might be scary is the thunderstorm; however, the characters just keep singing right through it. Older children may rather do something more exciting than watch this show.

Indiana Jones Adventure
A FASTPASS ATTRACTION

One of Disneyland's wildest rides is the Indiana Jones Adventure. Based on the popular movie character, this attraction is incredible. Guests enter through ancient ruins and make their way to the boarding area. Toward the end of the queue, you come to a room showing a movie hosted by Indy's trusty sidekick, Sallah. He explains the story line of the ride. You are in the temple of Mara, an Indian deity that can grant eternal youth, earthly riches, or knowledge of the future. However, don't gaze directly into the eyes of Mara or bad things will happen.

With that warning given, you are ready to board 12-person vehicles that will take you farther into the temple. These vehicles are very special in that they use hydraulics for all the motion during the ride. If you could see the road, it is perfectly flat and level. Computers control the bumps and rocking of the vehicles and allow for over 160,000 randomly generated combinations. Therefore, you will never get the same ride twice. Of course, someone in your vehicle has to look at Mara, so all of you are doomed. Luckily Indiana Jones is in the temple and helps you get through a variety of dangers, including a shaky suspension bridge over lava, a giant snake, mummies and skeletons, bugs, flying darts, and, of course, a giant rolling

Scare Factor

The Indiana Jones Adventure ride is very intense and rough. The height requirement of 46 inches is a good gauge of who will like this ride.

Helpful Hint

The queue for the ride is fun in itself as you make your way past booby traps that have already been sprung or are blocked for your protection. However, throw caution to the wind and touch or move things near the signs that warn you not to. In the spike room, shake the pole vigorously—it will seem as if the roof is about to cave in.

boulder. This ride is very intense and rough. The height requirement of 46 inches is a good gauge of who will like this ride. The queue on this ride can be up to two or even three hours long on busy days. Your best bet is to get there early and use the FAST-PASS station so you can bypass the long wait.

Fun Fact
The Indiana Jones Adventure contains lots of props from the original movies. For example, the truck near the entrance is the actual one used in *Raiders of the Lost Ark,* in which Indy falls off the hood and is dragged below it. Look for other props in his office in the queue area.

Jungle Cruise

This is one great ride that everyone we talked to enjoyed. There are lots of things to see along your cruise, and the spiel by the skipper of your boat makes it funny and entertaining. Guests board boats patterned after the *African Queen* and sail through jungles filled with lions, tigers, snakes, elephants, hippos, and even headhunters. The cruise, which takes about eight minutes, is fun for the entire family.

Helpful Hint
If it rains while you are at Disneyland, try riding the Jungle Cruise. The boats are covered, and the rain really adds to the ambience of being in a jungle.

Tarzan's Treehouse

Although veteran Disneyland guests may remember this as the Swiss Family Robinson Treehouse, it has been refurbished as the home of Tarzan. At the base of the tree is a camp area where children can explore and play with a variety of items, most of which create noise or other effects. Guests climb stairs up the tree and cross a suspension bridge to small huts built in the tree. As you go from hut to hut, the story of Tarzan unfolds. This attraction is primarily designed for children, though parents will have to help younger ones climb the stairs or even carry them. Older children will usually be bored unless they are taking their younger siblings through.

Fun Fact

The scientific name of the tree that houses Tarzan's Treehouse is *Disneyodendron semperflorens grandis,* which means "large ever-blooming Disney tree."

Shows

Young children will enjoy Aladdin and Jasmine's StoryTale Adventures. This takes place in front of Aladdin's Oasis and features the two main characters telling their story with the help of the audience. This shows daily during the summer and on most weekends during the rest of the year. The Trinidad Tropical Steel Drum Band plays near the entrance to the Jungle Cruise on select days throughout the year. Check the *Disneyland Today* schedule for times.

Character Greetings

Aladdin and Jasmine are available for photos and autographs at various times throughout the day near Aladdin's Oasis. Children can also meet them after their StoryTale Adventures.

Adventureland Tips

Head over to the Indiana Jones Adventure when the park first opens and the lines are short. On busy days, waits can be quite long—you may have to wait from two to three hours to come back with your FASTPASS.

Because of the popularity of the Indiana Jones Adventure, Adventureland can be quite congested. It is usually quicker to move through Frontierland when traveling between Central Plaza and New Orleans Square.

The Jungle Cruise and the Enchanted Tiki Room are good ways to spend time while waiting for an Indiana Jones Adventure FASTPASS slot.

Dining in Adventureland

Dining is somewhat limited in Adventureland. Bengal Barbecue serves grilled meat and vegetables on skewers with delicious sauces, along with breadsticks and pretzels. The Tiki Juice Bar, located by the Enchanted Tiki Room, carries refreshing pineapple spears, pineapple juice, and a whipped pineapple sorbet. Indy's Fruit Cart is where you can purchase fresh fruit as well as bottled drinks. For more details on these restaurants, including pricing and sample menus, see chapter 8.

Adventureland Shopping

Adventureland has some interesting shops that carry items appropriate for this area. The Adventureland Bazaar carries some of the jungle's best items, including plush animals and other jungle dwellers such as rubber snakes and spiders. At the Indiana Jones Adventure Outpost you can find fedoras like Indy's, clothing fit for an expedition, and even artifacts for your home museum. South Seas Traders carries more casual wear such as Hawaiian-style shirts and other comfortable items. Located next to the Jungle Cruise, Tropical Imports sells rubber snakes, skulls, and insects as well as other fun items kids love.

New Orleans Square

New Orleans Square is a unique area with a couple of Disney-land's most beloved attractions. As you stroll through this land, the air filled with the scent of Cajun cooking and the music of a Dixieland band, you can almost imagine yourself on Bourbon Street in the Big Easy. In 2003 Disney is releasing two feature films based on New Orleans Square attractions. *Pirates of the Caribbean* hit theaters in July, and *The Haunted Mansion* is to be released near the end of the year. Expect Disneyland to do something special during this time to help promote the films with activities in this area.

Pirates of the Caribbean
A FASTPASS ATTRACTION

This attraction is a favorite of many guests and fun for the entire family. Riders board boats and begin their cruise through a nighttime bayou complete with fireflies, croaking frogs, and even an alligator. Just as everyone is relaxing, a talking skull and crossbones warns of trouble ahead. The boat then drops down a couple of chutes, and you find yourself in a cavern filled with pirate treasure and the skeletons of its owners. After you view the cursed treasure, your boat is transported back a few centuries to a pirate raid on a Caribbean port town. It

Fun Fact

The name of the pirate ship is the *Wicked Wench*. The ship's pirate captain, with the braided beard, was modeled after the infamous Edward Teach, who was also known as Blackbeard. At the end of the ride, as you are headed up the ramp, take a look at the loot the two pirates are trying to make away with. The portrait is of Blackbeard, from the Disney movie *Blackbeard's Ghost*.

begins with broadsides by a pirate ship and return fire from the town's fort, with your boat sailing right in between the two and cannonball splashes all around. The cruise continues through the town as you watch the pirates plunder, pillage, and then burn the town down. Although this may seem violent and brutal, Disney has turned this raid into a musical, and the pirates themselves are more humorous than bloodthirsty. If you are not careful, you may even find yourself singing along to the song "Yo-Ho, Yo-Ho, A Pirate's Life for Me." At the end of the ride, your boat is carried up a ramp to the loading dock. Don't worry, there is not a large drop like on Splash Mountain; you are just being carried back up to the ground level. Although this ride is somewhat dark and the drops can be a bit wild, the ride is fine for children of all ages. Except for a tunnel you cruise through to the raid scenes, there is always something to look at, and once the singing starts any fears are cast overboard.

> **Helpful Hint**
> When you get to the front of the queue, ask the cast member if you can sit in the front row. He or she will usually ask you to wait for the next boat and then let you sit in front. Small children can see better in front, and there is also more room for legs and carry-ons such as backpacks.

Haunted Mansion
A FASTPASS ATTRACTION
Another favorite of guests, the Haunted Mansion is more humorous than frightening and is intended as a family attraction rather than one for only teens and adults. Guests enter through the front door of the mansion and are escorted into a

portrait chamber. The doors close, and the room appears to get taller. A hidden door then opens, and you walk through a gallery of spooky paintings to the Doom Buggies. These carry you around the remainder of the mansion.

During your journey, you will see the 999 inhabitants throughout the many rooms of the mansion as well as the graveyard outside. Near the end of the ride, you are warned against picking up hitchhiking ghosts. Before you know it, you look into a mirror and there is a ghost riding with you! There is a lot to see and great detail in this attraction. Therefore, if you have time, ride it two or three times, preferably close together, to try to see most of it. Although the ride was designed with children in mind, the part most children find scary is the darkness. Most of the ghosts themselves are actually funny looking. Children 4 and up who have no problem with the dark will be fine; 7 and up is more appropriate for other children.

As you go through the ride, you may notice several ravens. In the original plans for the attraction, the ravens would tell the story of the mansion. However, Disney decided to make it a musical so guests could enjoy it over and over again without getting tired of hearing the same old story. There were actually several story lines proposed for the ride, and in the end the develop-

Scare Factor

Children 4 and up who have no problem with the dark will be fine on the Haunted Mansion ride; 7 and up is more appropriate for other children.

ers combined them all to create the different scenes. There is one main story line that has several different versions. In one, a captain of a ship (note the clipper ship weather vane on top of the mansion) killed his fiancée on the day of their wedding (the ghostly bride in the attic) when he heard a rumor that she had been unfaithful. When he learned the rumor was false, he hanged himself (your host in the portrait hall at the start).

Beginning in October, the Haunted Mansion opens with a holiday theme. From October through New Year's, the attraction features Jack Skellington and other characters from the Tim Burton movie *The Nightmare Before Christmas*. The interior is modified for the new story line and features an all-new soundtrack as Halloween and Christmas come together

> **Fun Fact** Trivia
> The organ in the hall with the party is the one from *20,000 Leagues Under the Sea.*

in one ghostly holiday extravaganza. During this time, the attraction is a little less scary than with the original program, so younger children are not as likely to be scared. If you plan on visiting during this time period, be sure to have your family view the movie in advance so you know the background of the story. The attraction is usually closed in September, during its transformation, as well as in January, so it can be changed back.

Disney Gallery

Located directly above Pirates of the Caribbean, this was originally designed as an apartment for Walt Disney. Now it displays a number of works of art focusing on Disneyland attractions and conceptual works. The gallery contains a patio where guests are welcome to bring snacks and drinks to enjoy. Because not many people know about this spot, it usually is not crowded.

Shows

There is almost always some type of live performance taking place in New Orleans Square. You can find various types of bands, singing groups, and even mimes throughout the area.

New Orleans Square Tips

Although both the Haunted Mansion and Pirates of the Caribbean are popular attractions and are usually busy, they can both handle a lot of guests. With the addition of the FASTPASS system to each, you can always get a ticket and come back later for a shorter wait.

If you are not going to watch *Fantasmic!* go on the Haunted Mansion and Pirates of the Caribbean during the show. You can usually walk right into each attraction; if there is a queue, it is a very short wait.

There is no need to hit New Orleans Square first thing in the morning. Instead, do the rides that get the long lines (Splash Mountain, Indiana Jones Adventure, Big Thunder Mountain Railroad, etc.), then come here later in the day.

Dining in New Orleans Square

Some of the best dining at Disneyland can be found in New Orleans Square. The famous Blue Bayou restaurant offers a unique atmosphere and looks out at the bayou area of the Pirates of the Caribbean. The menu features a variety of meals, including seafood, prime rib, and the Monte Cristo sandwich. Reservations are highly suggested, and if you plan on dining here, get here early to make the reservations, which are same day only. The best

Money-Saving Tip
If you plan on dining at the Blue Bayou restaurant, do it before dinnertime. Although the menu remains relatively the same, the prices nearly double.

time to come here is during lunch, usually around 2 P.M. Café Orleans serves a variety of French- and Creole-inspired dishes, including sandwiches, salads, and other tasty dishes. French Market is a good spot for dinner. Here you can find jambalaya, fried chicken, and pasta. The prices are quite reasonable. Royal Street Veranda serves gumbo and clam chowder in bread bowls, while La Petite Patisserie offers waffles on a stick covered with a variety of toppings. If you just want to sip a mint julep (nonalcoholic) or snack on some fritters, try the Mint Julep Bar. For more details on these restaurants, including pricing and sample menus, see chapter 8.

New Orleans Square Shopping

New Orleans Square contains some very interesting shops where you can find all types of gifts and souvenirs. At the Disney Gallery, you can purchase reproductions of some of the art on display. Cristal D'Orleans carries a variety of crystal items. Jewel of Orleans sells antique jewelry, some dating back to 1850, as well as more modern pieces. For Christmas ornaments and other decorations year-round, visit La Boutique de Noel. La Mascarade carries sculptures and figurines, while L'Ornement Magique features the work of artist Christopher Radko. Le Bat en Rouge sells merchandise for the Haunted Mansion Holiday as well as gourmet food and Mardi Gras supplies. For the little cutthroats in your crew, Pieces of Eight carries all types of pirate items.

Critter Country

Formerly known as Bear Country, this land was renamed Critter Country when Splash Mountain opened. The area is rather small and can become quite congested by afternoon with all the guests wanting to ride Splash Mountain and the park's newest attraction, The Many Adventures of Winnie the Pooh.

The Many Adventures of Winnie the Pooh
A FASTPASS ATTRACTION

This new attraction is a dark ride similar to those in Fantasyland. Guests climb aboard hunny pots, each with its own unique name, and take a journey through some of Pooh Bear's more popular stories. As the hunny pots bounce around through the ride, guests will follow Pooh for a blustery day, save the hunny pot from the floody place, and even enter one of Pooh's dreams with Heffalumps and Woozles. This is a ride the entire family can enjoy, and most families can fit within a single hunny pot, since each seats four to five people. While this ride does offer a FASTPASS, because it is located at the end of Critter Country and is a good walk from the center of the park, pick up a FASTPASS for Splash Mountain, then wait in line and ride through The Many Adventures of Winnie the Pooh while counting off the minutes for Splash Mountain.

Splash Mountain
A FASTPASS ATTRACTION

Disneyland's one and only flume ride, Splash Mountain is themed with the characters from the Disney movie *Song of the South* and features Brer Rabbit as well as his nemeses Brer Fox and Brer Bear. Guests board log boats and are carried into the water-filled mountain. Inside, the characters sing as you ride through swamps and bayous, watching Brer Fox and Brer Bear try to catch Brer Rabbit. Finally, they do catch him and decide to throw him into the briar patch. At this point, your log races down a five-story drop into a pond below, surrounded by briars, and then heads back into the attraction for a musical finale. During the drop, your picture is taken, so try to smile. Many families even pose during this part and use it as a family picture. The photos can be purchased near the exit to the ride.

Most of the ride is fun and upbeat, with only one dark area where you go down a little drop. However, the scariest part of the ride is the drop down the tall chute. Although the ride has a height requirement of 40 inches and children must be at least 3 years old to ride it, it is probably best to wait until children are at least 4 or even 5 years old.

Helpful Hint

Believe the warnings around this ride that you will get wet. You really do. If you want to stay as dry as possible, ask the cast member at boarding to seat you at the back of the log. The people in front tend to get the wettest. Also, try to ride this attraction when the sun is shining and it is warm outside. You don't want to have children going around in the cold with wet clothes.

Time-Saving Tip

Splash Mountain can get very busy, and the queue can be up to two hours long or even more on very busy days. There is a FASTPASS system for this attraction, but when it gets busy you may have to come back three or four hours later! Therefore, try to get there by midmorning, when the FASTPASS returns are only about an hour away. Then come back and get on in 10 to 15 minutes.

Davy Crockett's Explorer Canoes

One of the best ways to travel the Rivers of America is in these canoes. Each canoe has two guides that help keep the craft on track while the guests have the opportunity to paddle nearly half a mile on their cruise around Tom Sawyer Island. Most children enjoy this ride because they get to help with the paddling. Although there is no height requirement, children under 6 must wear life jackets. This attraction closes at dusk and does not operate every day. Check the sign at the entrance to the attraction for operating hours.

Trivia

Fun Fact

When the canoes were first introduced to Disneyland in 1956, they were called the Indian War Canoes.

Character Greetings

Throughout most of the day, you can find Winnie the Pooh at the Thotful Spot near the Country Bear Playhouse. A cast photographer is on hand to take pictures that you can purchase on Main Street. Cast members will also be happy to take a photo for you with your own camera. Tigger and Eeyore also make appearances in front of the arcade at various times during the day.

Critter Country Tips

Because Critter Country can become very congested in the afternoon due to the crowds waiting for Splash Mountain, it is best to come here in the morning, if only to get a FASTPASS for later.

A good strategy for covering this land is to get here about an hour or two after the park officially opens. Get a FASTPASS for Splash Mountain and then ride The Many Adventures of Winnie the Pooh while waiting. If you have time, also try the canoes or browse around in the shops.

Dining in Critter Country

The Hungry Bear restaurant is a nice, quiet place to have lunch because most of the tables overlook the Rivers of America rather than the crowds. It serves hamburgers, sandwiches, and even onion rings. Harbour Galley offers only McDonald's french fries and drinks.

For more details on these restaurants, including pricing and sample menus, see chapter 8.

Critter Country Shopping

If you are looking for Pooh-inspired items, Pooh Corner has it all, from clothing to toys and even all types of household items with the cuddly little bear or his friends on them.

CHAPTER
6

Disney's
California
Adventure™

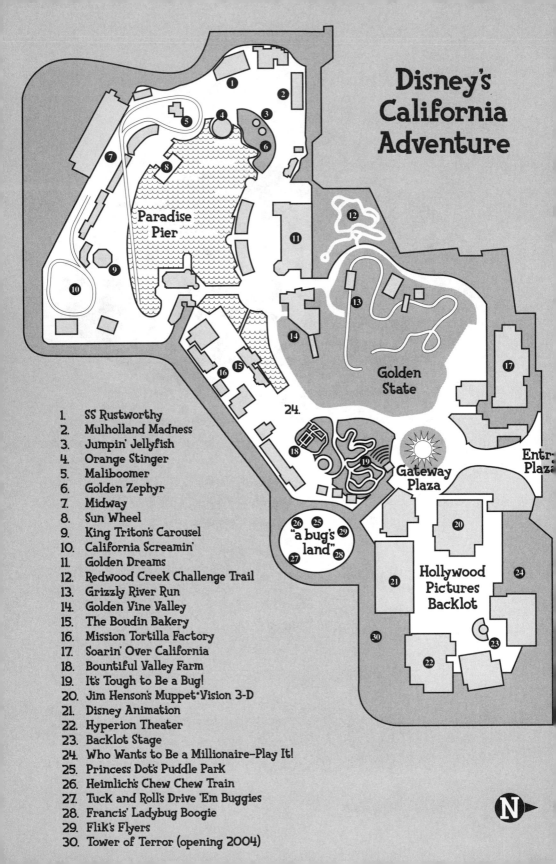

Disney's California Adventure

Paradise Pier

Golden State

Gateway Plaza

"a bug's land"

Hollywood Pictures Backlot

Entry Plaza

1. SS Rustworthy
2. Mulholland Madness
3. Jumpin' Jellyfish
4. Orange Stinger
5. Maliboomer
6. Golden Zephyr
7. Midway
8. Sun Wheel
9. King Triton's Carousel
10. California Screamin'
11. Golden Dreams
12. Redwood Creek Challenge Trail
13. Grizzly River Run
14. Golden Vine Valley
15. The Boudin Bakery
16. Mission Tortilla Factory
17. Soarin' Over California
18. Bountiful Valley Farm
19. It's Tough to Be a Bug!
20. Jim Henson's Muppet·Vision 3-D
21. Disney Animation
22. Hyperion Theater
23. Backlot Stage
24. Who Wants to Be a Millionaire–Play It!
25. Princess Dot's Puddle Park
26. Heimlich's Chew Chew Train
27. Tuck and Roll's Drive 'Em Buggies
28. Francis' Ladybug Boogie
29. Flik's Flyers
30. Tower of Terror (opening 2004)

This theme park, which opened on February 8, 2001, is the newest Disney theme park in the world. The main gate is located directly across from Disneyland's main gate, behind giant letters that spell out "CALIFORNIA." However, if you are guests at the Grand Californian or Paradise Pier hotels, private entrances are provided to help you bypass the lines at the main gate.

To Go or Not to Go— That Is the Question

One of the major decisions families with young children will make is whether they should spend a day at California Adventure or spend the time at Disneyland or another area theme park. California Adventure is designed primarily for adults and older children. Although there are some things for younger children to do, most of the time they may be waiting while their parents or older siblings ride the attractions.

Insider's Secret

As you tour California Adventure, be sure to note the names of the shops and restaurants as well as of the attractions. Many of the names are puns based on California cities, locations, or terms—for example, Maliboomer (Malibu), Baker's Field Bakery (Bakersfield), Bur-r-r Bank Ice Cream (Burbank), and so forth.

By the Numbers— Height Requirements

To help you decide, let's take a look at the numbers. California Adventure has 32 attractions, including shows and the parade. Of these, eight have height requirements. (We are not including the Redwood Creek Challenge Trail because only some of the challenges have height requirements.) Two attractions have a requirement of 40 inches, three require 42 inches, two require 48 inches, and one requires 52 inches. Therefore, right off, children under 40 inches cannot ride 25 percent of the attractions. Of the remaining 24 attractions, younger children will really enjoy only 10 to 12. The rest are either scary or designed for older children and adults, such as some of the shows and tours. Therefore, young children will enjoy only about one-third of the total attractions.

The Results

If you will be at the Disneyland Resort for only one day, you should know that single-day tickets allow entrance into either Disneyland or California Adventure—not both. However, Park Hopper tickets for two or more days allow you to come and go as much as you like between the two parks. In our opinion, and that of several families we have talked to, if your family consists of only young children, you can probably spend half a day in California Adventure and see everything you want. If all your children are older (around 6 years and up), then California Adventure should not be missed, and you will want a full day there. The tough decision comes for families with children in both age groups. If your young child is just a baby and would not do much at Disneyland anyway, go for California Adventure. Otherwise, try spending half a day at California Adventure with the older kids, which will still allow some time for the younger children at Disneyland. If the parks are staying open late, hit California Adventure in the evening, when the younger kids are tired and sleeping in the stroller. With Park Hopper tickets, there is no reason not to at least try California Adventure. If your family is not having a great time, then head next door to Disneyland for the rest of the day. Since California Adventure opened, Disney has added several new attractions targeted at younger children, making the park a much better experience for families with children of all ages.

Helpful Hint

Remember to do a parent swap when you have small children who cannot go on some attractions. Part of your family waits in line and goes on the attraction while the rest remain with the small children. When the first group gets back, the waiting group can proceed directly onto the ride without waiting. The parent swap option can also be used with the FASTPASS system.

Plan Your Day

Before you arrive at California Adventure, it is important that you take time to acquaint yourself with the park and plan your visit to help you avoid walking all over the park looking for specific attractions. For most families, plan an entire day at the park. You may want to add to or decrease that time depending on how busy the park is as well as the ages of your children.

Time-Saving Tip

If you need a stroller, you can rent one after entering at the front gate, near Engine-Ear Toys. This is usually the busiest spot to rent them, so you might try renting strollers at Fly 'n' Buy across from Soarin' Over California or at Souvenir 66 on Paradise Pier. These two latter spots are great if you are staying at either the Grand Californian Hotel or the Paradise Pier Hotel and use the private entrances for these hotels.

Touring Plans

To save time, as well as to see and do as much as possible, your family should have a general plan for the day.

The key to a good plan is to be prepared. A week or two before you leave on your vacation, you should get a map of the park to acquaint yourself with where everything is located. You can find a map on the Disneyland Web site at www.disneyland.com or request one by calling 714-781-4560. You can also use the map included in this book. Second, read about each attraction in the following section of this chapter. Once you are familiar with all the attractions and their locations, have the family create a plan.

California Adventure is smaller than Disneyland, and there are fewer attractions, making it easier to navigate. You can divide the attractions into three main categories: busy rides, FASTPASS rides, and all the rest. Try to hit the busy rides first thing in the morning until their queues begin to get long, then again toward late afternoon and evening. FAST-PASS attractions are great any time of day, as with the rest of the attractions.

The following lists divide the attractions according to the best times to do them. Throughout this chapter, we refer to younger and older children. Where the cutoff is depends on the child. At California Adventure, younger children are basically those not tall enough for the minimum height requirements. These children are usually 5 or 6 years of age or younger. Older children will make most if not all the height requirements and will enjoy the fast and wild rides while wanting to avoid the kiddie rides. They are 7 years or older. If you have children in both categories, then you will have to make compromises to keep everyone happy. Luckily, this is easier here than at Disneyland because the attractions for younger children are usually near the ones for the older guests. Now let's take a look at what to do when.

Popular Attractions for the Morning Lap

ℯ Younger Children (6 and Under)

"Playhouse Disney—Live on Stage!"

The Sun Wheel

King Triton's Carousel

Jumpin' Jellyfish

Golden Zephyr

"a bug's land" rides

The Ugly Bug Ball

❧ Older Children (7 and Up)

Soarin' Over California

Maliboomer

California Screamin'

Mulholland Madness

The Sun Wheel

Popular Attractions for the Afternoon Lap

❧ Younger Children (6 and Under)

Muppet*Vision 3D

Disney's Aladdin—A Musical Spectacular

Goofy's Beach Party Bash

Redwood Creek Challenge Trail

❧ Older Children (7 and Up)

Grizzly River Run

Orange Stinger

It's Tough to Be a Bug!

Muppet*Vision 3D

Disney's Aladdin—A Musical Spectacular

Redwood Creek Challenge Trail

Disney Animation

Who Wants to Be a Millionaire—Play It!

Popular Attractions for the Evening Lap

Disney's Electrical Parade

Paradise Pier rides

Anything you missed earlier or want to do again

Helpful Hint

Disney's California Adventure features a number of attractions where you can get wet. There are several little water parks where young children can get splashed, sprayed, or even downright drenched. Therefore, it is a good idea to take along a spare change of clothes for each child, just in case. However, on a warm day, your children will usually dry off fairly quickly—unless they are soaked to the skin.

These lists are general and intended to give you an idea of when to do each of the attractions. Following are some sample plans we have put together. Both are for a single-day visit, with the first designed for families with younger children and the second for those with older children. (*Note:* You may not have time to do everything on the plan. It is designed for a typical day. However, for days when it is very busy, you will have to cut some of the attractions.)

Sample Touring Plan (Children 6 and Under)

Morning

Pick up tickets for *Disney's Aladdin—A Musical Spectacular* at the Hollywood Pictures Backlot.

See *"Playhouse Disney—Live on Stage!"*

Head to "a bug's land" and ride the attractions there.

Head toward Paradise Pier.

Ride the Sun Wheel.

Ride the other kiddie rides in the Paradise Pier area.

Pick up a Happy Meal at Burger Invasion or have a snack.

Afternoon

Return to the Hollywood Pictures Backlot.

Pick up a FASTPASS for *Muppet*Vision 3D*.

See *Disney's Aladdin—A Musical Spectacular.*

See *Muppet*Vision 3D.*

See *Goofy's Beach Party Bash.*

Head over to and do Redwood Creek Challenge Trail.

Evening

Watch the parade.

Have dinner.

Ride the Paradise Pier attractions while they are all lit up.

Ride anything you missed earlier or want to do again.

Sample Touring Plan (Children 7 and Up)

Morning

Right at the start, head to Soarin' Over California.

Pick up tickets for *Disney's Aladdin—A Musical Spectacular.*

Continue to Paradise Pier and ride California Screamin'.

Ride Maliboomer.

Ride the Sun Wheel.

Ride Mulholland Madness.

Head to Grizzly River Run and pick up a FASTPASS.

Afternoon

Have lunch at the Pacific Wharf food court area.

Grab a FASTPASS for *It's Tough to Be a Bug!*

Ride Grizzly River Run.

Tour Mission Tortilla Factory and the Boudin Bakery.

See *It's Tough to Be a Bug!*

Head to the Hollywood Pictures Backlot.

Get FASTPASS for *Muppet*Vision 3D.*

See the shows.

See *Muppet*Vision 3D.*

Evening

Watch the parade.

Have dinner.

Visit Disney Animation.

Do any attractions you missed earlier or want to ride again.

Check out Paradise Pier at night.

More Than One Day at California Adventure

California Adventure can pretty much be visited in a single day. If it is really busy, you will have to use the FASTPASS system to shorten waits on the popular attractions. Even then, you may have to forgo a few of the attractions. Plan ahead of time which attractions you really want to do and which you could skip if short on time.

When visiting a second day, or half day, see as much as you can the first day. Then see what you missed or want to do again on the next day. California Adventure has a lot of neat shops and good restaurants to visit, and a second day will let you spend more time at these.

California Adventure FASTPASS Rides

As this book goes to print, California Adventure is currently offering the FASTPASS system on the following attractions:

- @ California Screamin'

- @ Soarin' Over California

- @ *It's Tough to Be a Bug!*

- @ Grizzly River Run

- @ Mulholland Madness

- @ *Muppet*Vision 3D*

- @ *Who Wants to Be a Millionaire—Play It!*

During the day, you should always have a FASTPASS for some attraction in your possession. That way you will be waiting for a quick entry onto or into an attraction while seeing or doing others. Also, be sure to pick one up before eating a meal. Two FASTPASS attractions are in the Hollywood Pictures Backlot, three are in the Golden State, and two are on Paradise Pier.

One strategy for using the FASTPASS system is to pick up one in the Golden State area on your way from Paradise

Pier to a show in the Hollywood Pictures Backlot. After the show, pick up another FASTPASS in the Golden State on your way to the first FASTPASS you picked up before the show. After hitting both attractions in the Golden State, head on back to Paradise Pier.

The Regions of California

Disney's California Adventure is divided into four main regions: the Hollywood Pictures Backlot, the Golden State, Paradise Pier, and the newest addition, "a bug's land." As you enter through the main gate to the Entry Plaza, the Hollywood Pictures Backlot is to your left, the Golden State is to your right, and Paradise Pier is on the other side of the Golden State. "A bug's land" is straight ahead and then to your left.

Insider's Secret

Just past the Golden Gate Bridge is the Sunshine Plaza. From this spot, and this spot alone, you can see into each of the three regions. However, once you enter a region, your attention will mostly be focused on just that region.

Entry Plaza

The Entry Plaza is inside the main gate of California Adventure. There are shops and places to eat, and the Sunshine Plaza is a central location where families can meet.

Shows

California Adventure features its own unique parade. The current parade as this book goes to print is Disney's Electrical Parade. This is pretty much the same parade that appeared at

Quick Guide to

Attraction	Location	Height Requirement
The Boudin Bakery	Golden State	None
Bountiful Valley Farm	"a bug's land"	None
California Screamin'	Paradise Pier	48 inches
Disney Animation	Hollywood Pictures Backlot	None
Disney's Aladdin— A Musical Spectacular	Hollywood Pictures Backlot	None
Flik's Flyers	"a bug's land"	None
Francis' Ladybug Boogie	"a bug's land"	None
Golden Dreams	Golden State	None
Golden Vine Winery	Golden State	None
Golden Zephyr	Paradise Pier	None
Goofy's Beach Party Bash	Hollywood Pictures Backlot	None
Grizzly River Run	Golden State	42 inches
Heimlich's Chew Chew Train	"a bug's land"	None
It's Tough to Be a Bug!	"a bug's land"	None
Jim Henson's *Muppet*Vision 3D*	Hollywood Pictures Backlot	None
Jumpin' Jellyfish	Paradise Pier	40 inches
King Triton's Carousel	Paradise Pier	None

0 Not scary at all.
! Might be somewhat frightening for some children. Usually either dark or a mild roller coaster.
!! Most young children will find this scary.
!!! This attraction may frighten some adults. This is usually reserved for high-speed roller coasters and other thrill rides.

California
Adventure Attractions

Duration of Ride	Scare Factor	Age Range
Approx. 8 minutes	0	All
N/A	0	All
3 minutes	!!!	7 and up
N/A	0	All
40 minutes	0	All
1 minute	0	All
1 minute	0	All
20 minutes	0	All
Approx. 10 minutes	0	All
2 minutes	0	All
12 minutes	0	All
3 minutes	!!	6 and up
2 minutes	0	All
Approx. 10 minutes	!	4 and up
Approx. 15 minutes	0	All
1½ minutes	!	4 and up
2 minutes	0	All

Quick Guide to

Attraction	Location	Height Requirement
Maliboomer	Paradise Pier	52 inches
Mission Tortilla Factory	Golden State	None
Mulholland Madness	Paradise Pier	42 inches
Orange Stinger	Paradise Pier	48 inches*
"Playhouse Disney— Live on Stage!"	Hollywood Pictures Backlot	None
Princess Dot's Puddle Park	"a bug's land"	None
Redwood Creek Challenge	Golden State	None**
Soarin' Over California	Golden State	42 inches
S.S. Rustworthy	Paradise Pier	None
Sun Wheel	Paradise Pier	None
Tuck and Roll's Drive 'Em Buggies	"a bug's land"	42 inches to ride, 48 inches to drive
The Ugly Bug Ball	"a bug's land"	None
Who Wants to Be a Millionaire—Play It!	Hollywood Pictures Backlot	none

* *There is also a maximum weight requirement of 200 pounds.*
** *Some challenges have a 42-inch minimum height requirement.*
 0 Not scary at all.
 ! Might be somewhat frightening for some children. Usually either dark or
   a mild roller coaster.
 !! Most young children will find this scary.
!!! This attraction may frighten some adults. This is usually reserved for
    high-speed roller coasters and other thrill rides.

California
Adventure Attractions

Duration of Ride	Scare Factor	Age Range
1 minute	!!!	7 and up
Approx. 6 minutes	0	All
2 minutes	!!	4 and up
2 minutes	!	6 and up
20 minutes	0	All
N/A	0	All
N/A	0	All
Approx. 8 minutes	!	5 and up
N/A	0	All
Approx. 6 minutes	0	All
2 minutes	0	All
10 minutes	0	All
20 minutes	0	All

Disneyland as the Main Street Electrical Parade several years ago. It begins at the Sunshine Plaza and makes its way through the Golden State to Paradise Pier and exits near the Maliboomer. On days when the parade runs twice, the second parade will follow the route in reverse. Sunshine Plaza is a great place to watch from because there are several places to sit. The amphitheater area across from Golden Dreams is another good spot for viewing.

Character Greetings

You can often find Mickey, Minnie, and other Disney characters dressed up for a California Adventure near the Sunshine Plaza or at other locations around the park. Flik and Princess Atta can be found in "a bug's land." For the hours, check the *Disneyland Today* guide for the day.

Entry Plaza Tips

If you plan on viewing the parade from the Sunshine Plaza area, get there at least a half hour early to stake out your spot. While part of the family or group holds the seats, the rest can visit the shops in the area or get a bite to eat and bring something back.

Dining at the Entry Plaza

There are only two snack stands at the Entry Plaza. Baker's Field Bakery offers a variety of baked treats as well as specialty coffees. Bur-r-r Bank Ice Cream features ice cream cones, waffle cones, and sundaes to help keep you cool in the California sun. Both of these are great places to hit for a bit while waiting for the parade.

For more details on these restaurants, including pricing and sample menus, see chapter 8.

Entry Plaza Shopping

The Entry Plaza also has two of the larger shops in California Adventure. Greetings from California is the main souvenir shop in the park. You can find everything here from shirts and other clothing to books and even snow globes and plush characters. Anything you can print a California Adventure logo on is here. Although there are other shops around the park, they usually only sell items themed to the region in which they are located. Engine-Ear Toys carries a number of items with a railroad theme, in addition to all types of toys.

Helpful Hint
The best time to hit these shops is while you are waiting for the parade or when you just want to take a break. Unlike the shops on Main Street at Disneyland, the shops in California Adventure do not always stay open after the park closes. This is particularly true on slow days or in the off season.

Hollywood Pictures Backlot

You enter the Hollywood Pictures Backlot, located to the east of the Sunshine Plaza, through a grand entrance. This puts you on Hollywood Boulevard, complete with lines down the middle of the street and even parking meters. Although it is only two short blocks long, the mural at the far end of the boulevard uses forced perspective to make it look as though it were much longer. By taking a left and heading north off Hollywood Boulevard, you will enter the backlot area. Here you see that several of the fancy buildings on Hollywood Boulevard are nothing more than false fronts for a movie set. Wandering about the area are several cast members dressed as stars, directors, agents, and other Hollywood types who will visit with the guests, looking for future stars.

Helpful Hint

While walking down Hollywood Boulevard, be sure to read the signs on the buildings. A Dr. Nippentuck runs a plastic surgery clinic called Gone with the Chin, and there is also an "epic" styling salon called Ben Hair.

Disney Animation

Located on Hollywood Boulevard, this attraction gives you a behind-the-scenes look at Disney animation. You first enter the Animation Courtyard. This lobby is surrounded by a number of screens on which various scenes and characters from Disney animated films are projected. From here you can continue into four different areas, each taking a different look at the process of creating an animated feature.

In the Animation Screening Room, you can watch a short film about Walt Disney and animation projects.

At Drawn to Animation, a real-life Disney animator (not an audio-animatronic) shows you how Disney characters are created and drawn. Guests can ask questions of the animator as they watch the process of creating a character.

The Sorcerer's Workshop contains three different interactive areas where you can get involved in animation. In the first area, you can try drawing your own animation. In the second area, the Beast's Library, guests sit at workstations where they can find out which Disney character they are the most like. A digital photo is taken of you, then you are asked a series of questions about your personality, such as, "Do you like to eat lunch with nice people, or do you like to eat nice people for lunch?" Your personality and face are then used to calculate which animated character you most resemble. Finally, in Ursula's Grotto, you provide the voice for a scene from a Disney movie. You can choose to either act or sing a part. Each family or group has its own workstation, so you need not worry about everyone else in the area watching your efforts.

Helpful Hint

You don't have to go into each of the four areas, especially if you are pressed for time. However, the Animation Screening Room movie is very good and only eight minutes long. Also, you should at least try the Beast's Library in the Sorcerer's Workshop. Kids and adults alike enjoy seeing which Disney characters they resemble.

The final area is the Art of Animation. This area is merely a display of artwork from Disney animated features, including preliminary sketches and storyboards.

Jim Henson's Muppet*Vision 3D
A FASTPASS Attraction

Remember the Muppet Show that used to be on television regularly? Well, at *Muppet*Vision 3D* you can experience the show firsthand and in three dimensions. While you are waiting to enter the theater, several Muppet characters provide a preshow on monitors throughout the lobby. Although most of the monitors are located in the front of the lobby, there are a few in the back right corner that are a bit lower and easier for small children to watch.

Once you are inside the theater, the real show begins. Statler and Waldorf, the two complainers from the television show, sit in a balcony making comments throughout the production. The show contains several 3-D gags with things reaching out toward you. However, there is nothing scary during the show. Dr. Bunsen Honeydew and his assistant, Beaker, create Waldo—the spirit of 3-D—who causes trouble throughout the show, which culminates in the destruction of the theater.

Younger children will enjoy *Muppet*Vision 3D,* especially if they already know some of the characters. If you think they may not like the 3-D part of the show, they can take off their glasses or just close their eyes.

Who Wants to Be a Millionaire—Play It!
A FASTPASS ATTRACTION

Have you wanted to be on the hit game show but haven't gotten a chance? Now is your time. This interactive show is a lot of fun. Guests from the audience are selected for the "hot seat" and get to compete for collectibles and other prizes. The rest of the audience gets to play along as well. Each seat has buttons so all guests can test their knowledge as the game progresses. The show takes about 20 minutes and is enjoyed by older children and adults. Younger children like to press the buttons but usually prefer other shows and attractions.

Insider's Secret
A new attraction will open in the Hollywood Pictures Backlot in 2004. The Twilight Zone Tower of Terror will be a thrilling ride set in the spooky halls of the Hollywood Tower Hotel. Guests retrace the steps of a group of previous visitors who disappeared one stormy night. Guests board an elevator and see strange apparitions as they ride to the top, only to drop 13 stories to the bottom. More information on this ride will be available at the Disneyland Web site once the ride opens.

Shows

California Adventure's main shows are located in the Hollywood Pictures Backlot. The Hyperion Theater puts on musical performances. As this book goes to print, *Disney's Aladdin— A Musical Spectacular* is currently playing. This Broadway-caliber musical is fantastic and will be enjoyed by guests of all ages. During the 40-minute show, the story of Aladdin from the hit Disney movie is told on stage, featuring great special effects that include a flying carpet and, of course, the hilarious Genie. Unlike other shows where you just wait in line, *Aladdin* has tickets that you can pick up in advance from a booth in the Hollywood Pictures Backlot. You should still return to the Hyperion at least 30 minutes before the show begins so you can get a good seat, though there are really no bad seats in the theater.

"*Playhouse Disney—Live on Stage!*" is a new show specially designed for young children. It features the popular characters from the Disney Channel's *Playhouse Disney.* There are no seats in this theater, so plan to sit on the carpeted floor. Although this may seem odd at first, once the show gets started, the children can stand up to dance along with the characters. Expect to see favorites from *Bear in the Big Blue House, Rolie Polie Olie, Stanley,* and *The Book of Pooh.* You will even learn how to do the "Bear Cha Cha Cha." Since the lines for this show can get rather long, try to see it as early as possible. Check the show times on the Web site or in the pamphlet you receive as you enter. The first show is usually about 30 minutes after the park opens, so if you head there first, you should have no trouble getting in.

The Hollywood Backlot Stage is an outdoor stage in the center of the region. *Goofy's Beach Party* is currently running. This show features humor, song, dance, and excitement as

Donald Duck directs Goofy and Max's latest father-son movie. Younger children will really like this.

Helpful Hint

During the day, especially with young children, you will need some time to sit down and take a break. The shows are a great way to do this. They provide a chance for parents to sit down and little ones to take a nap.

Character Greetings

Near Disney Animation, you can meet characters throughout the day from some of Disney's newest animated features. Often this is the only spot at which you will see these characters because they are usually not at Disneyland.

Hollywood Pictures Backlot Tips

The Hollywood Pictures Backlot region has no rides—just shows and showlike attractions. The best time to visit here is in the late morning or afternoon. Use this as your downtime for the day before hitting the rides again in the evening. While *"Playhouse Disney—Live on Stage!"* begins in the morning, *Aladdin* does not begin until afternoon. Get a FASTPASS for *Muppet*Vision 3D* or *Who Wants to Be a Millionaire—Play It!* before a show or while in Disney Animation. Try to see the earliest showings for the shows. The later showings are often busier.

Dining in the Hollywood Pictures Backlot

The Hollywood Pictures Backlot has a few places to find a snack or light meal. Award Wieners offers several types of hot dogs and sausage sandwiches. Fairfax Market is a fruit stand that also sells vegetables, nuts, and other healthy snacks.

Schmoozies is where you can find a variety of smoothies, juices, and specialty coffee drinks.

For more details on these restaurants, including pricing and sample menus, see chapter 8.

Hollywood Pictures Backlot Shopping

Don't forget to check out the shops for your Hollywood paraphernalia. Gone Hollywood is a fun shop to browse even if you don't plan on buying anything. It carries dress-up clothing as well as trendy items such as what stars might buy. Off the Page is located at the exit to Disney Animation. Here you can find a variety of items featuring Disney's animated characters as well as collectible items such as animation cels and other artwork. If the Muppets are more your speed, check out Rizzo's Prop and Pawn Shop, which features all types of Muppet-inspired items.

Golden State

The Golden State region is in the center of California Adventure; its districts represent the various parts that make up the state of California. Condor Flats represents the aerospace industry and is designed after a high desert flight test area. The Grizzly Peak Recreation area represents California's outdoors with a look of Yosemite and the Sierra Nevada mountains. Pacific Wharf offers the atmosphere of a seaside town such as Monterey. The Bay Area is designed with the art and architecture of the San Francisco area in mind. Finally, the Golden Vine Winery represents the wine country of California.

Soarin' Over California
A FASTPASS ATTRACTION

This is the only attraction in Condor Flats. However, Soarin' Over California is all this district needs. We overheard visitors

Insider's Secret

The themes in the various districts are very complete. As you are walking along the walkway in front of Soarin' Over California, notice the flashing blue lights that make it look like a runway. The path leading to Grizzly River Run is designed to look like a scenic highway complete with guard rails and cracks in the road. Notice the food and lodging sign by the entrance to the Grand Californian Hotel. Look at the cacti in this area: some have been trained to form a Hidden Mickey. Also be sure to read the signs in the windows of the Bay Area buildings.

exiting the ride state that this was worth the cost of admission by itself. We agreed. A large, hangarlike building houses the attraction. The queue area is filled with photos from California's aviation history. Riders are seated in 10-person rows, and once everybody is buckled in, the seats rise up into the air and position the riders in front of a large movie screen. The screen curves around the riders so that it fills their vision. You are supposed to be hang-gliding over the state and are taken along a river, up onto snowy mountains with skiers, over the coast, across an aircraft carrier, and much more. It ends with a flight over Disneyland. Pay careful attention as you are flying over the golf course. A golf ball will come flying up at you. Don't blink or you will miss a hidden Mickey on the ball. Also look for the fireworks at the end of the ride that form the familiar Mickey head.

As you fly over California, the seats move in synchronization with the movie. Gusts of wind from different directions add to the realism. Even your sense of smell is used. You smell orange blossoms while flying over an orange grove and pine trees while over the mountains and rivers. With all the effects put together, you really feel as if you are flying.

Soarin' Over California has a minimum height requirement of 40 inches. Most children who are tall enough will enjoy the ride. There is nothing scary except that the seats are lifted up into the air and your feet hang down. Some children who are fearful of heights may not like this. However, their attention will usually be on the screen, and they quickly forget about how high they are in the air. Most children 5 and up will be fine.

Grizzly River Run
A FASTPASS ATTRACTION

River rafting is a popular sport in California. With the Grizzly River Run, you can experience running the rapids with your family. Guests ride in circular rafts with everyone facing the center. The rafts are carried up a lift toward Grizzly Peak and then ride down the river flume through fast currents that buck the raft up and down. The rafts spin around a bit, so everyone gets an opportunity to be in front, where you usually get the wettest. The river is filled with boulders against which the rafts bounce, and the water is never calm. The rafts descend two steep drops; the latter one is a 22-foot waterfall.

Guests must be at least 42 inches tall to ride the Grizzly River Run. It is rougher and wetter than Splash Mountain at Disneyland. Some young children may find this ride too scary, especially if they do not like getting splashed with water. There are several places from which you can watch the ride. Let your children watch other people ride and then decide for themselves if they want to try it. Because of the roughness of the ride, children under 6 may find it too scary. Lockers are located near the entrance for this ride, across from the shop.

Use them to stow backpacks and other items you want to keep dry while you get wet on the river.

Scare Factor

Guests must be at least 42 inches tall to ride the Grizzly River Run. It is rougher and wetter than Splash Mountain, and some young children may find this ride too scary.

Insider's Secret

With the drops and other effects, Grizzly River Run is the tallest and fastest raft ride in the world.

Helpful Hint

If you follow a pathway off to the left of the entrance, you will come to a lookout point with an excellent view of the tall drop. This is a great place to take a picture of your family or group as they are rafting.

Redwood Creek Challenge Trail

Located across from the Grizzly River Run, this outdoor activity center is great fun for active children. There are towers and rocks to climb, cargo nets, bridges to cross, and even cable slides. Several Park Rangers are on hand to help out where needed. This area is a lot of fun, and kids enjoy the opportunity to run around, since so many other attractions require sitting or standing in line. If you go inside the bear cave, look around for a hidden Mickey created by an indentation inside the cave on the roof.

Some of the challenges have a minimum height requirement of 42 inches. However, there is something here for children of all ages.

Golden Dreams

This theater in the Bay Area district features a movie hosted by Whoopi Goldberg, who plays the goddess Califia, after whom the state is named. It traces a brief history of the region, from the Spanish missionaries through the Gold Rush, the movie industry, and agriculture all the way to the computer age. Don't expect a comprehensive history lesson in only 20 minutes. The movie highlights only a few spots in the state's rich heritage, with an emphasis on diversity.

Helpful Hint

If you're pressed for time, Golden Dreams is one attraction you can skip. Although it is somewhat educational, many children will be bored and would rather be doing something else.

Mission Tortilla Factory

Located in the Pacific Wharf district, the factory has a short tour. A cast member explains the history of making tortillas, and guests can watch video demonstrations of how tortillas used to be made at home during two different periods of time. The tour then leads to a modern factory setup. There you will see two machines, one making flour tortillas and the other making corn tortillas. At the end of the tour, you are treated to a sample tortilla, which you just saw being made. The tour is fairly short, and children often like the free sample at the end.

The Boudin Bakery

Right across from the tortilla factory, the Boudin Bakery features a longer and more entertaining tour. Hosted by Rosie O'Donnell and Colin Mochrie (from the television show *Whose Line Is It Anyway?*), this tour uses humor in explaining how sourdough bread is made. During the tour, you move from one station to the next as your hosts describe what you are seeing through the large windows into the bakery. Even if making bread is not your thing, the tour is actually quite fun. Plus you usually get a free sample of sourdough bread at the beginning. If you want another taste of what you watched being baked, step into the Pacific Wharf Café next door for some fresh sourdough bread.

Golden Vine Winery

Hosted by Robert Mondavi vineyards, this attraction features *Seasons of the Vine,* a movie about the wine industry and how wines are made. The winery contains everything for making wine. There is a small vineyard on site, and there are plans for the winery to produce its own label in the future. The area also features a wine-tasting room.

This attraction is not really designed for children. Instead, it is intended for adults. Unless you are really interested in the process of wine making, skip this attraction.

Shows

Inside the Redwood Creek Challenge Trail, the Ahwahnee Camp Circle features a storyteller throughout the day. Here children and adults alike can listen to *Stories of California.* These are based on Native American myths and legends from California. The stories are usually not very long, and the show is set up so you can come and go as needed. Children from about 3 to 10 years of age will enjoy the stories, and even adults find them entertaining because many are unfamiliar and the cast members do a great job by adding their own sound effects and joking around with the audience.

Character Greetings

At various times throughout the day, you can find Minnie dressed up as an aviator, as well as Mickey and the rest of the gang around the Golden State—usually dressed for the district in which they are located.

Golden State Tips

The Golden State region has a variety of attractions. There are six rides, two movie presentations, an activity center, and four demonstration areas or tours. Located between the Hollywood Pictures Backlot and Paradise Pier, the Golden State gets a lot of traffic. Three attractions use the FASTPASS system. Be sure to grab a FASTPASS for one of these when walking through the area. Or take the tours while waiting for a FASTPASS time. Try to hit Soarin' Over California and the Grizzly River Run in the morning before they get too busy. The afternoon or early evening is a good time to hit the rest of the attractions in this area because that is when the popular rides in the other areas are the busiest.

Time-Saving Tip

The tours and demonstrations can provide a good break between rides. However, if pressed for time, they can be cut.

Dining in the Golden State

The Golden State has some great places to eat. The Taste Pilot's Grill, located right next to Soarin' Over California, serves gourmet burgers, ribs, and other tasty meals as well as breakfast in the morning. At the Golden Vine Winery, the Wine Country Trattoria carries deli sandwiches and snacks, the Golden Vine Terrace offers appetizers, and the Vineyard Room serves four-course meals with or without wine.

The Pacific Wharf area contains a great food court that is sure to offer something to please each person in your family. The seating is all centrally located between the eateries. At the Pacific Wharf Café, you can get soup or salad in fresh-baked bread bowls as well as tasty desserts. Cocina Cucamonga serves tacos and nachos. The Lucky Fortune Cookery offers Asian-style food. Rita's Baja Blenders is a great place for a cool, refreshing fruity drink. Finally, the Pacific Wharf Distribution Company offers beer.

For more details on these restaurants, including pricing and sample menus, see chapter 8.

Golden State Shopping

The various districts in the Golden State have shops that feature merchandise themed to that particular area. Fly 'n' Buy in Condor Flats carries a variety of aviation-theme items, including shirts, hats, posters, and much more. Rushin' River Outfitters, right next to the entrance to the Grizzly River Run, carries outdoor-theme items, including hiking and camping wear, and lots of items emblazoned with the Grizzly Peak icon.

"a bug's land"

California Adventure's newest area, designed specifically for young children, provides guests with a bug's view of the world. Guests enter through a giant Cowboy Crunchies box and arrive in a land with benches made out of popsicle sticks, lights made out of drinking straws and fireflies, and shade provided by giant clover. This area also features five attractions.

Insider's Secret
"a bug's land" is shaded by 75 clovers. However, there is only one four-leaf clover in the mix. Can you find it?

Helpful Hint
"a bug's land" contains family bathrooms where a family, including all of the children, can go into a single, private room to take care of business. This is great for families with small children and for changing diapers.

Heimlich's Chew Chew Train

This is a slow ride where guests board a caterpillar train and "eat" their way through a garden. Heimlich provides a guided tour during which guests can use all of their senses. For example, while traveling through a watermelon slice, you can smell the watermelon and even get dripped on by "juice." This ride is best for children 6 and under. Any older and they may be bored.

Flik's Fun Flyers

This is a flying ride where guests climb into suspended gondolas that rise and fall as they spin. It is similar to the Dumbos at Disneyland except that riders here have no control over the height of the car. The gondolas are designed to look like boxes of apple juice, animal crackers, raisins, and even Chinese food.

Insider's Secret
The boxes the guests ride in rotate around a large tub of nondairy whipped topping. If you look at the nutrition label, you will see that the topping contains no fat, but 10 grams of fun per serving.

They are suspended from "balloons" created by bugs from twigs and leaves. Most children will enjoy this ride.

Francis' Ladybug Boogie

This is a fun spinning ride similar to the Mad Tea Party at Disneyland. Guests climb aboard ladybugs and then travel around in a figure 8 track. As they move, guests can spin their ladybugs as fast as they desire. There is also the added thrill of near misses at the intersection of the track as ladybugs almost crash into each other. This ride is good for children of all ages, since the guests can make the ride as thrilling or calm as they like.

Tuck and Roll's Drive 'Em Buggies

This attraction lets guests drive around in pillbug-shaped bumper cars. Each can seat two people and can be driven anywhere within the ring under the tent. For those who want to drive off the track or bump into other cars on the Autopia, Tuck and Roll's Drive 'Em Buggies allows them to do so without breaking any safety rules. Riders must be at least 42 inches tall for this ride, and drivers must be at least 48 inches tall. This is a fun ride for both younger and older children, even allowing them to ride together and bump into other cars. The ride is fairly gentle, so young children will not get bumped around roughly.

Princess Dot Puddle Park

This is a water play area for children of all ages but is targeted more toward the younger children. Water comes out of a fan sprayer at the end of a giant garden hose and also shoots randomly from little geysers in the ground. This is a great place to cool off on hot days and allows children to burn off some energy in the process. Adults will enjoy watching this attraction.

It's Tough to Be a Bug!
A FASTPASS ATTRACTION

Located just outside the area with the rides for younger children and featuring characters from *A Bug's Life,* this 3-D movie offers a number of special effects. Guests enter the theater through what looks like an ant hole. In the waiting area are several posters for movies with bug adaptations, such as *Antie, The Grass Menagerie,* and such. On entering the theater, guests sit on benches and then don their bug eyeglasses. Flik, the ant from the movie, is your host. He introduces a number of bugs that show you how they live. There is the spider who shoots quills, the termite who spits acid (you just get hit with water), and even a stinkbug who demonstrates his ability.

Just as the show is becoming educational, Hopper arrives. He doesn't like humans because they kill bugs, so he sends swarms of hornets and black widow spiders to get you.

Young children may find this show scary. In addition to the 3-D effects of things coming at you, the other special effects can be frightening, especially in the darkened theater. If you are unsure, sit in the rear of the theater on the right side so you can exit during the show if needed. Our 2-year-old daughter was a bit scared, but she made it through fine by hiding her eyes and holding onto a parent. By the time children are 4 years old, they should not be scared of the show.

Scare Factor

Young children may find *It's Tough to Be a Bug!* scary. In addition to the 3-D effects of things coming at the audience, the other special effects can be frightening, especially in the darkened theater.

Bountiful Valley Farm

California is an agricultural giant, and the Bountiful Valley Farm provides an interactive way to learn about it. There are gardens with all types of vegetables as well as groves of fruit trees. Children will enjoy playing in the water maze formed by sprinklers. Depending on the day, there are also demonstrations and exhibits on farming. The nice thing about this attraction is that you can spend as much or as little time here as you want. It is rarely crowded, and many children, as well as adults, enjoy seeing where their food comes from.

Shows

The Ugly Bug Ball is a cute show where Madame Butterfly teaches guests the latest bug dances, such as the Heimlich Maneuver and the Tarantula Tango. Children are even invited up on stage to dance along with Flik and Atta. This show is aimed at younger children.

Character Greetings

At various times throughout the day, you can find Flik the ant and sometimes other characters from *It's Tough to Be a Bug!* around the "a bug's land." If your children enjoy getting autographs, be sure to get these because they are not available at Disneyland.

"a bug's land" Tips

Since *It's Tough to Be a Bug!* is the only FASTPASS attraction in this land, pick up a FASTPASS as you enter the land and then hit the rides for younger children while you are waiting for your show time. The rides here are usually less busy first thing in the morning and toward evening.

Dining in "a bug's land"

"a bug's land" has some great places to eat. At the Bountiful Valley Farmers Market, you can find sandwich wraps and salads, with baked potatoes and chicken legs from nearby carts. Sam Andreas Shakes offers ice cream shakes and cones.

For more details on these restaurants, including pricing and sample menus, see chapter 8.

"a bug's land" Shopping

This area has limited shopping. The P. T. Flea Market sells candy and "a bug's life" products. The Caterpillar Cart sells a variety of toy tractors and trucks. (This is located by the farm exhibit, not by where *It's Tough to Be a Bug!* is shown.)

Paradise Pier

The fourth region of California Adventure is designed to resemble a classic boardwalk amusement park. As such, it contains a majority of the park's rides and tends to be one of the busier areas during the day. Everything here is intended to take you back to the glory days of the California surf scene. In addition to the rides, the restaurants and shops resemble their seaside counterparts and the air is filled with tunes from the Beach Boys and other similar groups but played on a pipe organ. Paradise Pier is a lot of fun during the day, and as the sun sets the area comes alive with thousands and thousands of lights, which further add to the ambience of the area.

Insider's Secret

Paradise Pier is built around Paradise Bay. If you take the time to look at the water, you will notice this is no placid lake. Instead, Disney Imagineers have designed a wave machine into the bay so the water is always moving—just like the real ocean.

California Screamin'
A FASTPASS ATTRACTION

Billed as the longest, fastest, and scariest ride at the Disneyland Resort, California Screamin' is a worthy addition to the resort's host of coasters. The ride is designed to resemble a classic wooden roller coaster. However, the experience is nothing like you would find on one of those rides. After riders board, their cars are halted on the tracks along the bay. The cars are then catapulted from 0 to 55 mph in only five seconds, giving the cars enough speed to climb the first hill without further chain assistance. If you have ridden wooden roller coasters at other parks, you know how they shake the riders up. Don't expect this on California Screamin'. This is a steel tube coaster, so the ride is smooth—at least as far as the track is concerned. The ride consists of several hills with steep drops, fast turns, and even a series of bumps that cause you to float above your seat for a moment. There is even a vertical loop—the first and only one at the Disneyland Resort. Most of the hills have scream tunnels. These are designed to amplify the intensity of the riders' excitement. So when you enter one of these tunnels, get ready to scream! You can even purchase a photo of your family coming down one of the drops, at California Scream Cam, located near the exit of the ride.

Insider's Secret

At the start of the ride, electromagnets are used to accelerate the cars to 55 mph so they have enough speed to climb the first hill without the need for a chain assist.

California Screamin' has a minimum height requirement of 48 inches. The ride is more intense than any other at California Adventure or Disneyland. So you'll want to be sure your children can handle all the other coaster-type rides before they try this one. Space Mountain is a good judge. If the kids liked Space Mountain, they will probably be fine on California Screamin'. Ages 7 and up is a good suggestion.

Maliboomer

This ride is imagineered to resemble the midway games that test a person's strength by having them swing a hammer to send a piece of metal up a slide to ring a bell. However, this time the riders are the object speeding up to ring the bell. The Maliboomer consists of three towers. Each tower has four rows of four seats. Riders are buckled into the seats and then shot 180 feet in the air. A bell rings at the top, and then the riders descend in a series of bounces. It is not a free-fall ride. Instead, the ascent is the thrill. Riders reach a maximum speed of approximately 55 mph.

Maliboomer has a minimum height requirement of 52 inches! The ride actually looks scarier than it really is. In fact, one adult we spoke with in the queue was about to chicken out. Afterward, he said he really liked it and would do it again. The main sensation is that of being pressed down into your seat during the ascent. The way down is controlled, and you never feel as if you are floating. The worst part of the ride

Helpful Hint
The Maliboomer does not offer a FASTPASS system. However, there is another way to expedite your way through the queue: There is a line for single riders. If you don't mind riding apart from your group, or if a parent has to ride alone while the other parent watches the children, this line moves much quicker. The cast member at the boarding area uses the people in this line to fill out each row of seats.

is the anticipation. The seats bounce up and down for a bit before launching skyward, keeping riders guessing as to when they will take off. Most children who meet the height requirement and like thrill rides will be fine on the Maliboomer. Ages 7 and up is a good guide.

Mulholland Madness
A FASTPASS ATTRACTION

This minicoaster is designed to represent Mulholland Drive, the winding road that leads from Hollywood to Malibu. Riders board small cars, some decorated as highway patrol cruisers, which then climb to the top of the ride. After a series of fast turns that make you feel like your car may leave the tracks, the ride takes you down a series of quick drops and climbs with more fast turns. From the outside, the ride appears fairly tame. However, when riding, you will experience more of a thrill than you expected. As you are looking at the large map mural on the ride, look for a Hidden Mickey. There is a swimming pool in the classic shape. You can also find Hidden Mickeys on the Mulholland Madness Billboard license plate.

The minimum height requirement is 42 inches. The Matterhorn Bobsleds is a good comparison for this ride. If your children liked the Matterhorn, they will have a good time on this ride as well.

Helpful Hint

Often when an adult rides with a young child on this type of ride, the safety bar does not hold the child in tight because it is limited by the size of the adult. Mulholland Madness has foam pads that can be placed over the child's section of the bar, keeping the child in safe and tight. Cast members usually put the pads over the bars. However, when it is busy, you may need to ask them for a pad.

Sun Wheel

The main icon of California Adventure, the Sun Wheel is a sight to behold. Before you dismiss it as nothing more than a run-of-the-mill Ferris wheel, take a look at the gondolas on it. Although the red gondolas (one out of three) are fixed to the outer edge of the wheel, the other two-thirds of the gondolas freely swing around on tracks built into the wheel. This provides an entirely new and thrilling experience to the ride. As the wheel rotates, these gondolas move around inside the wheel, taking some quick drops and then swinging wildly at the bottom.

Insider's Secret

The Sun Wheel provides a great view of California Adventure and the surrounding area. Try this ride during the day and then again at night when everything is lit up.

There is no height requirement for this ride. Families with young children should opt for the stationary red gondolas. The queue for these is often shorter, as well. The swinging gondolas are a lot of fun for older children. However, if you are not sure whether they would like it, take a ride in the red ones first, and watch what the other gondolas do during the ride.

Orange Stinger

The Orange Stinger is basically the common swing ride found at most fairs and carnivals but with a theme. Each of the swings is made to look like a bee. Riders then swing around to a buzzing sound inside a giant orange. The swings not only go around but also go up and down a bit.

The ride has a minimum height requirement of 48 inches and a maximum weight limit of 200 pounds. Although this may seem a bit extreme for a swing ride, it is because each rider sits individually in his or her own swing, preventing any parental help for small children during the ride. Children who meet the height requirement and want to go on the ride should not be scared and will enjoy the ride. Children 5 and under may find this ride too scary.

> **Scare Factor**
> Children 5 and under may find the Orange Stinger too scary.

Golden Zephyr
Based on another carnival-style ride, the Golden Zephyr consists of several rocket ships that swing around a central tower. As the ride picks up speed, the rockets swing out over the bay. This ride is similar to the Astro Orbitor at Disneyland, except that Golden Zephyr riders have no control over their rockets and the rockets are suspended on cables rather than an arm. This is a fun ride for children of all ages, with no height or age requirements. Use the Astro Orbitor as a comparison to judge whether your young children will like it or not.

Jumpin' Jellyfish
This ride is a scaled-down version of the Maliboomer. Riders sit in pairs under jellyfish-like parachutes and are taken up to the top and then descend back down to the ground in a series of bounces.

The minimum height requirement for this ride is 40 inches. Most children who meet this requirement will enjoy Jumpin' Jellyfish. However, those who are afraid of heights or are uncomfortable with their feet hanging during a ride should skip this attraction.

King Triton's Carousel
What theme park would be complete without a carousel? Paradise Pier's own version differs from most. Instead of riding

horses, guests climb up on various creatures of the sea, including otters, whales, dolphins, fish, and even sea horses. This is one of the favorites for young children at California Adventure.

S.S. Rustworthy

This water activity center is designed around a shipwrecked fireboat. Children can take part in a number of activities, including water cannons that can be squirted at targets or siblings, plus wheels to turn, bells to ring, and buttons to push. This is a great place to cool down and burn off some energy.

Helpful Hint

It is usually a good idea to have a dry change of clothes for your children after they play on this attraction, unless it is a warm day and they will dry off quickly.

Boardwalk Games

What boardwalk would be complete without some midway games? These games of skill and chance cost an additional fee—usually a couple of dollars per game. Winners receive prizes. For younger children, try the New Haul Fishery. Everyone receives a prize at this game.

Money-Saving Tip

If you have a limited budget or are pressed for time, skip the boardwalk games.

Paradise Pier Tips

Paradise Pier is usually the busiest region in California Adventure, with the afternoon generally being the worst time. Try to hit Paradise Pier first thing in the morning, or wait until late afternoon. Be sure to visit this area at night and enjoy the lights. It is quite spectacular. Even when the area is busy, you can use the FASTPASS system on California Screamin' and Mulholland Madness. Pick up tickets before you have lunch or dinner or while you are watching a show, then come back and get right onto the rides after a short wait.

Dining on Paradise Pier

Just like the rest of California Adventure, Paradise Pier has some great places to eat. Ariel's Grotto is the main restaurant in the area. It serves three-course meals with a set price. Guests can choose their appetizer, main course, and dessert. If you are just looking for a quick meal, Pizza Oom Mow Mow is the place for pizzas on surfboard-shaped crusts. Malibu-Ritos serves different types of burritos, while Strips, Dips, 'n' Chips offers chicken and zucchini strips with a variety of dipping sauces, as well as fish and chips. Corn Dog Castle is the home of large, meal-size corn dogs. Burger Invasion, hosted by McDonald's, serves the chain's usual fare, including Happy Meals and Big Macs. Finally, for a refreshing snack, Catch a Flave offers soft-serve ice cream cones with a variety of flavors swirled in.

For more details on these restaurants, including pricing and sample menus, see chapter 8.

Paradise Pier Shopping

Whether you need sunglasses, a T-shirt, or some Paradise Pier souvenirs, the shops here will have what you're looking for. Dinosaur Jack's Sunglass Shack is hard to miss—it is the large pink dinosaur. Pick up some shades to protect your eyes from the California rays and to look cool. Man Hat 'n' Beach carries a variety of surfing-theme clothing and, of course, all types of headwear. At Pacific Ocean Photos, you can insert your family into one of several scenes from California Adventure. These make great family souvenirs. Point Mugu Tattoo sells temporary tattoos as well as jewelry, while Sideshow Shirts has all types of T-shirts. Souvenir 66 is like a roadside shop where you can pick up souvenirs of your visit. For items themed after the classic boardwalks, check out Treasures in Paradise. Here you can find collectibles, toys, and even California Screamin' merchandise.

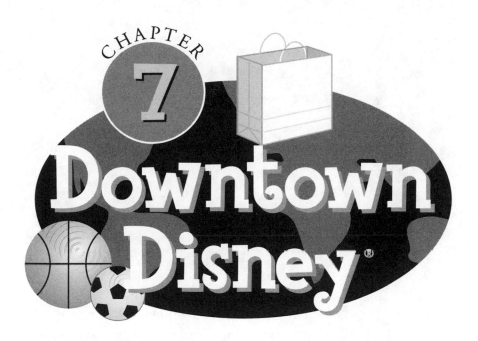

CHAPTER

7

Downtown
Disney®

Downtown Disney is an up-scale shopping area containing a variety of restaurants, shops, and entertainment venues. Located in between the main gates of Disneyland and California Adventure and the Disneyland Hotel, Downtown Disney further adds to the fun of a vacation at the resort.

Most of the venues in Downtown Disney are geared for older children and adults. However, there are a few places young children will enjoy. Downtown Disney remains open after the theme parks close—as late as 2 A.M. This provides fun activities after a day at the park, especially during the off season, when the parks close earlier.

Downtown Disney contains a monorail station near the Rainforest Café. This used to be the Disneyland Hotel monorail station. From here, guests with valid tickets can ride to the Tomorrowland station and back. A ticket stand selling passes to both Disneyland and California Adventure is located near the entrance to the monorail station. The monorail provides a quick means of getting from inside Disneyland to Downtown Disney for lunch or a break. Guests of the Disney hotels can also use it for getting back and forth to the park. Along the west side of Downtown Disney,

Insider's Secret
The monorail is one of the quickest ways to go from inside Disneyland to Downtown Disney for lunch or a break. Guests of the Disney hotels can also use the monorail for going back and forth to the park.

in between it and the Disneyland Hotel, a double-decker bus runs back and forth between the Pinocchio parking lot and the Paradise Pier Hotel—near where the Downtown Disney parking lot is located.

When you first arrive in Downtown Disney, be sure to pick up a "Getting Around Downtown Disney" pamphlet. It provides a map of the area, listing each shop and restaurant, and also provides a program of the various entertainment events scheduled during the week.

This chapter takes a look at the various entertainment venues as well as the shops. For information on the restaurants, see the Downtown Disney section of chapter 8.

Helpful Hint
Be sure to pick up a copy of the "Getting Around Downtown Disney" pamphlet soon after arriving in Downtown Disney. With it you'll have a map of the area, shop and restaurant listings, as well as a schedule for the various entertainment events.

Entertainment

Downtown Disney provides a number of entertainment venues, from sports to movies, with music thrown in as well.

AMC Theatres

Showing the latest movies, this 12-screen theater is designed in the style of Hollywood's golden era. If your family wants to catch a movie during your vacation, this is a great place to go. If you plan on seeing a show after leaving the parks in the evening, it is a good idea to purchase your tickets earlier in the day to avoid the lines in the evening and to ensure you get seats. For show times, call 714-769-4AMC or look them up at www.disneyland.com.

ESPN Zone

Think of this place as a sports bar gone mad. The lower level of the ESPN Zone features a gift shop and two restaurants. The entertainment is on the upper level. Here you can participate in a number of sports-related activities, including video games, a rock-climbing wall, laser skeet, hoop shooting, and much more. There is even a racing simulator where two guests can sit in actual-size cars and race against each other as well as computer-driven opponents. To play the games, you will need to purchase a Zone card. This is like a credit card that stores points. Each game requires a certain number of points to play. You buy a card with a set number of points, and you can add points to the card at ATM-like machines throughout the building. If you will be playing as a family or group, we recommend getting a single card for everyone, if feasible. That is because you get more points for each dollar spent: The more money you spend, the more points you get on that card. For example, $5 will get you a card with 15 points; $10, 40 points; and $100, 600 points. (*Note:* These prices may change after this book goes to print.)

In addition to the games, you can also catch the day's sporting events on the large-screen monitors down in the Screening Room. The largest has a 16-foot screen. For a schedule of events, either check www.disneyland.com or call 714-300-ESPN.

House of Blues

In addition to a restaurant, House of Blues features a theater that can seat nearly 1,000 people. Every night of the week, there is some type of entertainment here. Some big names even appear at House of Blues. Ticket prices range from $10 to $40 and up, depending on the show. Check the Web page from the www.disneyland.com site for shows, times, and ticket prices. If you plan on seeing a popular show, you can purchase tickets in advance by calling 714-778-BLUE (714-778-2583). In addition to blues music, House of Blues features rock, reggae, hiphop, Latin, and R&B. The Sunday Gospel Brunch offers an all-you-can-eat buffet along with live gospel music. Brunch and the show together is $32 per person.

Ralph Brennan's Jazz Kitchen

This establishment features live entertainment nightly at the downstairs restaurant, Flambeaux's. There is no charge, and although the music is intended for guests of the restaurant, you can sit outside the open-air dining area and enjoy it without having dinner. For a schedule of entertainment, check www.disneyland.com.

Shopping

Downtown Disney is filled with a large variety of upscale shops that carry all types of products from household items to apparel to toys and much more. Even if you don't have the money to spend, it is still fun to browse through them.

Basin

This London-based shop sells a variety of unique and fun bath and body products.

Build-A-Bear Workshop

This is a shop where you can actually create your own Teddy bear. Customers select from dozens of basic bears and then customize them with different outfits and accessories. This can be a fun experience, as you get to create your own souvenir.

Compass Books

Billed as the West's oldest independent bookseller, this shop sells books, magazines, and newspapers and includes a small café offering specialty coffees and baked goods.

Department 56

This shop carries collectibles and trendy knickknacks.

Hoypoloi

This gallery sells one-of-a-kind items created by artists from around the world. There is usually something here for everyone.

Illuminations

This shop sells all types of candles and accessories as well as aroma therapy products and home fragrance items.

Island Charters

This is a fun shop with a nautical-aviation theme. It sells clothing items as well as a variety of other items for your home or office.

LEGO Imagination Center

This shop is designed for kids and sells the entire line of LEGO products. Some of the products are often not available in local toy or department stores. The LEGO Imagination Center also has several workstations where kids can try out the building blocks before you buy them. LEGO-related items such as clothing and software are also available. This is a great place to pick up sets for children to play with in the hotel or for gifts.

Liquid Planet

This place carries all types of beach and surf wear and accessories. This can be a good place to pick up a souvenir from California.

Mainspring

If you have the time, stop by this shop, which sells watches of all types and styles.

Marceline's Confectionery

This is a standard candy shop designed like one from the past. It was inspired by Marceline, Missouri—Walt Disney's hometown. You can watch cooks make candies and other treats throughout the day.

Petals

This shop specializes in leather products ranging from coats to belts and handbags.

Sephora

This French cosmetics store not only sells all types of cosmetics and fragrances but also offers complimentary makeovers and demonstrations on applying the products.

Soliton

This trendy shop sells sunglasses in every shape and style you can imagine.

Something Silver

Something Silver carries all types of silver jewelry and accessories, including bracelets, necklaces, earrings, chains, and rings in a variety of styles.

Starabilias

This shop is filled with nostalgic memorabilia from the 19th and 20th centuries. This is a fun place to browse even if you don't plan on purchasing anything.

Walt Disney Travel Company

While you may think a travel office is the last place you would go during your vacation, this can actually be quite helpful. Not only can the staff book reservations for your next vacation, but they can also assist with any changes you may need to make to your current package. For example, if you want to add another day to your trip or add a character dining meal to your package, they can take care of it for you—often saving you money. This office can also make arrangements for visiting other Southern California attractions and even help you find transportation if needed.

World of Disney

Containing California's largest selection of Disney merchandise, this is essentially a super Disney Store. In addition to souvenir items for the Disney theme parks, you can find all types of apparel, household items, and more emblazoned with Disney characters, as well as plush characters, toys, books, videos, and much more.

Disney
Dining

During your vacation to the Disneyland Resort, your family will have to eat. No matter what your budget, you can eat some of your meals, if not all, at the resort. Therefore, we have included this handy guide to each and every restaurant at Disneyland, Disney's California Adventure, the Disney hotels, and even Downtown Disney.

Although many people think primarily of fast food such as burgers and hot dogs when they consider dining at a theme park, the Disneyland Resort offers much, much more. Of course, you can still find burgers and hot dogs, but because your family is on vacation, try taking a culinary vacation as well. Instead of eating the same quick foods you would at home, try something different. Several families we have talked to told us they plan where they want to eat even before they leave on their vacation.

There is a popular misconception that eating at the resort is extremely expensive. Although some things are higher, you can still find good deals to fit your budget. Fast-food items are probably the main thing that is higher. Although you can get a combo meal at McDonald's for $3 to $4, a similar meal at the resort may be $6 to $7. Keep in mind that you may also spend an extra 30 to 60 minutes walking out of the park, across the street to McDonald's, and then back into the park when you could have been riding attractions instead. You do pay for the convenience of some things. Some dinners at the restaurants are comparably priced to those outside the park. For example, one family told us they spent less on a big lunch at the Blue Bayou restaurant in Disneyland than they did on dinner at Tony Roma's the following night.

Eat for Less

There are several ways you can enjoy Disney dining without spending a lot of money. First off, schedule your meals so you eat only one or two at the park. If your hotel offers a complimentary breakfast, that takes care of one meal. If you leave the park during the afternoon to return to your hotel for naps or a swim, you can eat at an off-site place along the way. Or if the park closes early, you can eat dinner off site.

If you plan on dining at a nice restaurant in the resort, do so in the afternoon, usually around 1:30 to 2 P.M. This lets you choose from the less expensive lunch menu, and you also miss the lunch crowds. Because this will be your main meal for the day, you can get by with a light breakfast and light dinner.

Another way of saving money is to eat two meals and then have snacks in between. A late character breakfast with a buffet will last you into the afternoon. Precede it with some snacks in the morning, then more in the afternoon. Finally, have dinner a bit early before the crowds do and then have snacks or a dessert if needed later in the evening.

The key is to budget your meal expenses for the vacation as well as for each day. How strictly you adhere to this budget is up to you, but no matter what, it is a good starting point to saving money. For example, don't eat at a nice restaurant on the same day you do a character breakfast.

Money-Saving Tip

If you drink water with some of your meals instead of buying soft drinks, you can save a bundle over the course of your vacation. For example, a family of four can save $10 to $12 per meal by skipping the drinks.

Instead of buying a lot of snacks at the resort, bring some from home and carry them in a fanny pack or even a pocket. During warm weather, don't bring things that will melt, such as chocolate. Instead, bring nuts, dried fruit, granola bars, fruit snacks, pretzels, crackers, and cookies. Candy may recharge you quickly, but the energy you get is fleeting, and candy is not as filling as the snacks just mentioned. Don't forget drinks, either. Water bottles or juice boxes are much cheaper than buying drinks. In fact, we used our water bottles everywhere except at restaurants with table service.

Money-Saving Tip

You can also save money on meals by using the Disney Club card, American Express, or even an Annual Passport at various restaurants throughout the resort. Certain restrictions apply, so check with the appropriate card or club for more information.

Definitions for Restaurant Ratings

We've categorized and rated the Disneyland Resort restaurants based on the type of restaurant, price, whether you will need reservations, and the restaurant's suitability for children.

Types of Restaurant

Fast Food: Here you will find sandwiches, hamburgers, and other light meals. This category also includes snack or dessert places.

Buffeteria: Here you order a meal at a counter, pay for it, and then carry it to your table.

Buffet: This is an all-you-can-eat meal where you can choose from a variety of items and return for more as you like.

Restaurant: Here you are seated and someone takes your order and then brings the food to your table.

Price

$ *Inexpensive:* adult meals about $8 or less

$$ *Moderate:* adult meals about $9–$15

$$$ *Expensive:* adult meals about $16 and up

Reservations

Most restaurants in the theme parks do not accept reservations. However, most restaurants at the Disney hotels, as well as those in Downtown Disney, do. You can use the following notations to help make your decision:

Suggested: Although you can usually get in without reservations, especially if you come at an off hour, it is still a good idea to make reservations at restaurants that have this notation, to minimize the wait.

Recommended: You will need reservations here unless it is off season or you will be dining at an off hour.

Necessary: You will almost always need reservations here and may have to make them up to several days in advance.

Suitability for Children

The following icons in this chapter tell you how suitable an eating place is for children:

☺☺☺ This kind of restaurant is great for kids. It is informal and has several menu items that will appeal to kids. It has either some type of entertainment or even interesting and fun surroundings that will keep kids occupied while waiting for the meal to be served.

☺☺ This kind of restaurant is fairly casual and family oriented.

☺ This restaurant is designed mainly for adults. Although it may offer a children's menu, it is not really suitable for families with young children, or the menu does not really have children's items.

Disneyland Restaurant Descriptions

Bengal Barbecue	☺ $
Adventureland	**Fast Food**

The Bengal Barbecue serves skewers cooked over a flame for around $3 each. You can choose from beef in either a spicy or sweet sauce, chicken in a Polynesian sauce, bacon-wrapped asparagus, or just veggies. You can also get breadsticks, cinna-

Our Favorites

As we have visited the Disneyland Resort over the years and spent time at the various restaurants, we have developed favorites that we like to enjoy again and again. Here are some foods we look forward to when visiting the resort.

Food	Restaurant	Location
Monte Cristo Sandwich	Blue Bayou Restaurant	Disneyland
Crab Cakes	Blue Bayou Restaurant	Disneyland
Chip 'n' Dale's Breakfast	Storytellers Café	Grand Californian Hotel
Jambalaya	French Market	Disneyland
Pancake Breakfast	River Belle Terrace	Disneyland
Tacos del Mar (fish)	Rancho del Zocalo	Disneyland
BBQ Beef Sandwich	Rancho del Zocalo	Disneyland
Mint Juleps	New Orleans Square	Disneyland

mon twists, and Mickey Mouse pretzels here. For a meal, adults will probably want a couple of skewers or a skewer and a bowl of chowder or gumbo from the Royal Street Veranda. There are no children's meals here.

Kids' Picks

Our children have their favorite foods as well, so we thought we'd list them. Here is what our 3- to 6-year-olds look forward to:

Child	Food	Location
Beth	Churros	Carts around Disneyland and California Adventure
Sarah	Corn Dog	Corn Dog Castle at California Adventure
Connor	Ice Cream Cones	Disneyland and California Adventure

Blue Bayou   ☺☺ $$$
New Orleans Square   Restaurant

The Blue Bayou is Disneyland's most elegant restaurant. The dining area is located inside the boarding area of the Pirates of the Caribbean, and the tables overlook a bayou with the sounds of frogs croaking in the background. Reservations are highly recommended and can be made at the restaurant for the same day. You can also make advance reservations by calling Disney Dining at 714-781-DINE or from any resort pay phone by dialing *86. Therefore, if you plan on dining here, either arrive early or call ahead. Al-

though the staff does save some tables for stand-by, the wait can be quite long. If you plan to dine here on a busy day such as Thanksgiving, Christmas, or another holiday, make reservations well in advance.

The menus for lunch and dinner are similar and include crab cakes, jambalaya, prime rib, bronze chicken, steaks, salads, and seafood. A favorite is the Monte Cristo sandwich, which is turkey, ham, and Swiss cheese on bread. The sandwich is then dipped in batter, deep fried, and served with blackberry preserves. Lunch is served from 11 A.M. to around 3:45 P.M., with dinner immediately following. Lunches range in price from $11 to $17, and dinners are from $20 to $30. There are also a number of sides, such as calamari rings, shrimp cocktail, gumbo, clam chowder, and stuffed mushrooms. Desserts include crème brûlée, chocolate pecan pie, and other tasty treats. The kids' meal includes pasta, mini-corn dogs, or chicken nuggets. In addition, soft drinks are refillable (this is the only restaurant in Disneyland at which they are).

Insider's Secret

The lunch and dinner menus are nearly the same, except at dinner you will pay $6 to $9 more for the same thing. Even with reservations, the best time for dining at the Blue Bayou is around 2 to 3 P.M. This is after the lunch rush but still before the dinner prices go into effect. During holidays or in the summer, be sure to go to the restaurant first to make your reservations. Lines for reservations can get quite long. You can also look at the menu for the day to make sure everyone in your family can find something he or she would like.

Quick Guide to

Name	Description	Location
Ariel's Grotto	Three-course meals including soup or salad, entrée, and a dessert	Paradise Pier
Award Wieners	Hot dogs, sausage sandwiches	Hollywood Pictures Backlot
Baker's Field Bakery	Baked goods, specialty coffees	DCA Entry Plaza
Bengal Barbecue	Skewers with meat or vegetables; no children's meals	Adventureland
Blue Bayou	Fine dining; Cajun-style food, prime rib, seafood	New Orleans Square (inside Pirates of the Caribbean)
Blue Ribbon Bakery	Cinnamon rolls, muffins, scones, cookies, specialty coffees	Main Street, USA
Bountiful Valley Farmers Market	BBQ chicken, brisket sandwiches, salads, desserts	Bountiful Valley Farm
Burger Invasion	McDonald's burgers, sandwiches, fries, Happy Meals	Paradise Pier
Bur-r-r Bank Ice Cream	Ice cream cones, sundaes, shakes	DCA Entry Plaza
Café Orleans	Creole-style dinners; muffuletta sandwiches, salads, chowder	New Orleans Square
Captain's Galley	sandwiches, salads, boxed lunches, snacks	Disneyland Hotel

$ Inexpensive: adult meals about $8 or less
$$ Moderate: adult meals about $9–$15
$$$ Expensive: adult meals about $16 and up

Disneyland Resort Dining

Type	Price	Reservations	Kids	Details on
Restaurant	$$$	Recommended	☺☺☺	Page 271
Fast Food	$		☺	Page 272
Fast Food	$		☺☺	Page 272
Fast Food	$		☺	Page 244
Restaurant	$$$	Recommended	☺☺	Page 246
Fast Food	$		☺☺	Page 260
Fast Food	$		☺☺☺	Page 272
Fast Food	$		☺☺☺	Page 273
Fast Food	$		☺☺☺	Page 273
Buffeteria	$		☺	Page 261
Fast Food	$		☺☺	Page 281

☺☺☺ **Great for kids, informal, and fun.**
☺☺ **Fairly casual and family oriented.**
☺ **Mainly for adults.**

(continues)

Quick Guide to

Name	Description	Location
Carnation Café	Light breakfasts; sandwiches, salads, homestyle dinners	Main Street, USA
Catal and Uva Bar	Tapas bar, Mediterranean-style meals, soups, salads, sandwiches	Downtown Disney
Catch a Flave	Soft-serve ice cream with flavored swirls, also floats	Paradise Pier
Clarabelle's Frozen Yogurt	Frozen yogurt cones and cups, sundaes	Toontown
Club Buzz—Lightyear's Above the Rest	Breakfast; cheeseburgers, sandwiches, salads, fried chicken	Tomorrowland
Cocina Cucamonga Mexican Grill	Several types of tacos and nachos	Pacific Wharf
The Coffee Bar and Lounge	Specialty coffees, snacks, alcoholic drinks	Paradise Pier Hotel
The Coffee House	Baked goods, specialty coffees, drinks	Disneyland Hotel
Conestoga Fries	McDonald's French fries, drinks	Frontierland
Corn Dog Castle	Large corn dogs, corn dipped cheese stick, spicy corn dogs	Paradise Pier
Croc's Bits 'n' Bites	Chicken sandwiches and tenders, burgers, fries	Disneyland Hotel
Daisy's Diner	Individual-size pizzas, salads	Toontown

$ Inexpensive: adult meals about $8 or less
$$ Moderate: adult meals about $9–$15
$$$ Expensive: adult meals about $16 and up

Disneyland Resort Dining

Type	Price	Reservations	Kids	Details on
Restaurant	$		☺☺	Page 262
Restaurant	$$–$$$	Recommended	☺	Page 290
Fast Food	$		☺☺☺	Page 274
Fast Food	$		☺☺☺	Page 262
Fast Food	$		☺☺☺	Page 262
Fast Food	$		☺☺☺	Page 274
Fast Food	$		☺	Page 281
Fast Food	$		☺☺	Page 281
Fast Food	$		☺☺☺	Page 263
Fast Food	$		☺☺	Page 275
Fast Food	$		☺☺☺	Page 282
Fast Food	$		☺☺☺	Page 263

☺☺☺ Great for kids, informal, and fun.
☺☺ Fairly casual and family oriented.
☺ Mainly for adults.

(continues)

Quick Guide to

Name	Description	Location
Disney's PCH Grill	Character breakfast; pasta, pizza, seafood, steaks, and more	Paradise Pier Hotel
ESPN Zone	Salads, sandwiches, pizza, pasta, chicken, steak, seafood	Downtown Disney
Fairfax Market	Fruit, snacks	Hollywood Pictures Backlot
French Market Restaurant	Jambalaya, fried chicken, pasta, sandwiches; good value	New Orleans Square
Gibson Girl Ice Cream Parlor	Ice cream cones, sundaes, shakes, and frozen yogurt	Main Street, USA
Golden Horseshoe	Cheeseburgers, chili dogs, chili fries, chili in a bread bowl, desserts	Frontierland
Goofy's Kitchen	Character dining, buffet	Disneyland Hotel
Granville's Steak House	Formal dining; steaks, prime rib, chicken, seafood	Disneyland Hotel
Haagen-Dazs	Ice cream cones, sundaes, frozen drinks	Downtown Disney
Harbour Galley	McDonald's french fries, cold drinks	Critter Country
Hearthstone Lounge	Snacks, alcoholic drinks	Grand Californian Hotel
Hook's Pointe and Wine Cellar	Breakfast; pasta, pizza, seafood, steak, chicken	Disneyland Hotel

$ Inexpensive: adult meals about $8 or less
$$ Moderate: adult meals about $9–$15
$$$ Expensive: adult meals about $16 and up

Disneyland Resort Dining

Type	Price	Reservations	Kids	Details on
Restaurant	$$–$$$	Recommended	☺☺☺	Page 282
Restaurant	$$–$$$	Suggested	☺	Page 290
Fast Food	$		☺☺	Page 275
Buffeteria	$–$$		☺☺	Page 263
Fast Food	$		☺☺☺	Page 264
Fast Food	$		☺☺	Page 264
Buffet	$$$	Recommended	☺☺☺	Page 283
Restaurant	$$$	Recommended	☺	Page 284
Fast Food	$		☺☺☺	Page 291
Fast Food	$		☺	Page 264
Fast Food	$–$$$		☺	Page 284
Restaurant	$$–$$$	Recommended	☺☺☺	Page 285

☺☺☺ Great for kids, informal, and fun.
☺☺ Fairly casual and family oriented.
☺ Mainly for adults.

(continues)

Quick Guide to

Name	Description	Location
House of Blues	BBQ ribs, steak, chicken, seafood, sandwiches, pizza, salads, burgers; Sunday Gospel Brunch	Downtown Disney
Hungry Bear Restaurant	Burgers, chicken sand-wiches, salads, vegan patties available	Critter Country
La Brea Bakery	Soup, salad, sandwiches, pasta, chicken, seafood, baked goods	Downtown Disney
La Petite Patisserie	French pastries, drinks and specialty coffees	New Orleans Square
Little Red Wagon	Corn dogs; nearby cart sells tamales and chimichangas	Main Street, USA
The Lost Bar	Hamburgers, sandwiches, appetizers, alcoholic drinks	Disneyland Hotel
The Lucky Fortune Cookery	Sushi, rice or noodle bowls, dim sum, egg rolls, wonton	Pacific Wharf
Main Street Cone Shop	Ice cream cones, shakes, sundaes, sliced apples with caramel dipping sauce	Main Street, USA
Malibu-Ritos	Large burritos, desserts	Paradise Pier
Mint Julep Bar	Mint juleps, specialty coffees, fritters, baked goods, ice cream bars	New Orleans Square
The Napa Rose	Formal dining, seafood, steak, chicken, pasta	Grand Cali-fornian Hotel

$ Inexpensive: adult meals about $8 or less
$$ Moderate: adult meals about $9–$15
$$$ Expensive: adult meals about $16 and up

Disneyland Resort Dining

Type	Price	Reservations	Kids	Details on
Restaurant	$$–$$$	Necessary	☺	Page 291
Fast Food	$		☺☺☺	Page 264
Fast Food	$		☺☺	Page 293
Fast Food	$		☺☺	Page 265
Fast Food	$		☺☺	Page 265
Fast Food	$		☺	Page 285
Fast Food	$–$$		☺	Page 275
Fast Food	$		☺☺☺	Page 266
Fast Food	$		☺☺	Page 276
Fast Food	$		☺☺☺	Page 266
Restaurant	$$$	Necessary	☺	Page 286

☺☺☺ Great for kids, informal, and fun.
☺☺ Fairly casual and family oriented.
☺ Mainly for adults.

(continues)

Quick Guide to

Name	Description	Location
Naples Ristorante e Pizzeria	Gourmet pizzas, pasta, chicken, seafood, salads	Downtown Disney
Pacific Wharf Café	Soups and salads in bread bowls, pastries, bread breakfast	Pacific Wharf
Pizza Oom Mow Mow	Individual-size pizzas, calzone, salads	Paradise Pier
Plaza Inn	Character breakfast; fried chicken, pot roast, salads	Main Street, USA
Pluto's Dog House	Hot dogs, chips, drinks	Toontown
Rainforest Café	Breakfast; salads, sandwiches, seafood, pasta, steak, and more	Downtown Disney
Ralph Brennan's Jazz Kitchen	Three separate dining areas all featuring Cajun-style dishes; Sunday brunch	Downtown Disney
Rancho del Zocalo	Burritos, tacos, tostadas, BBQ ribs, chicken, sandwiches	Frontierland
Redd Rockett's Pizza Port	Pizza, pasta, salads	Tomorrowland
Refreshment Corner	Hot dogs, chili dogs, pretzels, drinks	Main Street, USA
Rita's Baja Blenders	Nonalcoholic margarita-style drinks	Pacific Wharf
River Belle Terrace	Breakfast; sandwiches, seafood, steaks, fried chicken	Frontierland

$ Inexpensive: adult meals about $8 or less
$$ Moderate: adult meals about $9–$15
$$$ Expensive: adult meals about $16 and up

Disneyland Resort Dining

Type	Price	Reservations	Kids	Details on
Restaurant	$$–$$$	Suggested	☺☺	Page 293
Fast Food	$–$$		☺	Page 276
Fast Food	$		☺☺☺	Page 277
Buffeteria	$–$$$		☺☺☺	Page 266
Fast Food	$		☺☺☺	Page 267
Restaurant	$$–$$$	Recommended	☺☺☺	Page 294
Restaurant and Fast Food	$$–$$$	Recommended	☺☺	Page 295
Buffeteria	$–$$		☺☺☺	Page 267
Buffeteria	$		☺☺☺	Page 268
Fast Food	$		☺☺	Page 268
Fast Food	$		☺☺	Page 277
Buffeteria	$–$$		☺☺	Page 269

☺☺☺ Great for kids, informal, and fun.
☺☺ Fairly casual and family oriented.
☺ Mainly for adults.

(continues)

Quick Guide to

Name	Description	Location
Royal Street Veranda	Gumbo, clam chowder, fritters	New Orleans Square
Sam Andreas Shakes	Ice cream shakes, soft-serve cones	Bountiful Valley Farm
Schmoozies	Fruit smoothies, juices, specialty coffees	Hollywood Pictures Backlot
Stage Door Café	Cheeseburgers, hot dogs	Frontierland
Storytellers Café	Character breakfast buffet; pasta, pizza, chicken, steak, seafood	Grand Californian Hotel
Strips, Dips 'n' Chips	Fried chicken or zucchini strips, fish and chips, dipping sauce, apples and caramel	Paradise Pier
Taste Pilot's Grill	Breakfast; burgers, BBQ ribs, salads	Condor Flats
Tiki Juice Bar	Pineapple spears, juice sorbet	Adventureland
Troubadour Treats	Individual-size pizzas, nachos, snacks; open only on days Mickey's Detective School shows	Fantasyland
Village Haus Restaurant	Individual-size pizzas, cheeseburgers, sandwiches, salads	Fantasyland
The Vineyard Room	Four-course meals, with or without wine	Golden Vine Winery
Wetzel's Pretzels	Pretzels, hot dogs, drinks	Downtown Disney

$ Inexpensive: adult meals about $8 or less
$$ Moderate: adult meals about $9–$15
$$$ Expensive: adult meals about $16 and up

Disneyland Resort Dining

Type	Price	Reservations	Kids	Details on
Fast Food	$		☺	Page 269
Fast Food	$		☺☺	Page 278
Fast Food	$		☺☺	Page 278
Fast Food	$		☺☺	Page 269
Restaurant	$$–$$$	Suggested	☺☺☺	Page 287
Fast Food	$		☺☺☺	Page 278
Fast Food	$–$$		☺☺	Page 279
Fast Food	$		☺☺☺	Page 270
Fast Food	$		☺☺	Page 270
Fast Food	$		☺☺☺	Page 270
Restaurant	$$$	Suggested same day	☺	Page 279
Fast Food	$		☺☺☺	Page 296

☺☺☺ Great for kids, informal, and fun.
☺☺ Fairly casual and family oriented.
☺ Mainly for adults.

(continues)

Quick Guide to

Name	Description	Location
White Water Snacks	Breakfast; sandwiches, burgers, pizza, snacks, desserts	Grand California Hotel
Wine Country Trattoria	Sandwiches, snacks	Golden Vine Winery
Yamabuki	Formal Japanese restaurant, sushi bar	Paradise Pier Hotel

$ Inexpensive: adult meals about $8 or less
$$ Moderate: adult meals about $9–$15
$$$ Expensive: adult meals about $16 and up

Blue Ribbon Bakery $
Main Street, USA   **Fast Food**

The Blue Ribbon Bakery is a great place to pick up breakfast while you are on Main Street waiting for the park to officially open. You can find all types of baked goods, including cinnamon rolls, scones, sticky buns, cake, cookies, and much more, all under $3. To wash it down, you can find several types of specialty coffees. You can also get sandwiches here on fresh folded bread. Although the bakery does not have a children's menu, kids like the baked goods and the crisped rice treats dipped in chocolate.

Disneyland Resort Dining

Type	Price	Reservations	Kids	Details on
Fast Food	$		☺☺☺	Page 288
Fast Food	$$		☺	Page 280
Restaurant	$$$	Recommended	☺	Page 288

☺☺☺ Great for kids, informal, and fun.
☺☺ Fairly casual and family oriented.
☺ Mainly for adults.

Café Orleans	☺ $
New Orleans Square	**Buffeteria**

This restaurant is usually open only on weekends during the off season and daily during holidays or the summer. It features a variety of Creole-style dishes, including muffuletta and other sandwiches, Cajun chicken Caesar salad, poulet de la maison, beef bourguignonne, and chowder. Prices range from $7 to $9. For children, there is a peanut-butter-and-jelly sandwich meal.

Carnation Café
Main Street, USA

 $
Restaurant

Although the Carnation Café is no longer sponsored by the Carnation Corporation, nor does it serve the ice cream treats as in the past, it is one of only two table service restaurants in the park. It offers light breakfasts, including continental, croissant sandwiches, French toast, waffles—all under $6— and delicious sticky buns and cinnamon rolls. For lunch and dinner, you will find a variety of salads, sandwiches, and some hot meals, such as beef stroganoff, chicken pot pie, or pot roast. All are between $7 and $9. Children can have a Mickey Mouse waffle for breakfast or macaroni and cheese, hot dogs, or peanut butter and jelly for lunch and dinner. All are about $5.50. You can dine indoors or outdoors.

Clarabelle's Frozen Yogurt
Toontown

$
Fast Food

This counter serves frozen yogurt by the cone, cup, or sundae, as well as soft-serve ice cream. This is a good place for an afternoon snack if you are in Toontown. Prices range from $2 to $3.

Club Buzz—Lightyear's Above the Rest
Tomorrowland

 $
Fast Food

For lunch and dinner, the Club serves cheeseburgers, chicken sandwiches, fried chicken, deli sandwiches, or Caesar salads, with prices ranging from $5 to $8. Kids' meals include mini-corn dogs or chicken nuggets. On most weekend evenings and during the week in summer, you can listen to live musical performances, and during the day the stage show *Calling All Space Scouts . . . A Buzz Lightyear Adventure* can be seen while

your family dines. You can also get breakfast at this venue; in fact, this is the location where you can redeem the breakfast-in-the-park vouchers that come with some vacation packages.

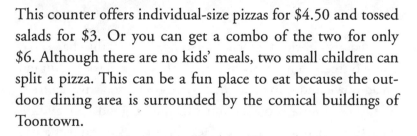

Conestoga Fries ☺☺☺ $
Frontierland **Fast Food**

This stand serves only two things: drinks and McDonald's french fries.

Daisy's Diner ☺☺☺ $
Toontown **Fast Food**

This counter offers individual-size pizzas for $4.50 and tossed salads for $3. Or you can get a combo of the two for only $6. Although there are no kids' meals, two small children can split a pizza. This can be a fun place to eat because the outdoor dining area is surrounded by the comical buildings of Toontown.

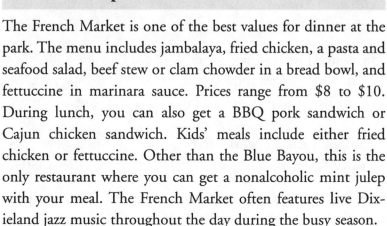

French Market Restaurant ☺☺ $–$$
New Orleans Square **Buffeteria**

The French Market is one of the best values for dinner at the park. The menu includes jambalaya, fried chicken, a pasta and seafood salad, beef stew or clam chowder in a bread bowl, and fettuccine in marinara sauce. Prices range from $8 to $10. During lunch, you can also get a BBQ pork sandwich or Cajun chicken sandwich. Kids' meals include either fried chicken or fettuccine. Other than the Blue Bayou, this is the only restaurant where you can get a nonalcoholic mint julep with your meal. The French Market often features live Dixieland jazz music throughout the day during the busy season.

Gibson Girl Ice Cream Parlor   ☺☺☺ $
Main Street, USA   **Fast Food**

This is a favorite of many guests and serves sundaes, cones, waffle cones, frozen yogurt, milkshakes, and even root beer floats. This is also the only place you can get the ice cream flavor Fantasia. It is a combination of cherry, pistachio, and banana ice creams (not all mixed together). Prices range from $2 to $5. Pick up a treat while you are waiting for a parade or on your way to the park exit.

Golden Horseshoe   ☺☺ $
Frontierland   **Fast Food**

Located inside the Golden Horseshoe Stage, this bar serves cheeseburgers, hot dogs, chili dogs, chili cheese fries, chili in a bread bowl, and some tasty desserts. Be sure to arrive 15 to 20 minutes before a show so you can find a good seat and get your food. It is also a great place for a snack during the day. Prices range from $3 to $6.

Harbour Galley   ☺ $
Critter Country   **Fast Food**

This counter located near the dock of the *Columbia* offers McDonald's french fries and ice-cold drinks. The seating looks out over the Rivers of America, making this a nice spot for a snack.

Hungry Bear Restaurant   ☺☺☺ $
Critter Country   **Fast Food**

This place right along the Rivers of America is a good place for lunch. The menu includes cheeseburgers, country-fried

chicken sandwiches, roast beef sandwiches, BBQ chicken salad, and even onion rings. Prices range from $5 to $8. Kids' meals include either mini corn dogs or chicken nuggets for $4. This is one of the few places where you can substitute a vegan patty for meat in the cheeseburgers.

Insider's Secret
This restaurant has a lower level right down by the river. The restrooms and telephones here are rarely busy because many people don't know they are even down there.

La Petite Patisserie	☺☺ $
New Orleans Square	**Fast Food**

This counter serves delicious French pastries. You can also find specialty coffees and other drinks. Prices are from $2 to $5. It is usually open only on busy days.

Little Red Wagon	☺☺ $
Main Street, USA	**Fast Food**

Located near the Plaza Inn, this red truck serves corn dogs and drinks—the only place in the park where you can get a regular corn dog. (Some places serve mini corn dogs in the kids' meals.) There is often a cart nearby that sells tamales and chimichangas. The Little Red Wagon is usually open only during busy days. Prices range from $3 to $5.

Main Street Cone Shop
Main Street, USA   ☺☺☺ $ Fast Food

This shop can be hard to find. It is located behind the fruit cart, by the lockers. It serves ice cream cones, milkshakes, sundaes, and sliced apples with a caramel dipping sauce. Prices range from $2 to $5.

Mint Julep Bar
New Orleans Square   ☺☺☺ $ Fast Food

This counter located near the French Market serves the famous Disneyland nonalcoholic mint julep as well as other drinks and specialty coffees. You can also get ice cream bars, fritters, and other baked goods here. Prices are from $2 to $4.

Plaza Inn
Main Street, USA    ☺☺☺ $–$$$ Buffeteria

In the morning, the Plaza Inn offers a character breakfast buffet with several Disney characters. It is $19 for adults and $11 for children, and the all-you-can-eat buffet includes an omelet bar, eggs, meats, potatoes, French toast, blintzes, waffles, fresh fruit, biscuits and gravy, bagels, muffins, and even cereal.

Helpful Hint
Although the price is a bit steep, especially for breakfast, you can make this the big meal for the day. Eat a late breakfast here after hitting a few attractions, then you can snack in the afternoon and later have dinner.

For lunch and dinner, the Plaza Inn becomes a buffeteria, serving fried chicken, pot roast, pasta, and salads for $10 to $13. Children can choose from chicken or pasta.

Pluto's Dog House	☺☺☺	$
Toontown		**Fast Food**

This counter serves only hot dogs with chips for around $4. With Daisy's Diner next door, they make a decent place to have lunch while in Toontown.

Rancho del Zocalo	☺☺☺	$–$$
Frontierland		**Buffeteria**

This restaurant is next to Big Thunder Mountain Railroad. It replaced two favorite Disneyland restaurants: Casa Mexicana and Big Thunder BBQ. As such, this place offers both Mexican-style food as well as a barbecue cuisine.

The menu features burritos, tacos (including chicken, beef, or even fish), tostadas, and quesadillas—all for $8 to $10. Most of these come with rice and beans. You can also get smoked ribs, BBQ chicken, or a combination of the two for $11 to $14. During lunch, the restaurant also serves a variety of sandwiches, including BBQ beef, chicken-fried steak, and a chicken verdugo. Each comes with a large pile of fries and coleslaw for around $9. Kids' meals include your choice of a bean-and-cheese burrito or a quesadilla, along with tortilla chips, a small cup of nacho cheese sauce, and a drink, all for $5.

This is a great restaurant for families. The portions are quite large, and most adults may have trouble finishing a dinner by themselves. Also, the nachos in the kids' meals instead of fries is a good change for kids during your vacation. We recommend

sharing an adult meal with a small child (especially if they like beans and rice) to save money.

Redd Rockett's Pizza Port	☺☺☺ $
Tomorrowland	**Buffeteria**

Redd Rockett's offers something for everyone. You can get a whole pizza for around $30 or by the slice for about $5. There is a selection of pasta dinners, for around $9, plus a kids' meal with cheese ravioli or spaghetti for $5. You can also find some interesting and tasty salads for $7 to $9. For dessert, try the cookie dessert pizza for $4. Children like the atmosphere at this place. The pizza slices are fairly large, so two small children could easily split one. If your family can agree on one type of pizza, get a whole one because this can be cheaper than buying pizza by the slice.

Refreshment Corner	☺☺ $
Main Street, USA	**Fast Food**

This place is also called Coke Corner. Here you can find regular or foot-long hot dogs and chili dogs for $4 to $5, as well as Mickey Mouse pretzels. This is a good place for a quick lunch or light dinner; there is often a pianist playing ragtime. Considering the entertainment, this is a good deal.

Helpful Hint

Across the street from the Refreshment Corner is a red truck (the Little Red Wagon) selling corn dogs (the only regular ones in the park except for the mini corn dogs in kids' meals) and a cart that sells tamales and chimichangas. You can pick these up, then return to Refreshment Corner for a drink and sit down to eat and enjoy the music.

River Belle Terrace ☺☺ $–$$
Frontierland Buffeteria

The River Belle Terrace serves a good breakfast. You can get pancakes or potatoes, eggs and meat for under $7, a large Mickey Mouse pancake for about $5.50, and even cinnamon rolls. The lunch menu offers sandwiches, including steak, chicken, turkey, deli, and even catfish—all for around $10. For dinner there is steak, catfish, and salmon as well as fried chicken, with prices ranging from $10 to $15. Children can find peanut-butter-and-jelly sandwiches or hot dogs.

Insider's Secret

Walt Disney used to enjoy eating Sunday breakfast at the River Belle Terrace. The outdoor seating also provides a good vantage point from which to watch *Fantasmic!*—if you get there early enough.

Royal Street Veranda ☺ $
New Orleans Square Fast Food

This counter serves steak or vegetable gumbo and clam chowder in bread bowls for $6. You can also find fritters and other sweet snacks here. Several families send a parent to go get dinner here while the rest hold a spot for *Fantasmic!*

Stage Door Café ☺☺ $
Frontierland Fast Food

Located next to the Golden Horseshoe, this counter serves hot dog and cheeseburger meals for around $5 each, as well as a kid's hot dog meal for $4.

Tiki Juice Bar    $
Adventureland   **Fast Food**

The Tiki Juice Bar is located at the Enchanted Tiki Room. If you don't like pineapples, don't come here. That is all they have. Choose from pineapple spears or pineapple juice for $2 each, or a very tasty pineapple Dole whip, which is a soft-serve sorbet, for $2.50. This is a good place for a refreshing snack, especially while waiting for the show. You can take your food in with you to watch the show as well.

Troubadour Treats    $
Fantasyland   **Fast Food**

Located near the Fantasyland Theatre, Troubadour Treats is usually open only on days when *Mickey's Detective School* is showing. Here you can find individual-size pizzas, hot dogs, and nachos, all for $4 to $5. If you just want a quick snack, get a funnel cake, a pretzel, or some popcorn for $2 to $3.

Village Haus Restaurant   ☺☺☺ $
Fantasyland   **Fast Food**

The menu here includes cheeseburgers, individual-size pizza meals that include a salad, sandwiches, and salads. All are $5 to $7. Kids' meals offer a choice of hot dogs or chicken nuggets for $4. If you decide to eat here, do it in the evening as Fantasyland begins to slow down. During the day it is usually quite busy, plus you have all the noise of Fantasyland around you.

California Adventure Restaurant Descriptions

When you decide to dine inside California Adventure, be prepared. It is nothing like Disneyland. Although you can still find the basic fast-food stand-bys, California Adventure offers a variety of different cuisines to tempt your taste buds, including Chinese, Japanese, and Mexican dishes. Just about everything here has a California flair.

Also unlike Disneyland, where no alcohol is allowed, California Adventure sells beer, wine, and cocktails at some restaurants. Guests purchasing these beverages must consume them at the restaurants where they buy them and may not walk around the park with them.

Ariel's Grotto	 $$$
Paradise Pier	**Restaurant**

Formerly Avalon Cove, this restaurant has been transformed into a family-friendly dining experience. Ariel, the Little Mermaid, greets the guests, making this a favorite of small children. The menu is unique to the Disneyland Resort because it offers set prices for lunch and dinner. Each consists of three courses, including soup or salad, an entrée, and dessert. Guests select from many options to create their own meal. Entrées include fish and chips, lasagna, hamburgers, and so forth. The price is reasonable, considering that it buys a full meal in a sit-down restaurant with character dining. Lunch is around $20 for adults and $15 for children, with dinner about $10 higher. Reservations are available and recommended, especially on busy days. Try to dine at Ariel's Grotto around 1:30 P.M. so you miss the lunch rush but still get the lunch price.

Award Wieners ☺ $
Hollywood Pictures Backlot — Fast Food

Located right on Hollywood Boulevard, this hot dog stand serves up some gourmet sausages. In addition to a chili cheese dog, you can also get a hot link, Caesar sausage, or Sicilian sausage on a bun with fries for $6. These are large meals, so expect to be filled up. Although there is no kids' meal here, you can get just a hot dog and fries for $5. However, the drink is not included.

Baker's Field Bakery ☺☺ $
Entry Plaza — Fast Food

This small bakery sells a variety of baked goods, including muffins, brownies, and other tasty treats, as well as specialty coffee drinks. This is a good place for a quick breakfast or a midday snack. Prices range from about $2 to $5.

Bountiful Valley Farmers Market ☺☺☺ $
Bountiful Valley Farm — Fast Food

This eatery serves a selection of barbecue favorites such as chicken, BBQ brisket sandwiches, and turkey legs. These meals come with coleslaw (and cornbread for the non-sandwich meals). There is also a Visalia Greek Salad for a lighter meal. These range in price from $7 to $8. Kids can choose a BBQ chicken-leg dinner or a unique *Bug's Life*–inspired meal consisting of peanut butter and jelly, marshmallow cream, crispy rice, and gummy worms all in a chocolate wrap. For

dessert, children love the Mix in Mud Kit, which is chocolate pudding with gummy worms, marshmallows, and cookie pieces to stir in. Prices for these are between $4 and $5.

Burger Invasion	☺☺☺ $
Paradise Pier	**Fast Food**

Don't let the name fool you. This is a McDonald's, pure and simple. You can get Big Macs, double cheeseburgers, or even Chicken McNuggets here. The meals include fries and run around $5. However, meals do not include a drink. You must buy that separately. Salads, fries, shakes, and even apple pies are also available at prices higher than you would pay at a Mc-Donald's outside the park. However, the Happy Meals are one of the best deals in California Adventure. Ranging from $3.50 to $4, they include your choice of hamburger, cheeseburger, or Chicken McNuggets, plus fries, drink, and a toy. This is usually cheaper than most kids' meals, and you can take the boxes with you if the parents and older children want to eat somewhere else in the park. Or, for a light meal, the whole family can get Happy Meals.

Bur-r-r Bank Ice Cream	☺☺☺ $
Entry Plaza	**Fast Food**

This ice cream stand located in the California Zephyr train is a great place for a quick treat, especially while waiting for the parade. In addition to standard scooped ice cream cones, you can also get waffle cones (dipped in chocolate or not) and sundaes. Cones range in price from $2 to $4, and the sundaes are between $5 and $6.

Catch a Flave   ☺☺☺ $
Paradise Pier   **Fast Food**

This ice cream stand sells vanilla soft-serve cones that are
swirled with your choice of flavor. It is not just limited to
chocolate either. You can also choose from cotton candy,
grape, orange, lemon, butter pecan, or bubble gum. Small
cones are $3, and large are $4. Ice cream floats in root beer or
another flavor of soda run around $3, or for $6 you can get it
in a souvenir mug. This is a good place for a snack, especially
on warm days.

Cocina Cucamonga Mexican Grill   ☺☺☺ $
Pacific Wharf   **Fast Food**

Located in the Pacific Wharf food court, this eatery serves a
plate of two tacos for around $6. You can choose from beef,
chicken, pork, or even fish. A plate of nachos will run you
around $7 with the same choice of meats—except fish. The
child's meal comes with chicken taquitos for $5. For dessert,
try the cinnamon rice pudding for $3.

Helpful Hint
The Pacific Wharf food court is a great place for
families to eat because it lets everyone choose
from a variety of menus, all located around a center
dining area. A good idea is to get a little something
from each of the surrounding eateries and then
share it as a family.

Corn Dog Castle $
Paradise Pier   **Fast Food**

Although you might first think $4 for a corn dog is a bit steep, those served at the Corn Dog Castle are large and a meal in themselves. In addition to the standard corn dog, this place also serves a cheese stick dipped in the batter and even a hot link corn dog. If you like spicy food, we definitely recommend the latter as an experience you will not likely find elsewhere. Unfortunately, this eatery does not have a kids' menu, and the corn dogs are probably too large for most small children and difficult to share between two. However, Burger Invasion's Happy Meals are close by.

Fairfax Market $
Hollywood Pictures Backlot   **Fast Food**

This stand is located right along the main strip and sells healthful snacks, including fresh fruit. Prices range from $2 to $4.

The Lucky Fortune Cookery   ☺ $–$$
Pacific Wharf   **Fast Food**

This eatery is in the Pacific Wharf food court and serves a variety of dishes from the Pacific Rim. The Dim Sum Platter goes for $9 and includes egg rolls, fried shrimp, and pot stickers. You can also get California rolls, a type of sushi, for $6.50 or a Chinese chicken salad for about $9. There are also rice or noodle bowls with beef or chicken that go for $8. The kids' meal is an egg roll on a stick for $4. This is probably not the best place for kids to eat unless your children like egg rolls. However, in the food court they can get something at one of the other eateries. Be sure to try the wonton for dessert. They come in three different flavors: lemon, apple, or chocolate raspberry.

Malibu-Ritos	☺☺ $
Paradise Pier	**Fast Food**

Located by the boardwalk games, this eatery serves chicken, beef, or bean-and-cheese burritos for $6 to $7. They are quite large and definitely a meal in themselves. There are also some tasty desserts here if you want to finish your meal with something sweet. There is no kids' meal offered; however, the bean-and-cheese burrito can be split between two children.

Pacific Wharf Café	☺ $–$$
Pacific Wharf	**Fast Food**

Located in the Pacific Wharf food court, this is part of the Boudin Bakery, which you can also tour. As such, it features soups and salads served in freshly baked bread bowls. Soups include clam chowder, corn chowder, or broccoli cheese for $6. The salads offered are chicken and apple, niçoise, or shrimp Louis and run from $8 to $9. The café also sells delicious cream puffs and other pastries. The café is also one of the few

Insider's Secret

Stop by this café and ask about Mickey Mouse–shaped sourdough bread. The bakers often make it at different times during the day. You can buy it hot out of the oven and take it home as a souvenir. These loaves run about $7. You can also purchase a hot loaf of round bread for about $4 to share as a family after the bakery tour.

places in Disney's California Adventure that serves breakfast. You can choose from scrambled eggs and bacon in a bread bowl, a breakfast croissant, and a bowl of oatmeal for $4 to $6.

Pizza Oom Mow Mow	☺☺☺ $
Paradise Pier	**Fast Food**

This pizza joint serves a variety of individual-size pizzas on surfboard-shaped crusts—all between $5 and $6. It also serves some delicious calzone for about the same price. If you would rather have a salad, a side Caesar is about $3 and a chicken Caesar is $8. The kids' meal features a peanut-butter-and-jelly pizza with drink for around $4. This is the only place for pizza in California Adventure. Although children may not care for the PB&J pizza with the kids' meal, two small children can share a regular pizza that may be more to their taste.

Rita's Baja Blenders	☺☺ $
Pacific Wharf	**Fast Food**

Located right in the middle of the food court, this is the place to get your drinks if you are eating in this area, or just to wet your whistle. These non-alcoholic margarita-style drinks come in a variety of flavors, including peach, pineapple-coconut, lemon-lime, and mimosa. Each drink costs around $4.

Helpful Hint
Rather than buying a soda at one of the eateries, just get the food and then buy your drinks from Rita's.

Sam Andreas Shakes $
Bountiful Valley Farm · Fast Food

This snack stand sells ice cream shakes for around $3.50. For $1 more, you can add topping and whipped cream. The toppings vary from crushed candy bars to healthy snacks such as dates. You can also get soft-serve cones here for around $2 to $4 depending on size and whether you want it dipped in chocolate. Because this stand is located right along the parade route and the main pathway through the Golden State, it is easy to stop by here and get some quick refreshment.

Schmoozies  $
Hollywood Pictures Backlot · Fast Food

This drink stand sells a variety of smoothies that come in several fruit flavors as well as a mocha. They go for $5 each. You can get specialty coffees and juices here as well.

Helpful Hint

If you are hitting the Baker's Field Bakery for a quick breakfast, slide on over to Schmoozies for a juice or other drink to wash down your baked goods.

Strips, Dips, 'n' Chips ☺☺☺ $
Paradise Pier · Fast Food

Located near Malibu-Ritos, this eatery serves four fried chicken strips with fries for $6. You have your choice of dipping sauce, including ranch, honey mustard, BBQ, or teriyaki. You can also find fish and chips here, as well as mozzarella

sticks for about the same price. For dessert, or just a yummy snack, try the apple wedges with a caramel dipping sauce. You can get this without chopped peanuts for around $3. Although there is no kids' meal here, a couple of children can easily share a meal of chicken strips and fries.

Taste Pilot's Grill	☺☺	$–$$
Condor Flats		**Fast Food**

This aviation-themed restaurant is a lot of fun and offers a great menu. Breakfast includes French toast sticks, biscuits and gravy, or a brioche roll breakfast sandwich—each for around $5. Kids' French toast is around $4.

If you come back later for lunch or dinner, you can choose from a chili burger, bleu cheese burger, or cheddar burger. This place also serves BBQ pork ribs and even hot wings. Prices range from $6 to $10, with the meals being quite filling. The kids' meals include chicken poppers or two miniburgers for around $4.50. This eatery contains an indoor dining area, making it a great area for a sit-down meal where you can also rest for a bit.

The Vineyard Room	☺	$$$
Golden Vine Winery		**Restaurant**

This fine restaurant serves four-course meals that include appetizer, pasta, entrée, and dessert. They run $42 for lunch and $50 for dinner per person with wine, or without wine, $28 and $36, respectively. A child's dinner is $14. The meals vary daily and feature a California culinary theme.

Reservations are highly recommended, especially during the busy season. You can make same-day reservations either at the location or by calling ahead. To save money, choose a late lunch rather than dinner.

This is not a good choice for families with young children. The children's meals are quite expensive, and the environment is not very family oriented.

Wine Country Trattoria	☺ $$
Golden Vine Winery	**Restaurant**

This eatery in the winery district offers sandwiches as well as lasagna and other baked pastas for $9 to $15. Reservations are available. You can also purchase bottles of wine at the nearby Terrace Wine Tasting. Because you are not allowed to carry the wine bottles around the park, you must buy them a few hours before you leave and then pick them up at the Package Express in the Entry Plaza.

Dining at Disneyland Resort Hotels

The three Disney hotels offer a variety of restaurants and places to pick up a quick bite. You do not have to be a guest at

Helpful Hint

Guests of the Disneyland Resort can make reservations at any of the hotel restaurants by dialing *86 from any resort pay phone. On some phones, there is an autodial for reservations. You can also make reservations before you leave on your vacation or while there by dialing 714-781-DINE. This number is good for all Disneyland Resort restaurants that take reservations, including those at the theme parks, hotels, and even Downtown Disney. For most of these restaurants, you can make reservations up to two months in advance.

one of the hotels to dine at any of these restaurants, so if you are staying at an off-site hotel, you are welcome to take either the monorail or tram over to the hotels and dine where you desire.

Captain's Galley ☺☺ $
Disneyland Hotel **Fast Food**

This poolside shop is more like a general store, offering sundries as well as food. The menu features sandwiches, salads, boxed lunches, and all types of snacks. You can even get a box of sushi (cooked, not raw). Prices range from $1 to $6, making this a quick and inexpensive place for lunch or a snack while at the pool or to pick up something on your way back to the hotel.

The Coffee Bar and Lounge ☺ $
Paradise Pier Hotel **Fast Food**

This counter serves specialty coffees, hot chocolate, and baked snacks as well as alcoholic drinks.

The Coffee House ☺☺ $
Disneyland Hotel **Fast Food**

This shop serves a variety of specialty coffees, hot chocolate, juices, and an assortment of baked goods, including bagels, muffins, scones, Danishes, and even brownies. Prices range from $1 to $5. This is a good spot to pick up a quick breakfast in the morning. Send one parent while the other and the kids are getting ready.

Croc's Bits 'n' Bites
Disneyland Hotel
 $
Fast Food

This counter serves hamburgers, BBQ chicken sandwiches, and chicken tenders. These are all around $4, or you can add a drink and fries for about $3 more. Children's meals include a hamburger, fries, and a drink for $5. This is basically the place for fast food at the Disneyland Hotel. It is also conveniently located for dining while at the pool.

Disney's PCH Grill
Paradise Pier Hotel
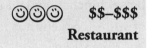 **$$–$$$**
Restaurant

The PCH Grill features the Minnie and Friends character breakfast from 6:30 to 11:30 A.M. The all-you-can-eat buffet includes an omelet bar, waffles, eggs, meat, and sweet rolls. There is also a traditional Japanese breakfast. While guests are enjoying their breakfast, Minnie and her friends sing and dance around before visiting with the guests at each table. The price is $19 for adults and $12 for children. This is the only character breakfast with a show. You should make reservations unless you plan on eating a late breakfast.

Insider's Secret
At the buffet, you can find granola bars and juice boxes. These are available for you to take with you to the parks. In fact, our waiter even invited us to take some boxes of cereal for our children. Cheerios and other cereals are a wonderful way of calming a fussy child when you're in a hurry.

The PCH Grill also serves a variety of dishes inspired by the Pacific Rim. These include salads and sandwiches, wood-

fired gourmet pizzas, seafood, pastas, steaks, ribs, and more. Prices range from $10 to $24. The kids' meal is about $6 and offers a choice of spaghetti, macaroni and cheese, chicken nuggets, hamburger, or make-your-own pizza. When kids order the latter, they are brought rolled-out pizza dough with sauce, cheese, and toppings. They then get to assemble the pizza before it is taken back for cooking. Reservations are a good idea for both lunch and dinner, to avoid having to wait.

This restaurant also provides the room service for the Paradise Pier Hotel. To save money, you can walk down to the restaurant and place an order to go. Either wait downstairs in the lobby or the gift shop or go back up to your room until it is ready. You'll avoid paying the higher room-service prices as well as the service charge and tip. Also, by taking out you can access the complete menu instead of the more-limited room-service menu. The smoked seafood chowder is delicious.

Goofy's Kitchen	☺☺☺	$$$
Disneyland Hotel		**Buffet**

Goofy's Kitchen features breakfast, lunch, and dinner with an all-you-can-eat buffet, complete with characters that come around and visit with the guests at each table. Breakfast (7 to 11:30 A.M.) is $19 for adults; lunch (noon to 2:30 P.M.) is $20; and dinner (5 to 9 P.M.) is $30. Children's meals are all $12. Breakfast includes a variety of typical favorites, such as waffles, eggs, meat, potatoes, cereal, fresh fruit, sweet rolls,

Money-Saving Tip

Lunch and dinner offer almost exactly the same dishes—including prime rib. However, adults save $10 by having lunch here rather than dinner. It is also usually less crowded for a late lunch.

and assorted breads. Lunch and dinner offer prime rib, chicken, fish, pizza, salad, fruit and sandwich bars, soup, and a variety of delicious desserts. You should try to make reservations here. However, the wait is not too bad if you drop by late for any of the meals. The lunch and dinner fare are similar, and you can save money by stopping at Goofy's for a late lunch around 1 or 1:30 P.M. You will miss most of the lunch crowd (usually smaller than the dinner crowd) and save $10 per adult. Since the restaurant is less busy at lunch, your family will get more personal attention from the characters. Once while we were having a late lunch here, Goofy sat down with our family for over 10 minutes and played with the children. That in itself was worth the price of the meal—and the food is great, too.

Granville's Steak House	☺	$$$
Disneyland Hotel		**Restaurant**

Granville's is a very formal restaurant that is open only for dinner—usually 6 to 10 P.M. The menu includes a variety of steaks, prime rib, filet mignon, chicken, lamb, lobster, and other fresh seafood. Dinners range in price from $25 to $35 and even higher for the lobster. You can also order a variety of salads and appetizers as well as desserts from $5 to $12. Because of the formal atmosphere and sophisticated menu, this is not a really good spot for families with young children.

Hearthstone Lounge	☺	$–$$$
Grand Californian Hotel		**Fast Food**

The hotel's lounge serves coffees and baked goods in the morning, then snacks and light meals during the remainder of

> ### Insider's Secret
> All of the woodwork in this lounge—the paneling and the counters—came from the same redwood tree, one that fell naturally rather than being cut down.

the day. It includes a fully stocked bar. You can even play checkers at some of the tables.

Hook's Pointe and Wine Cellar ☺☺☺ $$–$$$
Disneyland Hotel   **Restaurant**

Hook's Pointe serves breakfast in the morning, with the usual fare. The specialty is the omelets, which are about $8. For lunch and dinner, you can choose from a variety of pastas, gourmet pizzas, steak, chicken, and seafood. These range from $12 for the pizzas to $30 for some of the dinners. You can also order assorted appetizers, salads, and desserts. What makes this restaurant great for families is the wide variety of choices on the kids' menu. For about $6, they can choose from macaroni and cheese, pizzas, hot dogs, cheeseburgers, lasagna, or breaded mozzarella Mickeys.

On the lower level of the restaurant is the wine cellar, where guests may taste a variety of California wines and purchase them by the glass or the bottle.

The Lost Bar ☺ $
Disneyland Hotel   **Fast Food**

Although this is basically a bar serving alcoholic beverages for adults, it also offers hamburgers, chicken sandwiches, jalapeño poppers, and even a kids' hamburger meal. Prices range from

$5 to $7. You can get nonalcoholic mixed drinks here as well, which both kids and adults find delicious. Although parents can pick up a drink, we don't recommend it for families. After putting the kids to bed, one of the parents can head down to the Lost Bar for refreshments and bring them back up to the room to enjoy.

The Napa Rose	☺ $$$
Grand Californian Hotel	**Restaurant**

This fine restaurant offers a changing menu that highlights a variety of tastes in the California style. Appetizers include scallops, stuffed grape leaves, salads, and soups from $6 to $15. The entrées offer choices of seafood, prime rib, steak, chicken, pasta, and much more. Expect to pay from $20 to $30 for these. Desserts are along the same lines as the rest of the menu, with prices from $6 to $10.

The Napa Rose is designed to feature a host of California wines, with the atmosphere of the Napa Valley—California's wine country. As such, guests have the opportunity to not only have wine with dinner but also purchase various vintages to take home with them.

Because this is an extremely fancy restaurant, we don't recommend it for families with young children. They will find something more to their taste at the Storytellers Café. However, for couples, this is a great restaurant that offers views of the California Adventure park. Parents can enjoy a romantic dinner here alone while their children are supervised at Pinocchio's Workshop (also at the Grand Californian), a fun, entertaining, and safe environment.

> ## Helpful Hint
>
> If you would like a couple's night out and are stay-
> ing at the Grand Californian or one of the other
> Disney hotels, see about having your children su-
> pervised at Pinocchio's Workshop. This is open from
> 5 P.M. to midnight and runs $9 per child per hour.
> For more information, look under the Grand Cali-
> fornian in chapter 2.

Adjacent to this fine restaurant is the Napa Rose Lounge,
which offers a wide selection of California wines, full-menu
service, indoor and outdoor seating, and a crackling firepit.

Storytellers Café	☺☺☺	$$–$$$
Grand Californian Hotel		**Restaurant**

This is the main restaurant in the Grand Californian Hotel. In
the morning, Chip 'n' Dale host a character breakfast buffet.
It includes fresh fruit, eggs Benedict, bagels with a tray of toppings, Spanish sopas, potatoes, meat, an omelet bar, biscuits
and gravy, and all types of pastries and baked goods. Adults
eat for $19, children for $11. The meal includes beverages—
juices, soft drinks, hot drinks, and milk—even chocolate milk.

Lunch and dinner feature a traditional menu that includes
sandwiches, soups, salads, pastas, pizzas, seafood, chicken,
prime rib, and so forth. Expect to pay from $10 to $30 per
meal. The kids' menu includes burgers, chicken nuggets, macaroni and cheese, pizzas, and even quesadillas. All are around $7.

This restaurant also provides room service to the Grand
Californian Hotel, so just about anything on the menu can be
served in your hotel room for a bit higher price. Or if you
want to save money, you can walk down to the restaurant and

place an order to go and then take it up to your room by your-self. You pay the lower restaurant price and also avoid the room-service surcharge and tip.

White Water Snacks	☺☺☺ $
Grand Californian Hotel	**Fast Food**

This snack bar, located by the pool area, is a great place for midday or evening snacks as well as light meals. You can find breakfast sandwiches and French toast here in the morning for around $5. Later, chicken sandwiches, burgers, pizzas, and hot dogs are served for $5 to $6. In addition, there are a variety of prepackaged sandwiches, salads, desserts, and snacks, includ-ing Mickey Mouse pretzels and candy bars. You can even get kids' meals here. A small indoor dining area is provided, or you can grab some grub while your family is down by the pool or pick up dessert to take back to your room after a busy day at the parks.

Helpful Hint

If you have younger children who are tired from a long day at the parks, pick up their dinner here and take it back to the hotel room. Then when they crash, the adults can order room service and enjoy a nice, quiet dinner together.

Yamabuki	☺ $$$
Paradise Pier Hotel	**Restaurant**

Yamabuki is a formal Japanese restaurant that offers a variety of traditional cuisine. The restaurant features a sushi bar, a dining room, and tables where your dinner is cooked right in

front of you. The menu includes fresh sushi, tempura, teriyaki, seafood, and other Japanese favorites. Dinners range from $13 to $30. The children's menu includes teriyaki chicken or beef, tempura shrimp, udon noodles, and even chicken nuggets or corn dogs. They range in price from $5 to $8. Reservations are highly recommended.

If you don't want to take the entire family, Yamabuki offers takeout dining. On the way back to the Paradise Pier Hotel after a day in the parks, we stop in and place the order before heading up to the hotel room. They then give us a call when the order is ready, and one of us runs down to pick it up. For kids who do not like Japanese food, you can get takeout at the PCH Grill or somewhere else on your way back to the hotel.

Helpful Hint

If you just want some sushi for dinner but don't want to go to a restaurant, Yamabuki offers takeout. Just place your order, and the staff will put it together so you can take it back to eat at your hotel.

Downtown Disney Restaurant Descriptions

Downtown Disney is an area open to the public that includes a variety of shops as well as restaurants offering fare ranging from fine dining to snacks. Because Downtown Disney remains open several hours after the parks close, as late as 2 A.M., you can find a late dinner here after enjoying the day at one of the parks. Or you can have breakfast or lunch here during the day.

(For more information about the shops and the entertainment venues, please see chapter 7.)

Catal and Uva Bar   ☺ $$–$$$
714-774-4442   Restaurant

This restaurant actually offers two different types of dining. The dining room is located on the second floor, while the Uva bar is on the ground floor as well as out in the center of the Downtown Disney walkway. The outdoor bar serves coffees and pastries in the morning, then turns into a wine and cocktail bar later in the day, serving tapas-style food (small portions of appetizer-like food).

The Catal restaurant serves a variety of dishes with a Mediterranean theme. In addition to a variety of interesting soups, salads, and sandwiches at around $5 to $15, you can also order pasta, seafood, chicken, steak, and even lamb. The dinners are priced from around $12 to $25, making them quite reasonable for this type of restaurant. This is also a good place to come for a nice dessert.

Catal is not a very good choice for families with young children because of the atmosphere and menu. Reservations are recommended for the restaurant during dinner hours. For more detailed information, take a look at the restaurant's Web site at www.patinagroup.com/catal.htm.

ESPN Zone   ☺ $$–$$$
714-300-3776   Restaurant

The ESPN Zone features two different restaurants located on the ground floor. Both share the same menu but offer different atmospheres. The Studio Grill is set up more like a restaurant and is more appropriate for family dining. The Screening

Room is like a sports bar, featuring all types of games on monitors—including a giant 16-foot monitor.

The menu offers salads, sandwiches, and appetizers for $6 to $12. Entrées include steak, chicken, seafood, and pasta, with prices ranging from $9 to $25. Even if you're not in the mood for a meal, there are several delicious desserts to sample while watching a game.

This is not a great restaurant for families with small children because of the sports bar atmosphere and the noise level. However, if your children are older and enjoy sports, the ESPN Zone can be a lot of fun.

Haagen-Dazs	☺☺☺ $
	Fast Food

This ice cream shop serves ice cream cones, sundaes, and ice cream or frozen drinks as well as specialty coffees. Prices range from $3 to $6. This is a great place for a treat after the parks close, before you head back to the hotel.

House of Blues	☺ $$–$$$
714-778-2583	**Restaurant**

This restaurant feels a bit like a nightclub with a Southern atmosphere. The menu features a variety of choices—many with a Southern or Cajun flair. Appetizers include such tasty treats as catfish nuggets, crawfish cakes, BBQ duck, and others, most between $8 and $10. In fact, this is a fun place to just come in for an appetizer and beverage if you want to see what it is like but don't want a meal. Soups and salads are also available, with seafood gumbo, the steak salad, and a Caesar salad with salmon being some of the more interesting choices. They run from about $4 to $14. For a light meal, choose from several sandwiches, including a shrimp Po' Boy or a blackened-chicken sandwich. There are also burgers and pizzas. These run around $9. For the main entrées, you can try BBQ ribs, seafood, steak, chicken, or even pasta. Most are quite reasonably priced, starting around $12 but going up to $25 for some meals.

House of Blues also features a live entertainment area that is separate from the dining area. There is something going on there just about every night of the week. Because of the loud atmosphere, we do not recommend this restaurant for families with young children. However, teenagers usually have a great time.

Helpful Hint

On Sunday mornings, the House of Blues features an all-you-can-eat Sunday Gospel Brunch. Local gospel singing groups perform while you feast on a variety of brunch favorites. For families with older children who are not into the character breakfasts, this can be a fun alternative.

Reservations, especially for dinner, are recommended. If you want to dine here during a holiday or a busy night such as a Friday night or weekend, be sure to make your reservations several days, or even a couple of weeks, in advance.

One of the unique experiences at this venue is the House of Blues Gospel Brunch. Served just about every Sunday morning, this Southern-style all-you-can-eat buffet features jambalaya, eggs Benedict, prime rib, BBQ chicken, catfish, and more for guests to enjoy while listening to live gospel music. Be sure to reserve tickets in advance. For more information as well as a listing of the entertainment, visit the House of Blues Web site at www.hob.com/venues/clubvenues/anaheim.

La Brea Bakery
714-490-0233

 $
Fast Food

Besides breads and pastries, this bakery, which has outdoor seating, also serves soups, salads, and sandwiches ranging in price from $4 to $12. Also available are such entrées as pasta, chicken, and seafood for $10 to $18. A wine bar serves beer and wine by the glass. Unlike some restaurants in Downtown Disney, La Brea Bakery offers kids' meals of either a peanut-butter-and-jelly or grilled-cheese sandwich or chicken nuggets. Each includes fries for $4.

This is the closest place in Downtown Disney to the main gates of both theme parks. In the morning, stop by here for a hot drink and a muffin or another pastry; in the evening, get a dessert to take with you back to your hotel.

Naples Ristorante e Pizzeria
714-776-6200

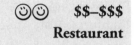 **$$–$$$**
Restaurant

This Italian restaurant is a great place for families and offers a comprehensive menu of unique as well as traditional Italian foods. One of the specialties are the wood-fired gourmet pizzas. These come in individual as well as family sizes, starting at $11 and going up from there. In addition to the traditional toppings, guests can also choose from seafood (not just anchovies), goat cheese, and several other things one might not think to put on a pizza. Soups and salads are available for $5 to $14. Several different types of pasta dinners are served, ranging from $12 to $18. You can also order entrées such as veal, chicken, and seafood for $15 to $25.

Although the prices seem a bit high for pizza, you may not find some of these pizzas served anywhere else, and they are quite filling. The prices of the dinners are in line with most restaurants in the resort area. The restaurant is family oriented. Older children will enjoy the place. Younger children can usually share a meal with an adult or with each other, and they can often find a pizza or meal that meets their tastes.

Reservations are recommended for dinner, especially on weekends and holiday periods. You can usually get them a day or two in advance or maybe even the same day. Try this restaurant for a late dinner after the parks close. Check out the restaurant's Web site at www.patinagroup.com/naples.htm for more information.

Rainforest Café	☺☺☺ $$–$$$
714-956-5260	Restaurant

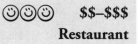

This restaurant, housed in what looks like an ancient Mayan pyramid, has a great atmosphere that continues inside. The Rainforest Café contains large aquariums around the dining area as well as other effects to make guests feel as though they are dining in a jungle.

The menu combines dishes from both North and South America and is quite varied. You can get several different types of salads, including tomato and onion or buffalo chicken, for $5 to $13. Appetizers feature pizzas, crab cakes, shrimp cocktail, chimichangas, and much more ($7 to $14). There are also soups, sandwiches, wraps, and pastas. There are a number of interesting seafood dishes, including coconut shrimp and Brazilian fish, as well as steak, chicken, pork chops, and even pot roast. These all range in price from $10 to $20 and even higher for lobster. A children's menu features smaller portions of some of the adult dinners, with prices around $7.

Rainforest Café is a great family restaurant, and we recommend it during your stay. Reservations, especially for dinner, are highly recommended, and you can even make them several days in advance by calling ahead. For more detailed information, check out the restaurant's Web site at www.rainforestcafe.com.

Ralph Brennan's Jazz Kitchen   ☺☺ $$–$$$
714-776-5200   **Restaurant and Fast Food**

This establishment is actually divided into three parts. The Carnival Club is located upstairs and offers fine dining. Flambeaux's, downstairs, has a more relaxed atmosphere and often has live entertainment. The Creole Café is the takeout eatery.

The Carnival Club is only open for dinner and offers a variety of Southern specialties. The menu changes regularly and includes turtle soup, seafood, poultry, and such. Entrées are priced from $20 to $30. However, you can also get entire meals that include an appetizer, an entrée, and a dessert for $30 to $40. These are actually a good deal, compared to ordering everything separately.

Flambeaux's serves several Cajun-style dishes, some with seafood. The menu here also changes regularly, but you can expect to pay from $13 to $25 for a dinner. In the evening, guests are entertained by live jazz music. Both Flambeaux's and the Carnival Club accept reservations. If you plan to dine here, be sure to reserve a table during the day or call ahead of time.

The Creole Café is great for a quick bite or for something to take back to the hotel. There are several types of sandwiches, including Po' Boys (shrimp, oyster, catfish, pork, and turkey). You can also get jambalaya, gumbo, red beans and rice, and even crawfish pies. These range from $4 to $10. If a

sweet dessert is more your speed, try the pecan pie (with chocolate chunks in it) or other tasty treats.

The restaurant offers a kids' menu and sometimes has specials where kids eat free before 6:00 P.M. The Creole Café's takeout also gives parents an option for taking meals back to the hotel while they pick up dinner elsewhere for the kids. In addition to lunch and dinner, Ralph Brennan's Jazz Kitchen also offers a Sunday brunch. You can find more detailed information at the Ralph Brennan's Jazz Kitchen Web site at www.rbjazzkitchen.com.

Wetzel's Pretzels	
	Fast Food

This is a typical pretzel stand like those often found in shopping malls. In addition to pretzels with a variety of toppings, you can also get hot dogs and drinks here. Prices range from $2.50 to around $4.

CHAPTER

9

Knott's®
Berry Farm

Knott's Berry Farm

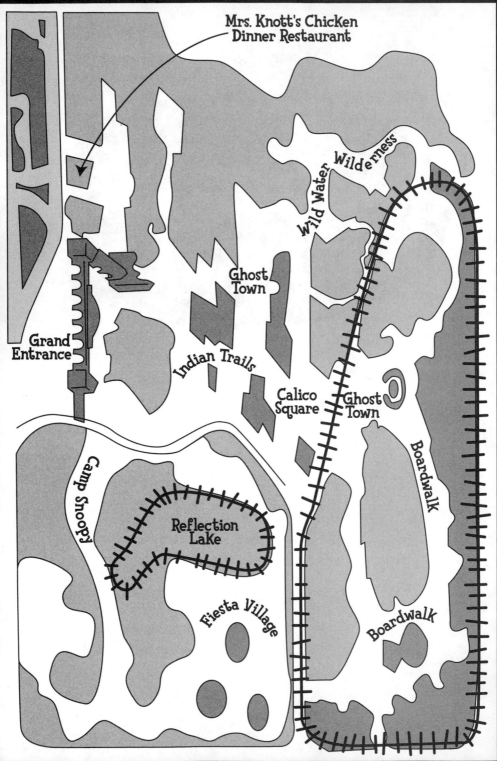

Mrs. Knott's Chicken Dinner Restaurant

Wild Water Wilderness

Ghost Town

Grand Entrance

Indian Trails

Calico Square

Ghost Town

Boardwalk

Camp Snoopy

Reflection Lake

Fiesta Village

Boardwalk

Knott's Berry Farm

Knott's Berry Farm is a unique Southern California attraction that takes the California Gold Rush and other historical eras as themes. Although many other theme parks offer more complex entertainment, Knott's Berry Farm has maintained a simpler, down-home appeal. In fact, the park advertises itself as "The Theme Park Californians Call Home." However, this does not mean only those visitors from California will enjoy themselves here. On the contrary, Knott's offers something for everyone.

Knott's Berry Farm actually did begin as a real berry farm. Walter Knott was the propagator of the boysenberry—a cross between the red raspberry, blackberry, and loganberry. During the Depression, to help make ends meet, his wife, Cordelia, began serving her chicken dinners on their wedding china to customers for only 65 cents. A few years later, the Knotts expanded their business into a restaurant. The popularity of the restaurant grew. In 1940 Walter Knott began bringing historical buildings to the farm as an attraction to entertain the thousands of customers lining up each day at the restaurant. These buildings became the basis for Knott's first theme park—the Old West Ghost Town. Since that time, the park has grown as more and more attractions, including rides, have been added. Five other areas joined the Ghost Town, making Knott's Berry Farm what it is today.

Although its rides and attractions don't always get the publicity and excitement of those at other parks, Knott's Berry Farm is truly a pioneer in the theme and amusement park industry. It not only was the first theme park (Disneyland opened several years later) but also featured the first log ride as well as the world's first 360-degree roller coaster.

Adjacent to Knott's Berry Farm is a separate water park, Soak City USA, which is modeled on the 1950s–1960s California surfing scene. Families can find a variety of wet fun here for all ages. Although it is aimed primarily at young to preteen children, there are a few high-speed slides for the older and more thrill-seeking visitors. There is more information on Soak City USA at the end of this chapter.

Knott's Berry Farm
8039 Beach Boulevard, Buena Park, California 90620
714-220-5200
www.knotts.com

Location

Knott's Berry Farm is located in Buena Park, only 15 minutes from Disneyland. Although it is easy to get there by car, check to see if your hotel offers a shuttle, as this can be convenient and save you the cost of parking. However, depending on how often the shuttle runs, you may prefer the flexibility of driving your own car.

If you are coming from the Disneyland area, take the I-5 (Santa Ana) Freeway north to the 91 (Riverside) Freeway west. Exit at Beach Boulevard, and turn left at the end of the exit ramp. Proceed south one mile to the auto entrance lanes on your right, past La Palma Avenue.

If you are coming from downtown Los Angeles, take the I-5 Freeway south to Beach Boulevard. Turn right at the end of the exit ramp, and proceed south two miles to the auto entrance lanes.

Admission

Admission to Knott's Berry Farm is similar to that of most of the other area theme parks. Single-day admission is $42 for adults and $32 for seniors (60 and over) and children ages 3 to 11 as well as expectant mothers. During the summer when the park is open past 6 P.M., you can purchase a discounted pass that allows you to enter after 4 P.M. Adults pay only $21, and it's $15 for seniors and children ages 3 to 11.

Tickets can be purchased at the ticket booths outside the main gates. You can also purchase tickets in advance at some hotels. Check with the front desk when you make your reservations. Discounted tickets can also be purchased from AAA. Several businesses or credit unions may

Money-Saving Tip

It is possible to see the park in only half a day. Therefore, the discounted admission after 4 P.M. can really save your family some money. Seriously consider this if you have small children who will be spending most of their time on the kiddie rides in Camp Snoopy or older children who will be hitting the coasters and other wild rides.

offer discounts to employees and members in the form of the Adventurers' Club or the Joe Cool Club. Each club has a card giving discounts not only on admission but also at several restaurants and shops in the park. Also check your hotel or local businesses for coupons. You should be able to save around $5 per ticket with coupons.

The cost for parking is $8 for cars and motorcycles and $12 for RVs. Don't forget to write down where you parked your vehicle before heading into the park. After a long day of fun, you don't want to have to wander around looking for your vehicle. There is free three-hour parking for people visiting the restaurants and shops located outside of the park.

Because Knott's has purchased a nearby hotel, several vacation packages are available at the Radisson Resort Knott's Berry Farm. This 321-room hotel features a pool, a spa, a kids' activity center, two lighted tennis courts, an exercise facility, and an arcade center. For families with young children, the hotel also offers 16 Snoopy-theme rooms and suites. Check the Knott's Web site for special packages and rates.

Operating Hours

Knott's Berry Farm is open daily, except for Christmas. During the summer, the hours are 9 A.M. to midnight. Nonsummer hours are 10 A.M. to 6 P.M., with later hours on the weekends and during holidays.

Amenities

Knott's Berry Farm's Information Center offers help and answers to all your questions. Guests with disabilities can pick up a guide at this location. This is also where the Lost and Found is located. If you get separated from one or more of your children, ask an employee for assistance. Separated children will be taken to the Lost Child Center located in Calico Square. Most restrooms offer baby-changing facilities. In addition, there are two baby stations: one at Camp Snoopy and the other in the California Marketplace. Both offer facilities for nursing.

Lockers are available in Ghost Town and near Bigfoot Rapids, allowing you to stash items such as dry clothes while getting wet. Strollers can be rented for $5 a day. However, if you will be visiting another theme park, it might be worth your money, and your child's comfort, to purchase an umbrella stroller before your trip. These can usually be found at large discount stores for a minimal cost.

If you are traveling with pets, you cannot take them into Knott's Berry Farm and there are no kennel services available on site. You will have to make other arrangements before your visit.

Suitability for Children

Knott's Berry Farm does a good job of providing something for everybody. Small children will enjoy Camp Snoopy as well as some of the milder rides throughout the park, such as the Log Ride and the Mine Ride. Also walk around Ghost Town to see the sights, and check out some of the shows.

Attractions

Knott's Berry Farm is divided into six themed areas. Each offers exciting rides and attractions, though some are designed for certain age groups in particular.

Ghost Town

This is where it all started. Ghost Town is the heart of Knott's Berry Farm. Ghost Town contains several shops, restaurants, and exhibits. It is fun to just stroll down the streets pretending

Quick Guide to

Attraction	Location	Requirement
Bigfoot Rapids	Wild Water Wilderness	46 inches
Boomerang	Boardwalk	48 inches
Butterfield Stagecoach*	Ghost Town	None
Calico Mine Train*	Ghost Town	None
Camp Bus	Camp Snoopy	None
Dentzel Carousel*	Fiesta Village	None
Dragon Swing	Fiesta Village	42 inches
GhostRider	Ghost Town	48 inches
Ghost Town and Calico Railroad*	Ghost Town	None
Gran Slammer	Fiesta Village	42 inches
Hammerhead	Boardwalk	48 inches
Hat Dance	Fiesta Village	36 inches
Jaguar!	Fiesta Village	42 inches
Kingdom of the Dinosaurs*	Boardwalk	None
Log Peeler	Camp Snoopy	32–48 inches
Log Ride*	Ghost Town	None

Guests under 46 inches must be accompanied by an adult.
**Guests between 36 inches and 54 inches must be accompanied by an adult.*

 0 Not scary at all.
  ! Might be somewhat frightening for some children. Usually either dark or a mild roller coaster.
 !! Most young children will find this scary.
!!! This attraction may frighten some adults. This is usually reserved for high-speed roller coasters and other thrill rides.

Knott's Berry Farm Attractions

Duration of Ride/Show	Scare Factor	Age Range
6 minutes	!	3 and up
1½ minutes	!!!	8 and up
6 minutes	0	All
8 minutes	!	5 and up
1½ minutes	0	All
1½ minutes	0	All
2 minutes	!	6 and up
2½ minutes	!!	7 and up
6 minutes	0	All
2 minutes	!	6 and up
Approx. 2 minutes	!!	7 and up
2 minutes	!	4 and up
2 minutes	!	6 and up
8 minutes	!	4 and up
1½ minutes	0	All
4½ minutes	!	3 and up

(continues)

Quick Guide to

Attraction	Location	Requirement
Montezooma's Revenge	Fiesta Village	48 inches
Mystery Lodge	Wild Water Wilderness	None
Peanuts Playhouse	Camp Snoopy	None
Perilous Plunge	Boardwalk	48 inches
Rocky Road Trucking Company	Camp Snoopy	None
Snoopy's Red Baron Airplanes	Camp Snoopy	32–54 inches
Supreme Scream	Boardwalk	52 inches
Tampico Tumbler	Fiesta Village	52 inches
Timberline Twisters	Camp Snoopy	36–69 inches
Waveswinger	Fiesta Village	47 inches
Wheeler Dealer Bumper Cars*	Boardwalk	36 inches
Wild West Stunt Show	Ghost Town	None
Wipeout	Boardwalk	42 inches
Woodstock's Airmail	Camp Snoopy	None
Xcelerator	Boardwalk	52 inches

*Guests under 46 inches must be accompanied by an adult.
**Guests between 36 inches and 54 inches must be accompanied by an adult.

0 Not scary at all.
! Might be somewhat frightening for some children. Usually either dark or a mild roller coaster.
!! Most young children will find this scary.
!!! This attraction may frighten some adults. This is usually reserved for high-speed roller coasters and other thrill rides.

Knott's Berry Farm Attractions

Duration of Ride/Show	Scare Factor	Age Range
36 seconds	!!	7 and up
20 minutes	0	All
10 minutes	0	All
1½ minutes	!!!	8 and up
1 minute	0	All
1½ minutes	0	3 and up
45 seconds	!!!	7 and up
1½ minutes	!	7 and up
1 minute	0	2 and up
2 minutes	!	6 and up
2 minutes	!	4 and up
20 minutes	0	All
2 minutes	!!	6 and up
1½ minutes	0	All
1 minute	!!!	8 and up

Time-Saving Tip

For families with children unable to go on some attractions, Knott's Berry Farm allows for parent
swapping. While one adult goes with part of the
group, the other waits with the young children.
Then when the first group returns, those who
waited can enter through a special entrance for immediate boarding. Be sure to speak with the attendant at the entrance to the attraction about
instructions for waiting and swapping.

you are back in the Wild West. Although you can quickly
move through this area on to other parts of the park, it can be
educational as well as entertaining to explore Ghost Town
with your children. Not all the sights here are listed on the
map of the park you receive when you enter Knott's Berry
Farm, so you will just have to browse around. Along the way
you will be able to peer into an old barbershop, a Chinese
laundry, and much more. The buildings here are either re-creations of historical buildings or actual buildings brought here
from around the United States. Visit the 19th-century one-
room schoolhouse from Kansas. Children will be impressed
with how it differs from their own classrooms. A "teacher" is
usually there from noon until 5 P.M. to answer questions and
describe how schools functioned over 100 years ago. You can
also watch a blacksmith work his trade.

The Birdcage Theatre, modeled after the original in
Tombstone, Arizona (remember the O.K. Corral?), offers seasonal entertainment. Several well-known performers got their
start here, including Steve Martin. At the far end of Ghost
Town, guests can pan for gold in sluice boxes for an additional

charge. However, it is worth the price for children who may never get such an opportunity again, especially those who have recently studied the Gold Rush in school. Be sure to visit Boot Hill, Ghost Town's cemetery. It is located behind some shops and is easily overlooked. The inscriptions on the tombstones are good for a laugh. Plus, don't forget to place a foot on the grave of the man buried alive. Somethin' is a-thumpin'.

There is a lot to look at in Ghost Town, and there are also several rides. Relive travel in the Old West by riding a real Butterfield Stagecoach around a track circling Camp Snoopy and Fiesta Village. This is the park's oldest ride and began in 1950. Because this ride can accommodate only a limited number of guests at a time, waits can be long. Hit this ride either early in the day or later in the afternoon as things begin to slow down. There is also the Calico Railroad. This steam-powered, narrow-gauge railroad originally operated on the Denver and Rio Grande line. During the ride, you may even experience a train robbery. Explain to children that this is just pretend so they are not frightened.

The Calico Mine Ride takes you into a mock gold mine, with miners digging deep into the earth in search of riches. Although there is no height requirement, young children may be scared of some of the dark parts of this ride. The entire family can go on this ride together, and even babies are fine. Nearby, the Timber Mountain Log Ride also offers a ride through a logging camp in one of the logs. Again, there is no height requirement, so children who could not ride Splash Mountain at Disneyland can ride this log ride. Be sure to smile on the way down the final chute. Your picture is taken here, and you can purchase them at a stand near the exit to the ride. Children under 10 must be accompanied by an adult on both the Mine and Log rides as well as on the Stagecoach and Railroad.

Ghost Town's newest attraction is the GhostRider. At 4,533 feet long and 118 feet high, it is the longest and wildest wooden roller coaster in the West. In fact, on A&E's top 10 list of the country's best coasters, GhostRider ranks number two! With an initial banked drop of 108 feet, this coaster includes 13 other drops and races out over Grand Avenue and into the parking area before returning. Riders must be at least 48 inches tall in order to ride this coaster.

Indian Trails

This small area is located in between Ghost Town and Camp Snoopy. It has a Native American tribes theme and offers crafts such as beadwork to observe and to try for yourself. There is a fee for materials. In addition, watch Native American song and dance or listen to storytellers pass on the legends of their tribes. Elementary school–aged kids will enjoy seeing an authentic Big House as well as tepees of the Blackfoot, Nez Perce, Cheyenne, Crow, and Kiowa tribes. The best time to visit this area is around show time so you can take in the show and look around before or after.

Camp Snoopy

If you have young children, plan on spending a good part of your day in Camp Snoopy. This 6-acre area features over 30 different attractions, all scaled for the little ones. Camp Snoopy is located just to the right of the main entrance. Snoopy himself is often around to meet children and take pictures with them.

Camp Snoopy is the home port for the *Walter K.* steamboat, which sails on Reflection Lake. The Grand Sierra Scenic Railroad also circles this lake and even crosses a drawbridge over the water. Both of these rides are fine for entire families; however, children under 10 must be accompanied by an adult.

Other rides in this area include the Balloon Races and the Red Baron, where riders pilot their craft around in a circle. Woodstock's Airmail is a pint-size version of the Supreme Scream, where riders are lifted up on a giant airmail letter and then released in short, quick drops. The Charlie Brown Speedway takes riders around a course with quick turns, and the Rocky Road Truckin' Co. features small trucks that meander around a trail. The Huff 'n' Puff puts children in little cars that they must propel themselves by pushing a lever back and forth. The Camp Bus takes riders up and down, as does the miniature Ferris wheel. For those too young to ride the big coasters, the Timber Line Twister provides some scaled-down thrills.

In addition to these attractions, there are also pony rides and a petting zoo. These two attractions have varying hours and usually don't open until later in the mornings and then usually close before the park does. The Peanuts Playhouse and the suspension bridge provide fun adventures, as does the Beagle Ballroom and the Snoopy Bounce. Also be sure to check out Edison's Workshop, where the inventor himself encourages guests to explore the hands-on experiments in this workshop.

Children ages 2 to 9 will enjoy most of the attractions here. A few attractions are wilder and may not appeal to the youngest, and some even have height requirements. These include minimum heights and/or maximum heights. The Red Baron and the Huff 'n' Puff require children to ride without adults because of the height requirements.

Fiesta Village

Fiesta Village reflects the Spanish-Mexican influence on the West. If you are looking for some wild rides, this area should be one of your stops. Jaguar! is a roller coaster that meanders all over Fiesta Village and around a Mayan temple. It even passes through the loop of Montezooma's Revenge. Although it has several quick turns as well as climbs and drops, it is not too fast and features no inversions. It is designed to simulate the stalking of prey by this big jungle cat. If children are unsure about this coaster, let them watch it and judge for themselves. Riders must be at least 42 inches tall for this coaster. Montezooma's Revenge is the other roller coaster in this area. Riders accelerate out of the station, reaching 55 mph in only five seconds, and immediately go through a 360-degree vertical loop before climbing vertically to a stop. Then the coaster heads back down through the loop again, in reverse, through the station and up another vertical climb. Finally, the coaster heads back down and ends at the station. Although this ride is short, it is intense. The minimum height requirement for this ride is 48 inches. This is one of the more thrilling coasters at the park. If children have no problem with Jaguar! or GhostRider, then they will probably enjoy Montezooma's Revenge.

Fiesta Village also features a number of carnival-style rides. The Waveswinger is a hanging swing ride that twirls you around. The Dragon Swing consists of a Viking longboat that swings back and forth. Up for a spin? Try the Hat Dance, where you control how fast you want to spin your sombrero. This ride is similar to the Mad Tea Party at Disneyland. The Gran Slammer is a swing-type ride. However, the platform that seats the riders always remains horizontal as the giant arms swing it up, down, and around. All four of these rides are fairly tame, though intended for older children and adults. For a bit more excitement, the Tampico Tumbler spins and twists riders all around as well as up and down.

Before leaving Fiesta Village, be sure to try the carousel. At more than 100 years old, this is one of the world's oldest working Dentzel carousels, and it offers rides not only on horses but also on lions, tigers, and even pigs.

Boardwalk

For those of you who haven't been back to Knott's in a few years, the old Roaring 20s area was remodeled as the Board-walk—a tribute to the California beach scene of the 1950s and 1960s. This area contains the wildest rides and is where teenagers will spend a lot of their time.

The newest Knott's ride is Xcelerator, a 1950s-themed coaster that launches riders to a speed of 82 mph in only 2.3 seconds. If that isn't enough to get your pulse racing, the cars use this speed to climb 205 feet up and then head back down in a 90-degreee drop. The entire ride takes about a minute and is definitely one of the most extreme rides at the park.

Another extreme ride is the Perilous Plunge. This is the tallest, steepest, and wettest ride on the planet. Riders take boats up to a height of 127 feet and then drop down a 115-foot water chute at a revolutionary 75-degree angle. The 45-foot splash at the bottom drenches not only the passengers but also any nearby observers. This ride is very intense and scary. Even many adults don't want to ride it. Just watching others go down the chute can be heart-stopping. Did we also mention you will get very wet? Although this ride is quite simple, it is the most thrilling ride at Knott's Berry Farm.

The Boardwalk offers further excitement. The Supreme Scream is a completely vertical ride. Riders are quickly carried 30 stories straight up in a matter of seconds. Then they drop all the way back down to the launch pad in only three seconds, reaching a speed of 50 mph and experiencing −1.5 Gs. The riders then rebound halfway back up the tower before return-ing to earth a final time. Another roller coaster in the area is the Boomerang. This one takes riders through a vertical loop as well as a boomerang corkscrew. Then the coaster reverses and takes the riders through the loops again backward. Riders experience six inversions and a lot of thrills, ranking this as one of Knott's more intense rides.

HammerHead is a rotating, swinging ride that lifts riders 82 feet into the air and then spins them head over heels in a 360-degree arc. All the twisting and turning makes this another intense ride. Wipeout is a spinning ride that's mild by comparison with those previously mentioned in the Boardwalk area. The Wheeler Dealer Bumper Cars are a lot of fun, and the Sky Cabin takes guests on a leisurely ascent to overlook the park and the surrounding community.

The only dark ride in the park, Kingdom of the Dinosaurs takes guests through the primeval world, with 21 fully animated creatures and special effects. Although the ride is not meant to be scary, the atmosphere can frighten young children because the ride contains several dark tunnels and some loud roaring. However, elementary school–aged children and up will usually be fascinated by the dinosaurs. Located near this attraction is the Charles M. Schulz Theatre, formerly known as the John Wayne Theatre and the Goodtime Theatre, which offers a variety of shows seasonally.

The Boardwalk also features midway games, arcades, and a Lazer Runner game where players can battle with one another using phasers and fiber-optic vests. There is a $3 fee for this attraction. You can even try rock climbing in the Boardwalk for a $5 fee.

Wild Water Wilderness

There is only one main ride in the Wild Water Wilderness area: the Bigfoot Rapids. This is a thrilling river-raft ride that takes guests down a whitewater river full of drops, bumps, spins, and lots of splashes. It's similar to the Grizzly River Run at Disney's California Adventure. The fact that this ride has its own lockers nearby lets you know that you will get wet on this ride. In fact, near the entrance to this ride you can even purchase ponchos to help keep you dry. This ride is fairly mild, and the height requirement is 46 inches. It is designed as a family ride, as long as your children are all tall enough, and is a lot of fun as you scream and get drenched together. If the air is chilly or you want to stay dry, skip this ride.

At the Ranger Station, a naturalist will introduce you to snakes, spiders, insects, and other creepy-crawly critters. Finally, be sure to check out the Mystery Lodge. We cover it in more detail in the following "Shows" section.

Shows

Knott's Berry Farm offers a variety of entertaining shows throughout the park. When you purchase your ticket or enter through the main gates, be sure to pick up an *Entertainment and Show Guide* listing all the shows as well as their times and locations. Most of the shows are performed several times each day. However, a few may only show once. If you want to see one of these shows, make sure you schedule it into your day and arrive early because everyone else who wants to see that show will have to go at the same time as well.

The Wild West Stunt Show

Located in the Wagon Camp Theater, this Western stunt show lasts about 20 minutes and is a lot of fun. If you are expecting something like Universal Studios Western stunt show, however, you may be disappointed. The Knott's show focuses on humor rather than amazing stunts. All ages will enjoy this show, but the sound of cap guns can startle some young children. Warn them in advance, and sit toward the rear of the theater to lessen the effect of the noise.

The Bird Cage Theatre

This theater features various seasonal performances. During the Christmas holidays, for example, Christmas plays are presented.

The Calico Saloon

Here you can sip a sarsaparilla while watching a variety of shows ranging from Old West singing to a cancan dance show. Most shows are around 20 minutes in length.

Indian Trails Native Song and Dances

This show, at the Indian Trails Stage, features both Native American and Aztec dancers, singers, and musicians who share their cultural heritage with the audience. The show can last from 15 to 30 minutes and is good for all ages.

Edison International Electric Nights

This nighttime spectacular blends pyrotechnics, animated lasers, water, and light effects with a stirring score of pop and American and *Peanuts* musical favorites. It is located out on Reflection Lake and shows during the summer when the park is open late.

Camp Snoopy Theatre

New for 2003, this theater will offer seasonal performances starring Charlie Brown and the rest of the *Peanuts* gang. It's inside Camp Snoopy and is aimed at young children and their families.

Charles M. Schulz Theatre

This large 2,100-seat theater hosts a variety of productions throughout the year. These include musical as well as ice shows that change seasonally. When the park is not open late, the shows are often only on Friday or Saturday.

Mystery Lodge

In this mystical, multisensory show, the Old Storyteller relates Native American folklore; the smoke from the fire illustrates the story. Lasting about 20 minutes, this show will keep all ages fascinated with the special effects as well as the stories.

Tips for Touring Knott's Berry Farm

Although Knott's Berry Farm is a fairly large park, it is possible to see and do everything in a single day. If you want to save some money and are content with just hitting certain types of attractions, such as just the rides for small children or just the coasters and wild rides, you can enjoy the park with the reduced admission after 4 P.M.

Time-Saving Tip

Most families spend only a single day at Knott's Berry Farm. That is all the time it really takes to see everything. Therefore, you will probably not want to leave the park to rest at your hotel and then return later. Instead, you can rest for a bit in the park. Try resting by hitting the shows, riding the train, or seeing Kingdom of the Dinosaurs. Or you can just wander around Ghost Town while sipping on a refreshing drink.

There are two main strategies for touring Knott's Berry Farm. The main difference is your focus. Do you want to hit all the roller coasters and thrill rides, or do you have small children and want to do only the attractions they can ride? Both strategies assume you will be arriving in the morning. A third strategy takes into account families with children of mixed ages, and there is a late-entry plan as well.

The Younger Children Plan

With younger children, a lot of your time will be spent in Camp Snoopy. The lines in Camp Snoopy never get really long because there are so many different rides from which to choose. Therefore, when you first get to the park, bypass Camp Snoopy and head straight back through Ghost Town toward the Stagecoach ride. Because this ride can have a long wait, hit it early. However, if there is already a long line, continue on to the Log Ride and the Mine Ride. Both can handle guests much quicker. After getting both of these out of the way, make your way back to Camp Snoopy. You can easily spend several hours here. When the children begin to get tired or hungry, pick up a snack and head off to one of the shows. This will give you a chance to sit down and rest for a bit. When you are ready to go again, you can try Kingdom of the Dinosaurs (if your children will be fine with the giant creatures) and/or Bigfoot Rapids to help cool you off on a warm day. By now it should be midafternoon. Consider eating an early dinner or strolling around exploring Ghost Town. If you missed the Stagecoach ride earlier, try it now as well as the steam train. Then go back and do any of the attractions again that the children liked and watch some more shows.

The Teenager Plan

If your children are older and want to hit the wild rides, this is a good way to do it. Right after going through the main gates, veer to the left and make your way to the GhostRider. It is the only coaster on the southern side of the park, so ride it early while you are already nearby. Next, march straight toward the Boardwalk area and try the Xcelerator, Supreme Scream, the Boomerang, and Perilous Plunge if you are feeling brave. Continue on to Fiesta Village for the Jaguar! and Montezooma's Revenge. By this time, you have hit all the major thrill rides and the lines for these are probably getting long. So ride all the smaller carnival-style rides now, as well as the Mine Ride, the Log Ride, and Bigfoot Rapids. During midafternoon, take in some shows or shop around Ghost Town. Then as people begin to leave and things start to slow down late in the afternoon, start going back to the coasters. The later it gets, the shorter the lines on most nights.

The Mixed Ages Plan

If you want to take in the roller coasters as well as the kiddie rides, you will have to use a plan combining the previous two. Start off with either GhostRider or one or two of the coasters in the Boardwalk area. The lines should be short, so the little ones won't have to wait long, especially if you do a parent swap. Next, try the Mine and Log rides before making your way through Fiesta Village to Camp Snoopy. Hit any rides with short lines along the way. As the little ones get tired, try a show or the attractions on the other side of the park, such as Bigfoot Rapids and Kingdom of the Dinosaurs. When things begin to slow down in mid- to late afternoon, the younger children will usually be content to munch on a snack as they watch the older children go on the wilder rides you skipped earlier.

This is actually one of the more difficult plans to follow because there are times when only part of the family is riding attractions. The key is to minimize the downtime for each age group. Try to go from thrill rides to kiddie rides and back, with family rides thrown in between.

The Late-Entry Plan

The late-entry plan is best suited to families with older children because after 4 P.M., most younger children are starting to get tired. If you want to save money with your younger children by coming late, make sure they get a nap and are well rested before entering the park. This plan does not work well for families with children of mixed-age groups because there is usually not enough time to see everything.

Unlike the other plans, the late-entry plan works in reverse. You begin by hitting the less popular rides first and then work your way to the coasters as the night progresses and the lines shorten. Because many of the shows do not continue late, see those you want early so you won't miss them. Also, because you don't want to waste time eating inside the park, have a good dinner before entering. Mrs. Knott's Fried Chicken Restaurant is a good choice. Get there around 2:30 P.M., and by the time your family is finished it will be time to enter the park.

Dining and Shopping

Knott's Berry Farm started out with a restaurant, so you should definitely try Mrs. Knott's Chicken Dinner Restaurant. In fact, this is probably the best meal deal you will find at a theme park during your vacation. This restaurant is located just outside the main gate in the California Marketplace. Lunches are around $5 to $7, and children's meals are $3 to $5. However, the best deals are the dinners, which are served from 11 A.M. to close. For around $12 you can get four pieces of fried chicken, a salad, your choice of chicken soup or an appetizer, mashed potatoes and gravy, vegetable, biscuits, and your choice of dessert (including boysenberry pie as well as other tasty treats). There is so much food that an adult can usually share a dinner with a small child. Instead of fried chicken, you can get ribs, chicken pot pie, pot roast, and other homestyle meals for the same price. Mrs. Knott's Chicken Dinner Restaurant is quite popular, and you don't even have to go to the park in order to eat here. In fact, you can park for three hours free near the restaurant.

Knott's Berry Farm also has other great restaurants and eateries. You can get fried chicken to go or in boxed meals at several locations in addition to the main restaurant. Auntie Pasta's Pizza Palace features pastas, pizzas, and salads for a reasonable price. Fireman's Brigade Barbecue has great chicken and ribs. Ghost Town Grill offers burgers, sandwiches, chicken, and even chili. All of these are located in Ghost Town. For south-of-the-border fare, head to Fiesta Village, where La Cocinita offers a Mexican buffet with tacos, burritos, and a fresh salsa bar, and the Cantina offers fajitas. Coasters, in the Boardwalk area, is a 1950s diner with burgers, fries, and thick shakes. Or try Hollywood Wok for Chinese favorites and pizza. In addition to these places, Knott's offers several others where you can find a quick bite or snack. Funnel cakes, somewhat like a Belgian waffle, are very popular and can be found in a number of places around the park

Part of the Knott's experience is the shopping. Although you can find typical souvenirs as at most theme parks, Ghost

Town offers some very unique and interesting shops. For example, you can purchase a pioneer bonnet, Native American beaded items, and other Western goods. Whether you buy anything or not, just browsing can be fun and a good way to rest during the busiest part of the day. Of course, you will have to go home with some Knott's Berry Farm preserves. Several shops in the park offer these goods, but it is best to wait and buy these in the California Marketplace outside the gates of the park, or, if you buy it in the park, when you are ready to leave. A few jars of jam can be quite heavy to carry around. Also the country-store-style shop in the California Marketplace offers a variety of preserves, including hard-to-find sugar-free selections as well as varieties not available in stores back home. Even if you are not going into the park, you may want to stop by the market to pick up gifts for others or yourself.

The Boysenberry Experience

When you visit Knott's Berry Farm, you have several opportunities to try one of the fruits of their labor—the boysenberry. Just about every restaurant and eatery offers some type of boysenberry product. Thirsty? Try some boysenberry punch. (You can also buy the concentrate to make it at home.) If you are eating pancakes in the morning or funnel cakes throughout the day, drizzle them with boysenberry syrup. Spread some boysenberry jam on your biscuits. There are several baked goods featuring the boysenberry, and for dessert try either boysenberry pie or boysenberry sherbet. Although boysenberry isn't the only flavor at Knott's, it is the most popular.

Visiting During the Holidays

If you will be visiting Knott's Berry Farm near Halloween or Christmas, be ready for some additional excitement. During

October, the park becomes Knott's Scary Farm. Camp Spooky combines daytime trick-or-treating, costume contests, fun mazes, Camp Snoopy Sidewalk Theater shows, and children's hands-on craft activities. For older guests, there is Halloween Haunt. Not recommended for children under 13, Halloween Haunt features hundreds of monsters, lots of mazes, and several scare zones, as well as creepy shows and entertainment. If you have teenagers who like to be scared and you will be in the area during this time, it is worthwhile to check this out. Then in late November and December, get ready for Knott's Merry Farm, when Ghost Town is transformed into the Christmas Crafts Village. There are Victorian carolers walking around and lots and lots of crafts. If you want to go just for the shopping during this time, you can purchase a separate admission to the crafts village for only $5 for adults. Children 11 and under are free. It makes for good Christmas shopping even if you don't want to see the other attractions, and you still get to experience Ghost Town and its shows as well. For more information on these and other seasonal events, check the Knott's Web site or call the number listed at the start of this chapter.

Soak City USA

Like many other Southern California theme parks, Knott's has an adjacent water park. Soak City USA's 13 acres host 16 speed, tube, and body slides leading down from four platforms between 39 and 62 feet high. In addition to the slides, Soak City USA has a large wave pool, a lazy river on which you can ride inner tubes, and a beach-house fun house with water activities for the entire family. For younger children, the lagoon area has a small pool and an activity area. There are changing rooms for men and women, as well as locker rentals. Meals and snacks can be purchased at two dining locations and from snack carts.

Soak City USA admission includes unlimited use of all rides and attractions in the park. Adults pay $22.95, and children 3 to 11 $16.95. After 3 P.M., adults pay $13.95 and children 3 to 11 just $9.95. The park is open from Memorial Day through Labor Day, 10 A.M. to 8 P.M. during the summer. The park closes earlier during the spring and at the end of summer. Private cabanas near the wave pool are available for an additional charge. For $55 on weekdays or $75 on weekends a family can rent a cabana with four lounge chairs, a dining table with four chairs, and a shade umbrella. Also included are free inner-tube rentals and walk-up food service, though food charges still apply. This price is for four people, but the cabanas can accommodate up to eight. It is just $5 for each additional person after the first four. For a family, especially on a weekday, the cabana can be a great place to set up camp. Knott's also operates Soak City USAs in San Diego and in Palm Springs.

CHAPTER

10

Universal Studios® Hollywood

Universal Studios Hollywood

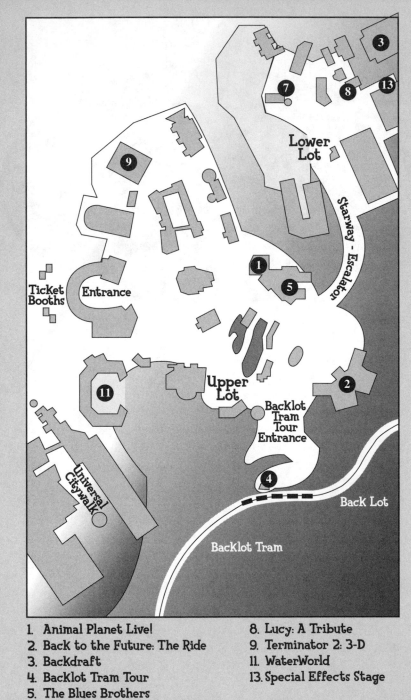

1. Animal Planet Live!
2. Back to the Future: The Ride
3. Backdraft
4. Backlot Tram Tour
5. The Blues Brothers
7. Jurassic Park: The Ride
8. Lucy: A Tribute
9. Terminator 2: 3-D
11. WaterWorld
13. Special Effects Stage

UNIVERSAL STUDIOS

SCENE 1

TAKE 17

Universal Studios is a fun-filled theme park that captures the glamour and thrill of Hollywood. Everything here is related to the moviemaking industry. In themes from some of the greatest Universal films, Universal Studios Hollywood features rides and attractions as well as live-action shows, taking guests from the prehistoric to the future.

When Carl Laemmle's movie studio Universal City opened in 1915, he invited the public to visit. It was such a success that he had special bleachers constructed so that for a quarter spectators could watch movies being filmed at the studio. This ended with the advent of the talkies because the spectators might make noise during the recording. Universal Studios Hollywood reopened in 1964, once again giving the public the chance to observe moviemaking firsthand.

What makes Universal Studios Hollywood so unique is that it is the only Southern California theme park that is also part of a working movie studio. Unlike other theme parks, the

Helpful Hint

Although you need not be a film expert to enjoy Universal Studios Hollywood, you will like most of the attractions more if you are familiar with a few of the films on which the attractions are based. Most of the attractions have things inside or even in the queue area that might be missed by someone who has not seen the movie. Here is a list of some of the movies with which you should be familiar: *Back to the Future* (I, II, or III), *Backdraft*, *Jurassic Park*, *Terminator 2*, and *WaterWorld*. If you have a chance, view these in the weeks before you visit the park.

rides are not the major attractions. In fact, there are only a few rides in the park. Instead, Universal Studios concentrates on making you feel like you are in the movies. The special effects are incredible.

100 Universal City Plaza
Universal City, CA 91608
818-622-3801
www.universalstudios.com

Location

Universal Studios Hollywood is located just off the Holly-wood Freeway (U.S. 101). Take the Universal Center Drive or Lankershim Boulevard exit, in between Hollywood and the San Fernando Valley.

Admission and Package Deals

Admission to Universal Studios Hollywood is similar to that of most other area theme parks. Single-day admission is $47 for adults and $37 for children ages 3 to 11. For only $79 per ticket, you can purchase Celebrity Annual Passports. These allow visits to Universal Studios Hollywood for 335 days, plus discounts at various shops within the park as well as on City-Walk. It also includes discounts at local hotels. Deluxe Celebrity Annual Passports are the same as the Celebrity Passports except there are no blackout dates. However, they are $20 more than the passport with the blackout dates. The Front of Line Pass runs $79 per adult, $69 per child and includes front-of-the-line privileges on all attractions and reserved seating at the shows.

For those big movie buffs, Universal Studios Hollywood offers the VIP Experience. For $129 per person, adult and child alike, guests are given a behind-the-scenes VIP guided tour of the studios, access to production facilities to see movies and television shows currently being filmed on one of the 35 soundstages, and priority boarding on all rides. The priority boarding allows you to go right to the front of the line for most rides and puts you ahead of other guests in a short-ened queue for the rest of the attractions.

If you plan on visiting SeaWorld in San Diego during your vacation, the Southern California Value Pass allows single-day admissions to both parks over a period of 14 consecutive days. It is a good deal and can save you money. These run $83 for adults and $63 for children. For those wanting to take in many of the local attractions, consider the Hollywood City-Pass. This provides one day at Universal Studios, plus single-day admissions to four other attractions. These include the Autry Museum of Western Heritage, the Hollywood Entertainment Museum, the Kodak Theatre Guided Tour, and the Starline Tours of Hollywood. These tickets run only $69 for adults and $49 for children. (For more information on these other attractions, see chapter 13.)

Adults wanting a night on the town can choose the City-Walk Nighttime Party Pass. This allows one-night admissions and priority entrance to B. B. King's Blues Club, Howl at the Moon, the Rumba Room, a $5 game card for Jillian's Hi Life Lanes, and two drink coupons. This can be purchased for only $15. Note that the Party Pass venues are for adults 21 years of age or older.

All these passes and tickets can be purchased at Universal Studios Hollywood from the Box Offices located near the entrance to the park. However, to save the time you would wait in line for tickets, purchase them online in advance from the Universal Studios Web site. At times, the studios run specials or offer discounts for online tickets. These may include an annual pass for the price of a single day or specials on upgraded tickets. Be sure to look early in the year for these specials, since they usually end in April or May, before the summer season begins. Universal Studios mails you the tickets purchased online, so you are ready to enter the park as soon as you arrive. Discounted tickets can also be purchased from AAA with discounts of around $10. Several businesses may offer coupons for their employees, or you can check at supermarkets in the area for coupons. The Box Offices open an hour before the park, so if you have to buy tickets there, try to get there early so you will have your tickets in hand when the park opens.

Over 75 acres of adjacent parking serve not only Universal Studios Hollywood and CityWalk but also the Universal Amphitheater. The cost is $8 for cars and motorcycles and $10 for RVs. You can also get preferred parking for $13. Before heading into the park, don't forget to write down where you parked your vehicle. After a long day of fun, you don't want to have to wander this large parking area looking for your vehicle.

Operating Hours

Universal Studios is open daily, except for Thanksgiving and Christmas. During the summer the hours are 8 A.M. to 10 P.M. Nonsummer hours are 9 A.M. to 7 P.M. The Box Offices open an hour before the park does and close at 5 P.M. during the summer and at 4:30 P.M. the rest of the year. Therefore, if you plan on arriving later in the afternoon, make sure you already have your ticket or get there before the Box Offices close.

Amenities

Universal Studios offers several amenities for its guests. At Guest Services, located near the main gate, you can find visitor information on the local area, guides for guests with disabilities, audio assist units, TDD phones for the hearing impaired, and travel assistance. This is also the location for the lost and found as well as for lost children. Any purchases you make during the day can be sent to Studio Styles, located near the main gate, to be picked up when you are ready to leave later in the afternoon. Lockers are available to store items you don't want to carry around all day. Strollers can be rented for $5 a day. However, if you will be visiting for more than one day or you will be going to another theme park, it might be worth your money and your child's comfort to purchase an umbrella stroller before your trip. These can usually be found at large discount stores for a minimal cost.

If you are traveling with pets, Universal Studios Hollywood offers a complimentary kennel. Just go to Guest Services at the main gate outside the park, and a representative will take care of your pet for the duration of your visit.

Universal Studios also has a Guaranteed Rain Check. On any day on which the park receives ⅛ of an inch or more of rain, all guests will be offered a rain check allowing them to return to the park anytime during the next 30 days.

Suitability for Children

Although there are some shows that children under 6 will enjoy, most will be bored for much of the day, waiting while their parents take turns doing things the kids can't. Many of the rides and attractions have either height requirements or are too intense for the little ones. However, children 6 and up, especially teens, will have a blast. If you have both young and older children, it is often a good idea to split up when doing age-appropriate attractions.

Attractions

Universal Studios Hollywood is divided into two main areas. You begin at Entertainment Center when you walk in through the main gates. Most of the shows as well as some of the attractions, including the Studio Tour, are located here. Down the hill is Studio Center. To get there you take the Starway. This series of very long escalators takes you down the hill and

Helpful Hint

Universal Studios Hollywood offers a great feature for parents with small children: You can check your strollers at two different locations. One is at the entrance to the Studio Tour boarding area. The second is next to the Starway at Studio Center. Because most of the attractions are close to each other on this level, small children can walk or be carried from place to place. The attendant will give you a claim tag for picking up your stroller when you are ready to go again. For the shows and attractions on the Entertainment Center level, there is plenty of stroller parking.

Helpful Hint

For families with children unable to go on some attractions, Universal Studios Hollywood allows for parent swapping. While one adult goes with part of the group, the other waits with the young children. Many of the attractions even have waiting areas for parents. When the first group returns, those who waited can then enter through a special entrance for immediate boarding. Be sure to speak with the attendant at the entrance to the attraction for directions to the waiting area and any other instructions for waiting.

over to the second area, where you will find several more rides and attractions. On most days, Studio Center opens an hour after the park.

If you are pushing a stroller, you can take it on the Starway escalators as long as you first remove the child and carry the child or have him or her walk next to you. There is an elevator for handicapped guests and strollers. However, because the Starway carries you over a distance as well as down, arrangements need to be made for a van to pick you up at the bottom and take you to Studio Center. This method can often take around 30 minutes. If you need to do this, there is an attendant by the elevator to assist and make the arrangements for you.

Entertainment Center

Entertainment Center is the main level of Universal Studios Hollywood. Its several streets have been made to look like streets from around the world. Although you begin on New York Street, turning one of the corners will take you to London,

Quick Guide to

Attraction	Location	Requirement
Animal Planet Live! Show	Entertainment Center Entrance Level	None
Backdraft	Studio Center Lower Level	None
Back to the Future: The Ride	Entertainment Center Entrance Level	40 inches
The Blues Brothers	Entertainment Center Entrance Level	None
Jurassic Park: The Ride	Studio Center Lower Level	46 inches
Lucy: A Tribute	Studio Center Lower Level	None
The Mummy Returns: Chamber of Doom	Entertainment Center Entrance Level	None
Nickelodeon Blast Zone	Entertainment Center Entrance Level	None
Shrek 4-D	Entertainment Center Entrance Level	None
Special Effects Stages	Studio Center Lower Level	None
Spiderman Rocks!	Entertainment Center Entrance Level	None
The Studio Tour	Tram Level	None
Terminator 2: 3-D	Entertainment Center Entrance Level	None
WaterWorld	Entertainment Center Entrance Level	None

0 **Not scary at all.**
 ! **Might be somewhat frightening for some children. Usually either dark or a mild roller coaster.**

Universal Studios Attractions

Duration of Ride/Show	Scare Factor	Age Range
15 minutes	0	All
Approx. 12 minutes	!	5 and up
4 minutes	!!	7 and up
20 minutes	0	All
5½ minutes	!!!	7 and up
N/A	0	All
N/A	!!	8 and up
N/A	0	All
11 minutes	!	All
Approx. 30 minutes	0	All
Approx. 15 minutes	!	All
Approx. 50 minutes	!	All
12 minutes	!!!	8 and up
15 minutes	!!!	8 and up

!! Most young children will find this scary.
!!! This attraction may frighten some adults. This is usually reserved for high-speed roller coasters and other thrill rides.

Paris, Cape Cod, or even the Old West. The streets are lined with restaurants and shops, with the shows and attractions located primarily along the periphery.

As you are wandering the streets, be on the lookout for famous universal stars. You may see Woody Woodpecker, Lucy, Groucho Marx and his brothers, Laurel and Hardy, Charlie Chaplin, Marilyn Monroe, as well as the Universal monsters: Dracula, the Wolfman, the Phantom of the Opera, the Mummy, and, of course, Frankenstein's monster. Some walk around, and others drive around in automobiles. All are willing to have their photos taken with you. For a great shot, get your picture taken next to the 24-foot hanging shark.

If you are interested in seeing the live taping of a television show, be sure to visit the TV Audience Ticket Booth. Here you can get free tickets to shows taped not only at Universal Studios but also at other studios in the area.

Terminator 2: 3-D

Unlike other 3-D movies, *Terminator 2: 3-D* incorporates Universal's well-done special effects and live actors. The attraction begins in a lobby of a robotics company named Cyberdyne. Your hostess welcomes you and begins to give a presentation on the company. However, the hostess's video introduction is interrupted by Linda Hamilton and Edward Furlong, playing their roles from the movie. After they warn the audience to "Get out while there is still time," the hostess regains control and opens the doors to the 700-seat theater. No one directs you to your seats, so try to sit right in the middle of the theater. Although sitting up front gives you a closer view of the actors, you have a limited view of the side screens and their action. Even if you have to sit in the very back, you will still be able to see everything. And don't worry, the 3-D effects will reach all the way to you, no matter where you sit.

The show includes loud gunfire, both on screen and live, explosions, lasers, smoke, jolting seats, and, of course, things coming at you from the screen. James Cameron, the director of the *Terminator* movies as well as *Titanic,* directed this production. The interaction between the screen and the live action is incredible. Be sure to watch as the Arnold Schwarzenegger look-alike rides a motorcycle through the screen and then enters the 3-D movie.

Although there is no age limit or height requirement, Universal Studios recommends the attraction for children 8 years and up. There is no blood and gore, and the violence is limited to the destruction of robots, but the show is quite intense and may frighten even older children. You should judge its appropriateness for your children based on the type of movies you let them watch.

Back to the Future: The Ride

In each of the three *Back to the Future* movies, the characters traveled through time in a highly modified DeLorean sports car. That is what you get to do, too. It turns out that Biff, the young one, has sneaked into Doc Brown's science center and stolen a time-traveling DeLorean and is running amuck through time. Your job is to follow him in your own vehicle and bump into him, bringing you both back to the present.

The queue area is themed like a science laboratory. Christopher Lloyd reprises his role as Doc Brown and informs you of the problem caused by Biff's joyride. Then guests are escorted to small rooms for the final wait. The Doc gives you some final advice, then the door opens to your waiting time machine. Each DeLorean holds up to eight people. Once everyone is secured in their seats, an attendant will close the doors and the action begins. The vehicles rise up out of their holding areas so you can see a large screen. The vehicles move in synch with the movie to create a virtual reality of flight and motion using flight simulation technology.

You begin in the present, and then you chase Biff to the year 2015, then back through time. You dodge traffic in the future, escape an avalanche during the Ice Age, are swallowed by a *Tyrannosaurus rex,* and even dodge lava and rocks inside a prehistoric volcano. Eventually, you bump into Biff and return to the present.

Back to the Future: The Ride has a minimum height requirement of 40 inches. However, it is a bit intense for most 4- and 5-year-olds. Children 8 years and up should enjoy it. For those in between, their enjoyment depends on how much motion and intensity they can take. If they like rough-and-tumble roller coasters, then they should be okay. The ride bumps and dips around, quite wildly at times. However, the combination of the motion and the movie tricks the brain into perceiving much more extreme movement such as falling. Because there is no way to get off during the ride, the best solution for children who get scared is to have them close their eyes. They will still feel some movement, but it won't be as scary. Compared to Disneyland's Star Tours ride, Back to the Future: The Ride is a bit scarier and seems to have more turbulence.

The Studio Tour

No one can go to Universal Studios Hollywood without taking the Studio Tour. In fact, for many years in the beginning, this was about the only attraction at the park. If you have not been to Universal Studios Hollywood in the last few years, you are in for a surprise. The trams are new and feature state-of-the-art audio and video technology, with celebrity guest hosts such as Ron Howard and Jason Alexander, whose career began on the Universal lot. Each tram is outfitted with four LCD flat-screen monitors (so everyone can see the tour guide), a state-of-the-art audio system, and a DVD playback recorder that stores numerous film clips and interviews. This adds a new dimension to the tour. After seeing some of the actual sets, guests can then see those sets as they appeared in the movie.

During the course of the 50-minute tour, the trams will take you all around the studios' production lot. However, this is no ordinary tour with the tour guide just pointing out buildings. In several areas, the guests get to experience Hollywood special effects firsthand. In addition, if you don't think a heavy, multicar tram could be shaken and jolted, you will be in for quite a surprise.

During the course of the tour, the tram enters a soundstage while the guide is explaining how the buildings are used for filming movies. This one is set up like a New York City street. All of a sudden a helicopter crashes right in front of you. As the tram tries to leave over a bridge, it begins to shake as a giant gorilla appears right next to the tram. Say hello to King Kong!

Another soundstage you visit is a re-creation of a modern subway station. Now for a California experience—a magnitude 8.3 earthquake. The pavement above cracks, and an 18-wheeler carrying flammables comes crashing down amid sparking power cables. Just when you think it has ended, a subway train comes speeding out of control into the tunnel and 60,000 gallons of water begin flooding the area.

Another shaker is a bridge that begins to collapse as the tram drives over it. However, after crossing over safely, look back and watch the bridge amazingly rebuild itself. The tour will eventually take you by Jaws Lake, which features an animatronic great white shark that terrorizes the lakeside village before swimming over to the tram and lunging up, with jaws wide open. At another part of the tour, you will enter the ruins of the lost Egyptian city of Hamunaptra, where you face the Curse of the Mummy's Tomb. Based on the movie *The Mummy,* the walls of the tunnel begin to rotate, causing the illusion of motion, as if the tram were beginning to tip to one side. However, the tram does not move at all. The guests are just experiencing vertigo. If the special effects are too stomach turning, just close your eyes and the magic of illusion disappears.

Speaking of vertigo, many of Hitchcock's classics were filmed at Universal Studios. The tour takes you by the Bates Motel and the house where the classic *Psycho* was filmed. Also, along the way you go through many sets from a host of movies. They allow filmmakers to represent many different locations worldwide and at different time periods. And, of course, you will even see the waters part for the tram so it can get through a flooded area.

Even though there are some pretty intense and amazing rides at Universal Studios Hollywood, many people say that the Studio Tour is their favorite part. We recommend it for all ages. Remind your children that none of it is real. It is just make-believe. Although some parts of the tour can be scary, it is mostly visual. Therefore, tell children who don't like it to just close their eyes. Most scary parts are over quickly. Our 2-year-old slept through the entire tour, and our 4-year-old just closed her eyes when she got scared. If a child does have a hard time, the tour guide will allow you to get off and will arrange a ride back to the start. Also, certain tours during the day are presented in Spanish.

To get down to the trams, you must descend an escalator to the boarding area. For those with strollers or wheelchairs, there is an elevator for getting down and back up again. There is a stroller check-in located at the entrance to this attraction.

Shrek 4-D

Brand new for 2003, Universal Studios presents a new 3-D movie in Ogre-vision. Shrek and Donkey are back for another adventure, and they are taking the audience along for the ride. Although the special effects are similar to *Terminator 2: 3-D* in that you not only see and hear the action but also feel the action, this attraction is a little less intense and can be enjoyed by the entire family. And although the 3-D effects and/or noise might be frightening for some children, most will enjoy it. A good judge of whether your children will like it is how they liked the movie *Shrek*. Also, if you are unsure, sit toward the rear and near an exit so you can leave in the middle of the show if necessary. However, some children can just close their eyes and avoid effects that might be frightening.

The Mummy Returns: Chamber of Doom

This walkthrough attraction is based on the Universal film *The Mummy Returns* and consists of a number of sets that take guests into an ancient Egyptian tomb of Hamunaptra. Expect scary mummies to jump out as you advance through this attraction. Many of the scenes are reproductions or pieces of the actual sets used in filming the movie. There are also several display cases of props used by the actors during filming. Think of this attraction as a house of horrors. Preteens and older will usually enjoy it, whereas younger children will just be scared. Again, use the original *Mummy* movies as a guide. If you would not want your children to see those movies, don't take them into this attraction.

Nickelodeon Blast Zone

Whereas many of the Universal Studios attractions seem to be geared toward older children and adults, the Nickelodeon Blast Zone is aimed right at younger children. Modeled on popular Nickelodeon animated series such as *SpongeBob SquarePants, Rugrats,* and *The Wild Thornberrys,* this area features fountains and other water activities, a fun house–type area with balls and other amusements, and even characters from the cartoons for the kids to meet and take photos with. For the preschool aged, there is the Nick Jr. Backyard, which is a bit slower paced and gives younger children their own area in which to play without having to worry about being run over by older children and preteens. Since many of the other attractions in the park require sitting and being still, the Blast Zone gives young children a place to run around and use up some of their energy. It is also a good place to cool down during a hot day at the park.

Coke Soak

Located near the exit to the *Terminator 2: 3-D* show, the Coke Soak is a series of fountains in which guests can cool off. Unlike the Jurassic Park ride, you can control how wet you want to get.

Studio Center

Located down the hill from the Entertainment Center, Studio Center contains several rides and attractions in close proximity to one another. This area often opens later than the upper level. Find out when it does open, and try to be down there as soon as possible thereafter because some of the most popular attractions are located here.

Jurassic Park: The Ride

Based on Steven Spielberg's popular movies, this ride is fantastic. Let me warn you now: You will not get wet—you will get soaked! One of our Studio Tour guides in fact recommended just jumping in the lagoon. "You will get just as wet and not

Helpful Hint

If you want to stay dry but don't want to pay for a poncho, check the locker room and waiting area. Often you can find a poncho there, left by a previous rider.

have to stand in a line," he said. As you are entering the queue area, there are some vending machines off to the right side. For 75 cents, you can purchase a poncho to wear to keep your clothes somewhat dry. Also, there is a locker room off to the left where you can store backpacks and other items you want to keep dry. A waiting area is adjacent to the lockers for guests with small children.

Guests board 25-passenger rafts for their trip through Jurassic Park. You pass by three-story-tall dinosaurs, and one suddenly rises out of the water right next to you. However, just as in the movies, something goes wrong. Your raft

Insider's Secret

When your raft takes a turn into the area where the dinosaurs have escaped, take a look at the ravaged raft to the left. Can you find the mouse ears from an unlucky tourist?

begins to drift through the back area of the park, where some dangerous dinosaurs have gotten loose. A truck comes falling down toward you, spitting dinosaurs launch water right at your face, and raptors lunge at you. However, for the finale a giant *T. rex* comes out at you just before an exhilarating 84-foot drop. By the time you reach the lagoon below, you are traveling nearly 50 mph and it feels as if someone has thrown a bucket of water at you. The drop is the fastest, steepest water-ride drop in amusement park history.

The ride has a minimum height requirement of 46 inches. However, even if your child is tall enough, the dinosaurs can be quite intense, not to mention the drop, which can be terrifying by itself. Children who were not scared by the movies and who like roller coasters should do fine. As usual, if they do get scared on the ride, just tell them to close their eyes.

Backdraft

This interesting attraction features a behind-the-scenes look at the making of the movie *Backdraft*. The attraction is narrated by the director of the film, Ron Howard, with help from some of the actors, including Scott Glenn and Kurt Russell. The attraction is a walkthrough, comprising three different rooms. In the final room, visitors are treated to an inferno in a chemical plant. It starts as a small fire in an office and gradually spreads until the whole stage is ablaze. Then at the end, the platform everyone is standing on jerks, as if it were about to collapse and throw everyone into the blaze below.

There is no age limit for this ride, and you can even take a stroller inside. The final scene can be quite intense, with loud explosions, and you can really feel the heat of the flames in front of you. However, most kids do fine in this attraction. The best time to hit Backdraft is just after riding the Jurassic Park ride. The heat in Backdraft will help dry you off.

Special Effects Stages

Another new attraction for 2003, the Special Effects Stages take you behind the scenes, immersing you in the magic of the movies. As guests progress through a series of stages, they are shown how different types of special effects are created for some of the biggest blockbuster hits—each stage showing a specific effect or technique. Movies featured as part of this attraction include *Gladiator, Jurassic Park, The Mummy, The*

Scorpion King, Shrek, U-571, and others. In many of the stages, guests will be shown firsthand how the effects are created. Volunteers from the audience are often used in the process. Once the guests learn how these effects are created, they are then shown how they appear in the actual movie. It is really amazing how some high-tech scenes in movies use very low-tech techniques for sound and visual effects.

Although certain scenes in these movies may be somewhat scary for young children, this attraction is usually fine for all ages, since children can see that the monsters and other scary things are not real but just pretend. If you want to be selected as a volunteer, show the staff that you are not afraid to act. Although they often pick teenagers, they also pick adults.

Lucy: A Tribute

Universal Studios Hollywood includes a great tribute to the undisputed Queen of Comedy. This walkthrough exhibit features clothing, awards, and other rare memorabilia from Lucille Ball and highlights her career with never-before-seen off-camera footage and photographs. Guests can view home movie and slide footage, her magazine covers, and even fan mail from various presidents of the United States. To top it off, the exhibit contains an interactive trivia game called "California, Here We Come." By answering questions about episodes of *I Love Lucy,* guests help Lucy, Ricky, Fred, and Ethel get to Hollywood. Lucy: A Tribute is fine for all ages, but most children both young and old will rather skip this exhibit.

Shows

Universal Studios Hollywood has just about as many shows as it does attractions, with anywhere from six to eight different shows each day. Currently there are five permanent shows with one or more that vary seasonally. Although most shows have plenty of seating, it is a good idea to get in line for the shows at least 20 minutes early. Once a show begins, no further seating is permitted. For show times, check the *Studio Guide* you received when you entered the park or look them up on one of the Digital Directories located around the park. All shows have several different times, so you should be able to catch all of them in between seeing the other attractions during your day. Most of the shows are also offered in Spanish. Check Universal's Web site for times and dates. The Spanish shows are usually run only on Sunday.

Spiderman Rocks!

Universal Studios Hollywood's newest show turns the *Spiderman* movie into a rock 'n' roll musical. The audience watches as the meek and lowly Peter Parker is transformed into the web-slinging hero. As with any of the shows at Universal Studios, you can expect great special effects. This one includes some awesome aerial acrobatics as Spiderman battles against the Green Goblin—all to the heart-pounding musical beat complete with dancing and singing. Although the show is aimed at the preteen and older crowd, most younger children will enjoy it as well. The Green Goblin and the explosions can be scary for some children, but there are a lot of other things happening on which they can fix their attention, such as the trio of dancer-singers who help the story flow along. If you liked the movie, you will enjoy this show.

WaterWorld: A Live Sea War Spectacular

Based on the Kevin Costner movie, *WaterWorld* is Universal Studios Hollywood's biggest show and features some great action and special effects. The audience witnesses a battle featuring the Mariner and Helen (the good guys) against Deacon and his cronies. The stunt-filled battle uses firearms, cannons, jet skis, hovercraft, and much more. The show is filled with gunfire, explosions, and pyrotechnics, including giant fireballs rising 50 feet into the air, then cascading down to create a wall of fire. The finale includes a seaplane that comes swooping down over the audience, skidding across the water to an explosive crash landing, all up close to the audience. You will be amazed at what Universal has fit into a 15-minute show.

The loud gunfire and explosions in this show make it unsuitable for most small children, who will often be frightened by all the fighting. As for the violence factor, the actors shoot at each other with guns—the show is basically a big battle. Therefore, you should decide on this show based on the type of television programs and movies you deem appropriate for your children. Also, the green seats in the front rows are colored for a reason: If you sit in them, you will probably get wet. This show is quite popular and fills up quickly. It is important to get in line early, not only so you can get a good seat but also just so you can get in.

Animal Planet Live!

Unlike many of the animal shows you see at other parks or zoos, the *Animal Planet Live!* show is pure entertainment. Don't expect to learn how animals are trained. Instead, get ready for a fast-paced show featuring over a hundred animals of various types. Most of these animals have starred in motion pictures. The cast includes Babe, Beethoven, Jethro the Orangutan from *The Flintstones,* and many more. A few volunteers are selected from the audience to take part in some of the acts. Usually the younger children are the ones who get to participate. Although the show is 15 minutes long, it leaves most people wanting more.

This show is great for all ages, and everyone seems to love it. In fact, several families go to more than one showing during the day because the kids want to see the animals again. The show holds a lot of people; however, because of its popularity, get in line early so you can get a good seat.

The Blues Brothers

Jake and Elwood Blues have just arrived from Chicago, and they are getting the band back together. This rhythm-and-blues show is a lot of fun. If you liked the movies, you will love this show. It is appropriate for all ages. The younger children enjoy the music and dancing.

Tips for Touring Universal Studios Hollywood

If you have Internet access, you can begin planning your visit before you even arrive. Go to the Universal Studios Hollywood Web site and look up the show times up to a week in advance. Decide which shows you would like to see and when to see them. If you have enough time before you leave on your vacation, purchase your tickets online so you don't have to wait in line at the park.

If you have to purchase tickets at the park, get there early. The Box Offices open an hour before the park. Even if you already have your tickets, still arrive early so you can get a good parking spot and then get in line to enter the park when it opens. Use the time you wait in line for planning. Too often families walk into the park and then stop to plan what they will do first. If nothing else, at least know where you want to go first when you get through the main gate.

As soon as you enter the park, head over to *Terminator 2: 3-D,* if you have decided to do it, or *Shrek 4-D.* Later in the day, these attractions can have long waits. Then while waiting in line to get in, check the *Studio Guide* you get at the main gate to see when Studio Center at the lower level opens. During the summer or other busy times, you'll want to head down the Starway as early as possible.

After *Terminator 2: 3-D* and/or *Shrek 4-D,* head over to Back to the Future: The Ride if you have enough time before the lower level opens. With the main attractions at Entertainment Center taken care of, take the Starway down to Studio Center. If you don't have time to catch Back to the Future: The Ride now, you can ride it later in the afternoon.

As soon as you get down to Studio Center, take a left and go to the Jurassic Park ride. This is usually the longest wait, so get on early. You might even be able to ride it a second time if the line isn't long yet. You are already soaked, so a little more water won't hurt.

While at Studio Center, catch all the attractions here. Be sure to catch Backdraft, the Special Effects Stages, and the Lucy exhibit. By now it is probably lunchtime. If you are going to eat at the Jurassic Cove Café, do it now. Otherwise, head back up the Starway.

Back up at Entertainment Center, take in a show or two, then head for the Studio Tour. Because it lasts nearly 50 minutes, it gives families a chance to rest from the busy morning. In addition, younger children can use this as a nap time. After

Time-Saving Tip

You should try to see everything down at Studio Center all at once. The trips down and back up the Starway can take a lot of time. Therefore, do only one trip if possible, especially if you're on a tight time schedule.

Helpful Hint

If you plan on eating lunch on CityWalk, head there after finishing up on Studio Center. Then you can experience Entertainment Center when you get back to the park.

the tour, catch another show or two or walk through the Mummy Returns: Chamber of Doom. Although you can plan to go from one show to the next, most children may get restless with all the sitting. Stop by the Nickelodeon Blast Zone or the Coke Soak to let them burn off some energy.

After you have done everything you want, you can either hit some of the attractions or shows again, spend some time on CityWalk, or head on to your next vacation adventure.

Dining and Shopping

Universal Studios Hollywood offers a variety of dining options from a quick hot dog to nice sit-down restaurants. Between the park itself and Universal CityWalk, you need not leave the studios to find a meal.

Within the park, there are some good choices. Carleon and Sons features Chicago-style pizzas as well as monster hot dogs, salads, ice cream, and homemade pies. Along those same lines, Roman Noodle #1 offers brick oven pizzas and pasta. As for Louie's Pizza and Pasta, the name says it all.

If you're not hungry for Italian, then try the Jurassic Cove Café. Here you can find some good ribs and rotisserie chicken as well as hamburgers and other fast-food items. Cybergrill also features rotisserie chicken, along with barbecue beef and made-to-order salads and sandwiches.

Doc Brown's Fancy Fried Chicken is great for a quick homestyle meal featuring fried chicken and all the fixin's. Mel's Diner, from the movie *American Graffiti,* offers burgers, milkshakes, and even onion rings. If you're looking for Mexican, try the Hollywood Cantina.

Kids' meals are available at most of the restaurants, with Roman Noodle #1 being the main exception. In addition to the restaurants just listed, there are several spots where you can pick up fast food or a quick snack.

In addition to the dining venues at the park, Universal CityWalk contains several great restaurants. Because it is just outside the main gate, it's easy to leave the park for lunch or dinner, then return to the park for more excitement. With nearly 30 choices from fancy dining to fast food, there is something for everybody.

Although most families think of having a quick lunch, then a nice dinner, while you are at Universal Studios Hollywood, the reverse is a better idea. Most of the nice restaurants, especially on CityWalk, get busy in the evening because many local residents go there to eat and that is when most tourists have their main meal. Instead, have your main meal of the day in the early afternoon, usually after 1:30 P.M. By that time the lunch crowd is leaving, so you don't have much of a wait, and the lunch menu is often less expensive than the dinner menu. Then in the evening, have your quick meal while everyone else is dining. Because lunch is later, either take some snacks along to tide the children over or get a pretzel or popcorn in the park.

Universal Studios Hollywood has a lot of fun shops where you can buy souvenirs of your visit. All of the main attractions have a shop dedicated entirely to the attraction and movie. In fact, *Terminator 2: 3-D* exits right into the T2 Gear and Supply shop. You can also find places to purchase videos and DVDs of Universal movies, all types of clothing, and anything else the Universal logo can be put on. A favorite souvenir is the Universal Studios clapboard. All the merchandise can also be purchased from home through the Universal Web site. So you can either browse to see what you want in advance or see what you like while you are there and purchase it after you get home.

Universal CityWalk

Universal Center Drive
Universal City, CA 91608
818-622-4455

Located just outside the main gate to Universal Studios Hollywood, Universal CityWalk is a glamorous promenade featuring dining, shopping, and entertainment establishments. CityWalk does not require admission, so you can come back later and easily spend half a day there.

Along the walk, you can find many different types of restaurants, including the Hard Rock Café, B. B. King's Blues Club, Gladstone's, Wolfgang Puck's Café, and Tony Roma's Ribs. In addition, there are also several fast-food venues and snack spots.

You will also find a number of shops on CityWalk. Most of these are "fun" shops, in addition to being places to buy treats or souvenirs. With all the different types of shops, there is something for everyone. Even if you don't want to spend any money, just browsing around CityWalk is enjoyable in itself.

If Universal Studios Hollywood is not enough for you, CityWalk also includes several entertainment venues. There is an 18-screen movie theater, an IMAX theater, a virtual-reality

NASCAR racing arcade, and much more. Wizard's Magic Club offers dinner and a magic show. B. B. King's Blues Club, the Rumba Room, and Howl at the Moon feature nightclub entertainment for those 21 and older.

Universal Amphitheater

100 Universal City Plaza
Universal City, CA 91608
818-622-4440

The Universal Amphitheater is also located in the Universal Studios area. It features concerts and other types of shows. Before you leave on your vacation, check Universal's Web site to see if anything will be going on while you are there. You can also purchase tickets online or by calling the Universal number.

CHAPTER

11

Six Flags®
Magic
Mountain

Magic Mountain

Magic Mountain's slogan, "Where the rides ARE the attraction," pretty much says it all. Even though there are some shows and the park features the Looney Tune characters as well as DC Comics superheroes, the main reason people come here is for the rides. Self-proclaimed as the "world's first and only Xtreme Park," Magic Mountain features some of the world's greatest roller coasters, and to stay on top it is always adding bigger, faster, and better rides. Currently it has 16 coasters and a number of other thrilling rides.

> 26101 Magic Mountain Parkway
> Valencia, CA 91385
> 661-255-4111 or 818-367-5965
> www.sixflags.com

Location

Six Flags Magic Mountain is located west of Interstate 5 in Valencia. Take the Magic Mountain Parkway exit. It is about an hour and a half drive from Anaheim, depending on time of day and traffic.

Admission and Package Deals

Admission to Magic Mountain is similar to that of most other area theme parks. Single-day admission is $45 for adults, $30 for seniors and for children under 48 inches tall. Children 2 years old and younger are free. A combo ticket allowing admission to both Magic Mountain and the Hurricane Harbor water park on the same day is $55. For only Hurricane Harbor admission, it is $22 for adults and $15 for seniors and for children under 48 inches tall, with children under 2 years old getting in free.

Magic Mountain also offers a season pass good for the calendar year. With this, you get unlimited admission not only to Magic Mountain but also at all the other 14 Six Flags theme parks throughout the United States and even the parks in Amsterdam, Holland, and Mexico City. The season pass does not include Hurricane Harbor or any other water park. If you plan on spending more than one day at Magic Mountain or will be visiting any of the other Six Flags theme parks

Money-Saving Tip

If you plan ahead a bit, you should never have to pay full price for admission to Magic Mountain. Many employers, credit unions, and travel clubs offer coupons for admission. Many local supermarkets or fast-food restaurants may also have discounts. Some will save you from $15 to $18 off each adult admission to Magic Mountain and around $4 for Hurricane Harbor. These discounts can really add up for families.

during the year, the season pass is often the way to go. Because the season pass is only good for the calendar year, its price falls as the months go by. Either check the Six Flags Web site or call for the current pricing, and then decide whether it is worth it.

Tickets can be purchased at the gate or online. For online purchases, you can either have your tickets mailed to you or pick them up at the Will Call window. Magic Mountain also features ATM-like ticket dispensers that take either credit cards or some ATM cards. Although this is usually a quick way to avoid the lines at the ticket booths, the ATM machines do not accept coupons or discounted admission.

There is a large parking lot at Magic Mountain. However, it is a good walk from the lot to the main gate, especially if you have to park at the far end of the lot. A tram provides transportation from the lot to the gate, though it is often quicker to walk. The cost for parking is $8. Don't forget to write down where you parked your vehicle before heading into the park. After a long day of fun, you don't want to have to wander around looking for your vehicle.

Operating Hours

Magic Mountain is open daily April through September. During the rest of the year, it is open only on weekends and some selected weekdays. Either call or check the Web site for hours

Helpful Hint

To ensure the safety of their guests, Magic Mountain has metal detectors near the main gate. So leave all pocketknives, even the little ones on key chains, and other potential weapons in your car. All backpacks and bags are also searched.

and dates. It usually opens at 10 A.M., but the closing time varies. Therefore, if you are staying in Anaheim, you don't have to get up very early to get to the park as it opens.

Amenities

Magic Mountain offers several amenities for its guests. At Guest Relations, located near the main gate, you can pick up a copy of the *Guests with Disabilities Guidebook,* which provides detailed information on the accessibility of rides and other attractions. Here you can also find audio assist units and TDD phones for the hearing impaired. This is also the location for the lost and found as well as for lost children. Lockers are located behind the Guest Relations building. Strollers can be rented for $6 a day, with a $10 deposit. Wheelchairs are also available for rental.

If you are traveling with pets, Magic Mountain offers free pet boarding. Just go to the kennel located in the parking lot, and a representative will take care of your pet for the duration of your visit.

Although food cannot be brought into the park, Magic Mountain provides a picnic area in the parking area if you want to bring your own meals.

Suitability for Children

When deciding whether to include Magic Mountain as a part of your family's vacation, it is important to know that over half of the rides at the park have a minimum height requirement. Although there are shows and kiddie rides, if all of your children are under 42 inches tall, it isn't worth the drive or the cost to visit Magic Mountain. However, if you have teenagers who love the thrills of roller coasters, they will usually want to try out the latest and greatest rides here. For families with children, both young and old, you can divide into two groups and let the older kids hit the coasters while the younger ones do the less intense rides.

Attractions

Magic Mountain is divided into nine themed lands, arranged in a circular pattern. The park contains four main types of rides. There are the monster roller coasters, which are scattered about the park. Filling in the spaces between the coasters are carnival-style rides. Then there are kiddie rides and, finally, the water rides. Unlike most theme parks that have only one or maybe two water rides, Magic Mountain has five!

New for 2003!

In 2001 Six Flags Magic Mountain set a world record when it opened its 15th roller coaster. Before any other park could catch up, Magic Mountain broke its own record in 2003 by opening its latest extreme ride, Scream! The name really says it all. Riders board trains connected to a track below. However, there are no floors, so the riders' feet hang in the open air. Starting with a 150-foot drop, the ride reaches a speed of 65 mph and immediately enters a 128-foot vertical loop, the first of seven inversions, including a high-speed helix and two

Helpful Hint

For all the roller coaster rides, you can choose where you want to sit in the cars. The queues widen out at the boarding area, letting guests get in line for the different seats. The line for the front is usually the longest. Although sitting in the front gives you a better view of what is ahead, the best ride is usually in the back. Plus, the line for the back is usually short.

interlocking corkscrews. With 4,000 feet of track, this three-minute ride is indeed extreme and will have you screaming. Riders must be at least 54 inches tall for this ride.

Six Flags Plaza

Once you enter Magic Mountain through the main gate, you are in Six Flags Plaza. Here you can find a few rides, including the Grand Carousel. The Looney Tunes characters also roam around this area and are available for pictures with guests.

The Flashback is the only roller coaster in this land. It features six steeply banked vertical 180-degree hairpin drops, giving riders a powerful free-fall experience. Unlike other coasters, this one has a stacked design and even has a gravity-defying 540-degree upward spiral. The minimum height requirement for this ride is 48 inches. This land also has one of the water rides, Log Jammer. Guest take hollowed-out logs for a twisting and turning ride that includes two near-vertical drops. Children under 42 inches can ride this as long as they are accompanied by an adult.

If you don't feel like walking all the way up to Samurai Summit, you can ride the Orient Express. This people mover takes you from Six Flags Plaza to the top of the hill.

High Sierra Territory

The next land, as you go around the park counterclockwise from the entrance, features most of the rides for young children. The hallmark of this land is the General Sam Tree. At 140 feet, this is the largest man-made tree in the world. A tunnel at its base allows you to walk through it to Bugs Bunny World, where you can find a number of kiddie rides. There is a Tour Bus ride that takes kids up and down. Taz's Lumber Co. is a car ride. Plus, there are airplane and balloon rides, mini spinning cups,

Quick Guide to

Attraction	Location	Requirement
ACME Atom Smasher	Gotham City Backlot	42 inches
Batman: The Ride	Gotham City Backlot	54 inches
Buccaneer	Colossus County Fair	None*
Circus Wheel	Colossus County Fair	None*
Colossus	Colossus County Fair	48 inches
Cyclone 500	Cyclone Bay	58 inches
Déjà Vu	Cyclone Bay	54 inches
Dive Devil	Cyclone Bay	48 inches
Flashback	Six Flags Plaza	48 inches
Freefall	Movie District	42 inches
Gold Rusher	Movie District	48 inches
Goliath	Colossus County Fair	48 inches
Goliath Jr.	High Sierra Territory	must be under 54 inches
Grand Carousel	Six Flags Plaza	None*
Granny Gran Prix	High Sierra Territory	48 inches*
Grinder Gearworks	Gotham City Backlot	42 inches
Jet Stream	Cyclone Bay	None*
Kiddie rides	Bugs Bunny World	None

Guests under 42 inches must ride with an adult.
**Guests under 48 inches must ride with an adult.*
***Guests under 54 inches must ride with an adult.*

Magic Mountain Attractions

Duration of Ride	Scare Factor	Age Range
1½ minutes	!	6 and up
2 minutes	!!!	8 and up
2 minutes	!!	6 and up
2 minutes	!!	6 and up
2½ minutes	!!	6 and up
3 minutes	!	9 and up
2½ minutes	!!!	8 and up
2½ minutes	!!!	9 and up
1½ minutes	!	7 and up
1 minute	!!	8 and up
2½ minutes	!	6 and up
3 minutes	!!!	8 and up
1½ minutes	0	6 and up
2 minutes	0	All
3 minutes	0	4 and up
1½ minutes	!	6 and up
5 minutes	!	5 and up
Varies	0	All

0 Not scary at all.
 ! Might be somewhat frightening for some children. Usually either dark or a mild roller coaster.
!! Most young children will find this scary.
!!! This attraction may frighten some adults. This is usually reserved for high-speed roller coasters and other thrill rides.

(continues)

Quick Guide to

Attraction	Location	Requirement
Log Jammer	Six Flags Plaza	None*
Ninja	Samurai Summit	42 inches
Psyclone	Cyclone Bay	48 inches
Revolution	Baja Ridge	48 inches
Riddler's Revenge	Movie District	54 inches
Roaring Rapids	Rapids Camp Crossing	42 inches
Sandblasters	Movie District	42 inches***
Scrambler	Movie District	36 inches
Scream!	Colossus County Fair	54 inches
Sierra Twist	High Sierra Territory	42 inches
Speedy Gonzales Mouse Racers	Baja Ridge	None
Spin Out	Movie District	36 inches
Superman: The Escape	Samurai Summit	48 inches
Swashbuckler	Colossus County Fair	42 inches
Tidal Wave	Movie District	42 inches
Viper	Baja Ridge	54 inches
X	Baja Ridge	48 inches
Yosemite Sam Sierra Falls	High Sierra Territory	None*

* Guests under 42 inches must ride with an adult.
** Guests under 48 inches must ride with an adult.
*** Guests under 54 inches must ride with an adult.

Magic Mountain Attractions

Duration of Ride	Scare Factor	Age Range
4½ minutes	!	5 and up
1½ minutes	!!	6 and up
2 minutes	!!	7 and up
2 minutes	!!	6 and up
3 minutes	!!!	9 and up
3 minutes	0	5 and up
3 minutes	0	5 and up
2 minutes	!	6 and up
3 minutes	!!!	9 and up
2 minutes	!	6 and up
2½ minutes	0	All
1½ minutes	!	6 and up
1 minute	!!!	9 and up
2 minutes	!	5 and up
2 minutes	!	5 and up
2 minutes	!!!	8 and up
3 minutes	!!!	8 and up
N/A	!	5 and up

0 Not scary at all.
! Might be somewhat frightening for some children. Usually either dark or a mild roller coaster.
!! Most young children will find this scary.
!!! This attraction may frighten some adults. This is usually reserved for high-speed roller coasters and other thrill rides.

and even a fun house. To help get the youngsters ready for the big coasters, Bugs Bunny World offers two small coasters. The Canyon Blaster is a mini roller coaster with some small hills and easy drops. Both parents and children can ride this one together. Goliath Jr. is also designed for younger children and only goes about 10 mph with a maximum height of 10 feet. It is quite tame, and riders must be under 54 inches tall. For children 7 and under, Bugs Bunny World is the favorite, with all its small rides. Young children will also enjoy Critter Canyon, a petting zoo with a variety of farm and exotic animals.

In addition to the kiddie rides, there is also the Granny Gran Prix, which allows guests to drive around in electric antique cars. Although this may seem like a ride for small kids, they must be 48 inches to drive alone or 42 inches if riding with an adult. Yosemite Sam Sierra Falls is the water ride in this land. You ride in two-person rafts down a water slide. It is pretty tame compared to the other water rides in the park.

Colossus County Fair

This land is home to Goliath. This behemoth was billed as the first large coaster of the millennium. Riders begin when their car climbs to the top of the first hill, which is 255 feet high. Even though the car climbs quickly, it seems as if you just keep going up and up. The biggest thrill occurs as you cross over the top and begin your descent down at a 61-degree angle. To increase the drop even further, the track at the bottom goes underground for 120 feet. However, riders—now traveling at 85 mph—will hardly notice the tunnel before heading back up again to float over camel backs and speed down through a spiraling curve and breathtaking dives. This is one of the most intense coaster at the park. The minimum height requirement for this ride is 48 inches.

The namesake of this land, the Colossus, is a dual-track wooden roller coaster that takes riders up and down hills over a two-mile track. Compared to the other coasters at the park, this one is pretty tame and a good introduction for kids to this type of thrill once they are tall enough (48 inches). The Buccaneer, a swinging pirate ship ride, and the Swashbuckler, a spinning swing ride, round out the attractions here.

Gotham City Backlot

This land is themed after Batman. As such, its featured coaster is Batman: The Ride. What makes this ride so unique is that you ride in ski-lift-style cars suspended from the track above with your feet hanging in thin air. For this ride, you want to try to sit in the front. Otherwise, all you see is the back of the people in front of you. Seeing where you are going makes it more fun as you go through vertical loops, corkscrews, and a heart-line spin. Because your feet hang, visitors wearing sandals or other footwear that may come off must carry them on the ride. If you have to do this, just sit on them. The attendants will not let you leave your shoes behind at the station. This ride is moderately intense, with a minimum height requirement of 54 inches.

Also in Gotham City Backlot are the ACME Atom Smasher and the Grinder Gearworks, a couple of carnival-style rides. For a good picture-taking spot, stop by the replica of the Batmobile near the entrance to Batman: The Ride.

The Movie District

This land continues the Batman theme with Riddler's Revenge. What makes this ride different from the rest is that the riders stand up while riding this coaster, which includes loops and drops. It is currently the world's tallest and fastest stand-up coaster. It also has a minimum height requirement of 54 inches. The second coaster here is the Gold Rusher. This was the first coaster at Magic Mountain and is quite tame compared to the rest. There are no loops, just drops and tight turns, which make this another good introductory coaster. Riders must be at least 48 inches tall. Freefall is a unique ride in that the seated guests are raised to the top of a 10-story tower, then drop unrestricted, reaching 55 mph in only two seconds. The minimum height requirement is 42 inches.

In the Movie District you will find yet another water ride, the Tidal Wave. This simple ride takes 20-passenger boats up a hill, then plunges them down a 50-foot waterfall, getting everybody wet as the boat creates a wall of water at the bottom. You must be at least 42 inches tall to ride this. Finally, you can take in a few more carnival-style rides here, including bumper cars.

Samurai Summit

Located on top of the hill at the center of the park, Samurai Summit is a challenge just to get to. If you decide to get to the top on foot, it is a steep walk. Pushing a stroller is really difficult. Therefore, if you have small children, take the Orient Express from Six Flags Plaza or the Metro Monorail.

If you are up for a big thrill, try Superman: The Escape. This is the world's tallest, fastest, and most technologically advanced thrill ride. Using electromagnetic force, guests in 15-passenger vehicles accelerate from 0 to 100 mph in only 7 seconds, rocketing to the top of a 41-story tower where they experience 6½ seconds of weightlessness before heading back down backward to the station. Riders on this intense coaster must be at least 48 inches tall.

Also at the top of the hill is Ninja. Riders sit in cars suspended from an overhead track. Although there are no loops and the ride is fairly tame, the cars swing 180 degrees from side to side as the coaster goes around fast turns. The minimum height for this ride is 42 inches. Towering 38 stories above the summit, the Sky Tower gives visitors a scenic view of the park and surrounding hills. The elevator ride to the top is a lot of fun by itself.

Cyclone Bay

This land, themed like a California boardwalk, is the home of two coasters. The Psyclone is a classic wooden coaster modeled after the one at Coney Island. Although this coaster has no loops and doesn't go as fast as the steel coasters, it is one of the roughest rides in the park. During the course of going up and down hills, then making fast turns, riders are shaken, thrown side to side, and jostled around. Some teenagers we talked to really liked it, but some other riders said it was like torture and they couldn't wait until it was over to end their suffering. Riders must be at least 48 inches tall.

Déjà Vu, the other coaster in the land, is a boomerang-style coaster with vehicles that hang from the track above, similar to a ski lift. The coaster starts off by carrying the riders, with their feet dangling in the air, backward up a 196-foot tower and then drops them in a 20-story vertical free fall face-down. Reaching a speed of 65 mph, the coaster then takes riders around the outside of a 102-foot vertical loop, followed by a butterfly turn, after which it climbs a second tower, 200 feet tall. Then the riders descend backward down the drop, going through the turn and loop again in reverse before stopping at the station. This is another intense ride and requires riders to be at least 54 inches but under 76 inches (6 feet 4 inches) tall.

The Jet Stream water ride can also be found in this land. Riders board colorful jet boats that take them up the hillside and circle around the area before taking them down a 57-foot plunge into Jet Stream Lake. Small children can ride this if they are accompanied by an adult.

Cyclone Bay also features a couple of attractions that require an additional fee. The Dive Devil combines the thrills of hang gliding and bungee jumping as riders are attached to a cable, hoisted up 150 feet, then released to swing forward, reaching speeds of 60 mph. Guests 48 inches or taller can ride solo or with up to two other people. The price for a single person is $28 and goes up from there. Reservations are required, and the ride is weather dependent. The other attraction is the Cyclone 500. This raceway lets riders drive small gas-powered race cars. Drivers must be at least 58 inches tall, and the price is $6. Finally, for $5, guests can practice their rock climbing on a climbing wall.

Rapids Camp Crossing

This land has just one ride, the Roaring Rapids. Guests ride in 12-passenger boats along an artificial whitewater river. Expect waves, crosscurrents, and even rapids. This is a fun ride for those at least 42 inches tall. As with most of the water rides, expect to get wet.

Baja Ridge

Completing the Magic Mountain circle, this land features the Viper and X. Voted California's number one coaster, Viper is the world's largest looping roller coaster. Riders experience a breathtaking 18-story drop, three vertical loops, a double-barrel boomerang, and a classic corkscrew with speeds approaching 70 mph. To ride the Viper, riders must be at least 54 inches tall. It is very intense, with one loop, turn, or drop after another.

The other extreme coaster in this land is X, the world's first fourth-dimensional coaster. What makes X unique is that the riders can rotate 360 degrees independently of the vehicle's motion. Unlike most rides, the seats are positioned off to the sides of the track rather than directly over or under the track. Along with the rotations of the seat, riders do not know what to expect next, thus increasing the thrill. The ride reaches speeds of 76 mph and includes a 200-foot first drop. Since there is no other coaster like this around, you should definitely try it—if you dare! Riders must be at least 48 inches tall to ride this extremely intense ride.

Also in this area is the Revolution, the first 360-degree looping steel coaster ever built. This is a moderate coaster and a good introduction to loops, with some fast turns and steep drops thrown in for thrills. The minimum height requirement for this ride is 48 inches.

Shows

Magic Mountain offers several shows throughout the day. Located at the Looney Tunes Pavilion in Six Flags Plaza, the *Warner Bros. Kids' Club* is a game show hosted by Bugs Bunny with challenges involving the whole family. Also, during the summer months you can catch the Looney Tunes Nite Parade as it passes through this area. *Just Wingin' It* takes place at the Carrot Club Theatre in High Sierra Territory and features several beautiful exotic birds in an entertaining show.

All the shows are seasonal and subject to change. The best way to see what shows are on is to check the Six Flags Web site. Also, many shows seem to take Tuesday off. Others may only be put on during the summer or only on weekends.

Tips for Touring
Six Flags Magic Mountain

If you plan on hitting the roller coasters at Magic Mountain, you should get there early. Unlike other parks where the lines get longer during the day and then shorter toward night, the roller coaster lines here get longer as time goes by. Because Magic Mountain attracts a lot of local residents, especially teens and young adults who either get out of school or off work in the afternoon, the coasters can be quite busy at night.

However, if you don't plan on riding the coasters, you don't have to feel rushed to get there. Most of the carnival-style rides and some of the kiddie rides don't begin running until an hour or more after the park opens. This is especially true during off-peak weekdays.

Magic Mountain is a big park. The way it is arranged in a circle around the center hill makes getting from one point to another time consuming. To minimize the time spent walking, there are two strategies for taking in Magic Mountain.

If your family has small children, plan on making one lap around the park. As you get to each land, do everything you can there before moving on to the next area. The only downside to this strategy is, if you want to do some

Helpful Hint

For families with young children, we recommend a stroller. All the walking you must do at Magic Mountain will soon wear out little legs and feet. Having to carry a tired child will quickly wear out parents. Although you can rent a stroller at the park, a lightweight umbrella stroller will work just as well.

of the rides that are not yet running when you get there, you will have to come back. Right at the beginning, head to High Sierra Territory and hit the kiddie rides at Bugs Bunny World. This is fairly close to the main gate, so you can get the kids riding right away. Then make your way around the park in a counterclockwise fashion, following the guide listed earlier in this chapter. After you do the kiddie rides, the rest of the rides around the park should begin opening. After making a full circuit, then you can head back to Bugs Bunny World for a repeat of the kiddie rides before leaving the park, if the kids are not too worn out.

The second strategy applies to older children who want to take in all the coasters. This will require two trips around the park. As soon as you get to the park, head straight to Scream! Because it is the newest coaster, its line is usually the longest. Skip Colossus for now and instead head to Goliath, then make your way around the park in a counterclockwise direction, hitting Batman: The Ride, Riddler's Revenge, Superman: The Escape, Ninja, Déjà Vu, and Psyclone, until you get to the Viper and X. These are all the rides that will get long lines later in the day. Once you have ridden them all, make another lap around, taking in the rides you skipped the first time, including the older coasters, the water rides, and the carnival-type rides.

It can get quite hot at Magic Mountain, even when it is cool in the Los Angeles area. Therefore, be sure to drink lots of fluids. Several of the dining venues offer refillable sports bottles. Although it costs to refill them, this is cheaper than buying drinks all day long. It is also a good idea to take along some water bottles of your own. These can be refilled at drinking fountains as needed. Nighttime can get cold at the park, even if it was hot during the day. If you are staying until closing time, you may need jackets or sweatshirts. Keep these either in the car or in the lockers, and get them when needed.

Dining and Shopping

With one exception, most of the dining venues at Magic Mountain offer primarily fast-food fare, such as burgers, pizza, chicken, and the like. For visitors who want more of a sit-down meal, head to the Mooseburger Lodge. Guests can order off the menu or choose the buffet for lunch and dinner. This is hands down the best place to eat in the park. The restaurant also features entertainment, music, and air conditioning. The latter can be a real bonus on hot days. Because most guests will hit the restaurant around noon or 5 to 6 P.M., the best time to go is between 2 and 3 P.M. Eat a hearty breakfast before you arrive at the park, then have a good lunch with a light meal or snacks in the evening.

If you want to bring your own lunch, there is a picnic area in the parking lot area. This can save you some money. Don't try to leave the park to eat—there is nothing close by. The walk to the car, the drive to the off-site restaurants, the wait to get back into the parking lot, and then the walk back to the park can take a big chunk out of your day.

Magic Mountain offers a number of shops throughout the park. In addition to the standard theme park souvenirs, guests can also purchase Looney Tunes and DC Comic Super Hero paraphernalia.

Hurricane Harbor

Located right next to Magic Mountain, Hurricane Harbor is a water park with water slides and other related rides for the whole family. Tickets for the park are available at the same booths as for Magic Mountain. The prices for admission, including a combo ticket for both parks, are listed earlier in this chapter, along with those for Magic Mountain.

Hurricane Harbor is divided into a number of areas and features seven towers with over 20 slides among them. Black Snake Summit features five speed slides, including two of the tallest fully enclosed speed slides in Southern California, as well as two enclosed twisting slides and a near-vertical open drop slide. The Bamboo Racer has a six-lane slide where riders race head first down the slide to the finish line. Reptile Ridge is another tower, with three twisting slides, a straight drop slide, and a gentle slide. Taboo Tower has three slides: a 45-degree straight drop, a bumpy slide, and a spiraling slide. Lighting Falls has three twisting and turning slides. Tiki Falls takes riders down three slides that end with the rider coming out through the mouths of three tikis. Finally, the Lost Temple Rapids puts guests into four-passenger rafts and sends them down an ancient-looking aqueduct. Black Snake Summit, Reptile Ridge, and Taboo Tower each have 48-inch minimum height restrictions. However, anyone can ride the rest. Some slides require rafts; others are body slides.

Helpful Hint

If you plan on wearing shorts over your swimsuit, make sure they don't have rivets or metal buttons. These are not allowed on the slides because they might get caught on the way down.

In addition to the water slides, Hurricane Harbor has several other attractions. Castaway Cove is for children under 54 inches in height. It has small slides, waterfalls, a fortress, swings, and even a tide pool at Octopus Island. Shipwreck Shores is for families with children of all ages. There are over

Helpful Hint

You should always be safety conscious, especially with small children. Even though there are lifeguards all around, it is hard for them to keep track of every child, especially when it is busy. Stay close to your children. If you let your older kids go off on their own, make sure they use the buddy system and go in a group of at least two.

30 interactive activities here. The River Cruise takes guests in rafts along a lazy 1,300-foot river past many of the park's sites. The Forgotten Sea is a wave pool with a constant tide of two-foot waves. This pool begins at a depth of zero and goes down to six feet.

Rafts can be rented for the day. However, all the rides that require rafts have them available for use. If you rent rafts, you then have to keep an eye on them and drag them around with you. There are men's and women's changing rooms with showers and lockers located near the entrance plaza and lots of lounge chairs throughout the park.

If you are going to be in the area for Magic Mountain, Hurricane Harbor is great fun for the whole family. There is something here for all ages. The park also has a number of dining venues with fast-food fare on the menu.

CHAPTER
12

LEGOLAND®
California

LEGOLAND

LEGOLAND California is one of the most unique theme parks in Southern California. Unlike most other parks, LEGOLAND is designed especially for children under 12. In addition, most attractions are interactive. That means kids get to take part in the fun, instead of just being passive riders or observers.

If you are not familiar with LEGOs, they are colorful building blocks that children use to create all types of things, from spaceships to castles and everything in between. Ole Kirk Christiansen introduced the first LEGO bricks in 1958, in Denmark. They were first introduced to the United States in 1961. Since that time, they have spread around the world and are a favorite of children everywhere. In fact, *Fortune* magazine designated LEGO "Product of the Century" in the toy category. The word *LEGO* was formed by contracting the Danish words *leg godt,* meaning "play well." Later, it was learned that LEGO in Latin means "I put together" or "I assemble." The first LEGOLAND opened in Billund, Denmark, in 1992. It was such a huge success that a second one was opened, in Windsor, England, in 1996. LEGOLAND California, which opened in 1999, is the third park.

Although the park has only been open a few years, LEGOLAND California has become a popular family attraction. We find that most families who have visited LEGOLAND have one of two opinions: either they love it or they feel they should have spent the day elsewhere. There are several factors that affect a family's enjoyment at LEGOLAND. One is the age of the children. Although LEGOLAND was designed for children from 2 to 12 years of age, 3 to about 10 years is a bit more realistic, according to the families we talked to, although children up to 12 will still be fascinated if they are really into LEGOs. Older children will probably be bored unless they enjoy taking their younger siblings around the park. Another factor affecting enjoyment is expectation. There are only 15 rides in the park, and all are quite mild. Not one is scary. Therefore, many families used to the large number of fast, wild rides at other parks will be disappointed if that is what they expect at LEGOLAND. The final factor is LEGOs themselves. Because everything at LEGOLAND is based on the toy-building system, children who are not

Insider's Secret

If you will be spending several days in the Disneyland area and are interested in visiting LEGOLAND California, we recommend you try it midweek or in the middle of your vacation. LEGOLAND is much slower paced than the rest of the theme parks and provides a wind-down day for young children, as well as parents.

familiar with the product will miss out on some of the excitement at this park.

One nice aspect of LEGOLAND is that it has a much slower pace. Because it is intended for families with young children, there are no teenagers running around.

One LEGOLAND Drive
Carlsbad
CA 92008
760-918-LEGO
www.legoland.com

Location

LEGOLAND California is located about 45 minutes south of the Disneyland area and 30 minutes north of San Diego. Take I-5 to Carlsbad and exit at Cannon Road. Go east, following the signs to LEGO Drive.

Admission

Admission to LEGOLAND California is similar to that of most other area theme parks. Single-day admission is $42 for adults and $35 for seniors and children 3 to 12. LEGOLAND offers discounts to AAA members; ask your employer or credit union about discounts as well.

LEGOLAND has a large adjacent parking lot. The cost is $7 for cars and $8 for RVs. Preferred parking is available for $12. Remember to write down where you parked your vehicle before heading into the park. Although the parking lot is not as big as at other theme parks, with tired children you don't want to have to search all over for your vehicle.

Operating Hours

LEGOLAND is open daily from 10 A.M. to 8 P.M. from the end of June to the end of August. During the rest of the year, the park closes at 6 P.M. on weekends and 5 P.M. during the week. LEGOLAND also closes on Tuesday and Wednesday throughout most of the year except during spring break, summer, and the last weeks of December. Therefore, be careful to check the Web site for the days the park will be open before heading down to LEGOLAND. Nothing is more frustrating than taking the hour drive from Anaheim, only to discover the park is closed. However, during the summer, Tuesday and Wednesday tend to be the least busy days.

Amenities

LEGOLAND offers a number of services for its guests. Lockers can be rented for $3 at the Marketplace, near the entrance. Strollers, wheelchairs, and electric wheelchairs are also available. A single stroller or wheelchair is $6, a double is $12, and the electric wheelchair rents for $30. LEGOLAND also offers loaner digital cameras. They are free to use at the park, and you can burn the pictures to a CD for a fee at the end of the day to preserve your memories. Cameras are limited and can be found at the Marketplace, Brick Brothers, and the Big Shop. This is a fun way to allow children to take their own pictures, which are great souvenirs of their visit.

Following LEGOLAND's focus on families with young children, you will find many things at the park designed with children in mind. All the restrooms have low sinks for washing

Helpful Hint
You'll be hard pressed to find much shade at LEGO-LAND, especially when waiting in lines. Therefore, remember to bring hats and sunscreen. Several of the food stands sell drinks in souvenir sports bottles. Although the price may seem high, around $9, you can refill them over and over again throughout the park at the various places to eat.

LEGOLAND Vocabulary

To help you better understand the LEGO lingo, here are a few terms with which you should be familiar:

Model Citizen: A LEGOLAND employee. The park security personnel are known as Park Rangers.

Block: LEGOLAND is divided into several themed areas known as Blocks.

Buddy: The life-size LEGO man that wanders around LEGOLAND greeting guests.

DUPLO: The series of LEGO toys designed for younger children.

Mindstorms: LEGO's product line that allows builders to create actual working robots.

LEGO Maniac: Anyone crazy about LEGOs.

small hands as well as diaper-changing stations in both men's and women's restrooms. There are also family restrooms at various locations. In all the interactive attractions, buttons and other controls are at lower levels, and even the restaurants have low counters, allowing children to push their own trays and see what is available without needing an adult to pick them up. The Family Care Center, located in Fun Town, provides a microwave, high chairs, rockers for nursing mothers, and diaper-changing facilities. Entire families are welcome, and there are LEGO stations where children can play while their baby brother or sister is being fed. If you run out of diapers or happen to forget them, the Family Care Center provides complimentary size-3 diapers and diaper wipes. If you are traveling with pets, you can check them into the kennel located to the east of the front gate. There is no charge for this service.

Attractions

LEGOLAND is divided into nine "blocks." Two of these blocks, The Beginning and The Garden, contain only shops or restaurants. The Beginning is just inside the front gates, and The Garden is across from The Lake, with an overlooking view of both The Lake and Miniland. Now let's take a look at all the fun in each of the other blocks.

Explore Village

Located just to the left of The Beginning, Explore Village is designed for younger children. The Safari Trek takes guests around in little jeeps through a jungle, savanna, and waterway where they will see over 90 life-size animals made entirely out of LEGOs. These include lions, monkeys, flamingos, crocodiles, and even elephants. Fairytale Brook is a boat ride that takes guests through scenes from classic fairy tales with music and animation. Several of the stories have a modern twist. Look for Prince Charming with a cell phone and the Big Bad Wolf with a boom box.

The rest of Explore Village uses DUPLO bricks as its theme. At the Water Works, children can play with water without getting wet. All the activities here are interactive. By pressing buttons, turning handles, and pulling levers, children shoot water cannons that animate various characters and animals when the water hits the target. The DUPLO Playtown features 13,000 square feet of fun. Children can climb on and explore several different types of buildings in the town, go through a maze, and activate various features such as lights and sirens, or talk on a phone. The DUPLO Train is just the right size for toddlers and takes them around a little farm. They can even ride it on their own. This is where children ages 3 to about 6 will want to spend some time.

The Ridge

The rides at The Ridge are kid-powered and allow guests to view the entire park from this overlook in the center of the park. The Sky Cruiser lets riders pedal their way down a track that wraps around The Ridge. If you get tired, don't worry. An electric motor will take over and keep your vehicle moving. Also at The Ridge, the Kid Power Towers seat two guests and allow them to pull themselves up to the top of 30-foot towers. When the rope is released, the guests return to the bottom in a controlled free fall. Because their legs dangle below the seat, younger children may find this ride too much, especially if they do not like heights.

Fun Town

Fun Town is where children go to do adultlike activities in a town scaled down to their size. One of the most popular rides here is the Driving School. Children from 6 to 13 years of age can drive electric cars through a layout of roads. There are stop signs and traffic lights to obey, and the drivers actually steer, accelerate, and apply the brakes as they drive around without the confinement of tracks. For children 3 to 5, there is the Junior Driving School, where these youngsters drive smaller, slower cars around an oval, also without tracks. A Model Citizen is right there to help teach the children how to operate the cars and to help keep them going around the course. At the Skipper School, guests ride propeller-powered boats through a maze of buoys. As with the cars, the boats are not on tracks and can be steered freely within the confines of the course.

For young aviators, Fun Town offers two rides that let them take to the sky. The Sky Patrol features helicopters with two joysticks that allow the riders to control the helicopter as it goes up and down and also turn it right and left. On the Flight Squadron, children pilot small planes, controlling their up-and-down motion as they fly around in a circle.

Fun Town also contains a couple of interesting walk-through attractions. The LEGO Factory shows guests how the popular bricks are manufactured and boxed into sets. The self-tour even has "quality control" games. The Adventurer's Club is also a lot of fun. Guests wander through a jungle, an ancient pyramid, and even the Arctic on a quest for keys. The club is filled with interactive games. Some areas of the club are dark and may frighten younger children.

Castle Hill

Castle Hill is themed after the popular castle series of LEGOs. It is also where the park's only two roller coasters are located. The Dragon is near the castle. The ride begins with a tour of the castle featuring Merlin as your host. As riders are treated to an animated depiction of life in a castle, they will suddenly come across a large dragon guarding the treasure. Riders are then whisked out of the castle, and the roller coaster part of the ride begins. This coaster is quite mild compared to most coasters elsewhere and consists of one climb, after which it twists and turns back down to the end of the ride. The Spellbreaker is a hanging coaster where riders enter two-person cars that are hoisted up to the top of a tower. Once there, two cars are released at the same time, on different tracks, and race to the bottom. Although the ride is mild, children fearful of heights may not like the fact that there is nothing below them.

A fun ride for children 12 and under is the Royal Joust. Each child mounts his or her own horse, which trots along a track through a knight's training area. At the end, they charge against another knight as their picture is taken. These photos can be purchased near the exit of the ride. Near the Royal Joust is the Hideaways. This giant jungle gym castle contains towers to climb up, balance beams, curvy slides, and net and wall climbs. For younger children who cannot climb up into the castle, there are several types of equipment to play on. The Enchanted Walk is a short nature path where guests can view indigenous plants of the California foothills and mountains, as well as LEGO re-creations of the wildlife that lives in those regions. Finally, at the Builder's Guild, children 5 years and older can build with LEGO castle products, while younger ones can play with DUPLO blocks. During the year, there are contests and seminars on building. Check your daily program to see if any will be held during your visit.

Miniland

For anyone who has ever built with LEGOs, both young and old, Miniland is something you can't miss. New Orleans; New York City; Washington, D.C.; the California Coast; and a New England Harbor are all re-created here with LEGO bricks in 1:20 and 1:40 scale. In addition to just standing fascinated at the detail of these models, guests can press buttons or turn handles to animate scenes or activate sounds. Often Model Builders will be adding new features to Miniland during the day. Or to see what new projects they are working on, check out the Model Shop, where you can watch the Model Builders in action. They will also show you the basics of building models.

Imagination Zone

The Imagination Zone offers a variety of attractions for all age groups. New to the park is the BIONICLE Blaster. Based on the popular line of action toys, this attraction features 12 cars, each of which can hold up to five guests. As the cars spin around on large platforms, riders can make the ride even wilder by spinning the wheel in the middle as fast as they desire. This ride is similar to the Mad Tea Party at Disneyland. The LEGO Technic Test Track is a roller coaster that features a number of tight turns and quick drops; the cars are designed like life-size Technic vehicles. The Aquazone Wave Racers is the first power-ski water ride in North America. Riders board power ski craft that move around in a circle on the water. The riders can steer the craft left and right, allowing them to weave through water blasts triggered by spectator stations outside the ride. Children too small for this ride still have a lot of fun pressing the buttons for the water blasts as they try to get the riders all wet. Also new to this area is the LEGO Sports Center. Here guests get to test out their soccer, basketball, and football skills as they view life-size models of NBA athletes such as Shaquille O'Neal and Chris Webber. While in the area, be sure to stop in at the LEGO Show Place and see *LEGO Racers 4-D*. This 12-minute 3-D movie features a number of special effects along with computer animation to make the audience feel like they are racing along with Max Axel.

The main part of the Imagination Zone is the building area. Here all ages of children, and even adults, can get their hands on LEGO products. For youngsters under 6 years of age, the DUPLO Play Area provides thousands of DUPLO bricks and toys for playing and building. At the Build and Test, children build cars with LEGO TECHNIC elements and then test them for speed. In the Maniac Challenge, visitors can use LEGO software in a learning center environment. Finally, for the older children and adults, LEGO Mindstorms teaches them the basics of robotics and provides an opportunity to build and program a simple robot. All these building areas can be reserved by schools and groups. However, there is always lots of time left for all guests to use these facilities. See the signs in the area for availability.

The Lake

The only attraction at The Lake is the Coast Cruise. Large boats take guests around a lake on a short cruise. The cruise is the only way you can get a close-up view of some of the models and areas in Miniland.

Shows

LEGOLAND offers a variety of shows throughout the park. Each show has at least one day off during the week, so you may not get to see every show on a single day. Shows can vary seasonally, but there is usually a ventriloquist show in Explore Village. Fun Town features *The Big Test,* a great show filled with both slapstick comedy and acrobatics. The show includes a working fire truck, which keeps the younger children entertained. Plus, there are inside jokes that make the adults laugh as well. For a merry medieval show, be sure to see *Medieval Merriment* at Castle Hill. It includes fun tales of life in times past. Most shows average between 15 and 20 minutes, which make them a good time to sit down and rest. Be sure to check the show schedule you receive at the front gate to see which shows are playing during your visit as well as their start times. It is usually a good idea to get seated 15 to 20 minutes before the start of the show on busy days because seating is limited. However, on slow days, 5 minutes is plenty of time. When LEGOLAND is open late, such as during the summer and on holidays, the park will have a night show using lights, lasers, and pyrotechnics. Be sure to catch this show if available.

Tips for Touring LEGOLAND California

The best time to visit LEGOLAND is on a weekday. Weekends can be much busier because that is when the park gets a lot of local visitors with their annual passes. However, during the summer any day can be busy. On a slow day you can take your time and still be able to see and do everything you want. Busy days take a bit more planning. Normally the busiest time is between noon and around 4 P.M., so try to avoid the more popular attractions during these hours any day.

Most families, when they enter the park, will take a left at The Beginning and head straight to Explore Village. Be different and go right to the Imagination Zone. If you have older children that want to do any of the activities in this area, such as the Mindstorms, be sure to make reservations and check to see when the other activities will be open. Then continue up Castle Hill. Because the Dragon and the Spellbreaker will have some of the longest lines, hit them first. Next head on to Fun Town for the Skipper School, followed by the Driving Schools. Continue on to The Ridge to ride the Sky Cruiser and the Kid Power

Time-Saving Tip

If you plan on eating at LEGOLAND, it is a good idea to get a snack around 11 A.M. to tide the family over for a few hours. Then around 2 P.M., as most guests have finished their lunch and are heading back to the rides, have your meal. By doing this, you will not spend time eating when the park is slow and you will also miss the lunch rush at the restaurants.

Towers. You want to try and go on most of these rides before noon if possible. Between noon and 4 P.M., visit Explore Village, Fun Town, Miniland, and the Imagination Zone. This is also a good time to see the shows, though you will need to arrive early. Then as things begin to slow down in the late afternoon, you can head back to the more popular rides to do them again.

Dining and Shopping

When you decide to have a meal at LEGOLAND, be prepared for a change: Most of the food is fresh and made to order. This continues LEGOLAND's philosophy of nourishing the child in all areas of development—including nutrition. LEGOLAND has four sit-down restaurants and numerous eateries and kiosks. Ristorante Brickolini in Explore Village offers pastas, salads, and wood-fired pizzas. Fun Town Market serves salads, sandwiches, pastas, and ice cream. The dining area is decorated with antique toys from the LEGO collection. The Garden Restaurant overlooks The Lake and Miniland. Here you can find soups, sandwiches, and specialty breads, as well as salads and desserts. The Knight's Table Barbecue offers smoked Danish spareribs and roasted rosemary chicken. These dinners come with all the fixin's as well. You will pay between $5 and $14 for a meal at LEGOLAND.

There are also several places where you can pick up snacks such as fruit, baked goods, ice cream, and so forth. One of LEGOLAND's specialties is Granny's Apple Fries. The fried apple strips are rolled in cinnamon and sugar, then served with a whipped cream dipping sauce. These are delicious and make a great snack. Of course, you can also find the fast-food stand-bys. Hamburgers and hot dogs are available at most places as well. For an entertaining snack break, try the

LEGO Maniac Clubhouse. This ice cream and soda fountain features a LEGO robot band and is popular with children of all ages.

LEGOLAND has several shops offering all types of items with the LEGO brand on them. In addition to the usual clothing and other types of souvenirs, you can even buy LEGO play sets. The Big Shop at The Beginning offers just about every current LEGO toy the company makes. You will find sets here that most stores never carry, such as LEGO lines for girls and bags of extra parts you would normally have to special-order direct from LEGO. A LEGO set makes a great souvenir that will get used more often than most. In addition, lots of families do shopping for birthdays or holidays while they are at the park. The prices here are comparable to most major stores outside the park. A new feature is the LEGO Bricks by the Pound. At the LEGO Clubhouse in Fun Town, guests can choose from over 400 different bricks in all colors of the rainbow and pay for them based on weight. This is great for those who need certain pieces that may have been lost or who want to create a new masterpiece back at home. Also at the LEGO Clubhouse, you can buy a LEGO Mosaic. A digital photo is taken, and the Brick-o-lizer then transforms the photo into detailed instructions allowing you to create your own portrait from LEGO bricks. The entire kit, including bricks, sells for about $30.

Helpful Hint

There is also a LEGO shop located in Downtown Disney, so if you don't have time to purchase items at LEGOLAND, you can also find them near Disneyland.

CHAPTER
13
Other
Los Angeles Area
Attractions

The Los Angeles area is filled with great things for families to do in addition to the major theme parks. If you have an extra day or two in your vacation, consider visiting some of the places described in this chapter.

Orange County

Orange County offers several attractions besides the Disneyland Resort and Knott's Berry Farm. You can see most of them within a few hours.

Medieval Times

7662 Beach Boulevard, Buena Park
800-899-6600 or 714-521-4740
www.medievaltimes.com

This fun and entertaining dinner theater takes you back to the days of knights and their ladies. The seating is arranged around an arena where guests watch performances by Andalusian stallions as well as authentic jousting matches and hand-to-hand combat between knights using medieval weaponry. Audience participation is a part of the show as guests cheer for their favorite knight. Although the show may be a bit loud for very young children, the atmosphere is designed for families and children love to watch the pageantry from nearly a thousand years ago.

The cost is $43.95 for adults, $30.95 for kids 12 and younger (includes tax but not gratuity). You can find discount coupons at most hotels and can even print one out online from the hotel Web site. The admission includes the show and a meal (an appetizer, soup, roasted chicken, spareribs, potato, dessert, and a beverage). It is a good idea to make reservations in advance, especially on weekends or during the busy season, and be sure to call for hours and show times. Depending on the season, there are usually two to three shows a day. Also check for matinees, which often have discounted rates.

Insider's Secret

For a great listing of just about everything to do in Orange County, from attractions to hotels and restaurants, request *The Anaheim/Orange County Official Visitor's Guide* by calling 888-598-3200 or from the Web site at www.anaheimoc.org. You can also find deals and even printable coupons at this Web site.

Movieland Wax Museum

7711 Beach Boulevard, Buena Park
714-522-1155
www.movielandwaxmuseum.com

This is a great place to see some of your favorite stars in memorable scenes from their movies or television shows. From Charleston Heston in *Ben Hur* to William Shatner and the crew from *Star Trek,* there is something for everyone. The museum continues to add new exhibits with the latest stars, including top names from the music industry such as Michael Jackson. A popular area for teenagers is the Chamber of Horrors, which features scary scenes from a number of scary movies. This part of the museum is off by itself, so families with small children can skip this and still tour the remainder of the museum. This is a good place to visit after a day at Knott's Berry Farm or when doing other nearby attractions on Beach Boulevard. Also consider it on rainy as well as hot days as a break from one of the theme parks.

Admission for adults is $13, seniors $10.50, and children (4 to 11) $7. Many Anaheim-area hotels offer discounted tickets. It's also possible to get a combo ticket that includes Ripley's Believe It or Not! Museum (adults $16.90; seniors $13.95; kids $9.75). Discounts are available at most area hotels and often online at the Web site. Movieland is open every day of the year from 9 A.M. to 8:30 P.M., although it has shorter hours on some holidays. Call ahead to get the hours during your vacation.

Ripley's Believe It or Not! Museum

7550 Beach Boulevard, Buena Park

Billed as an Odditorium, this collection of real-life phenomena and curiosities makes for an interesting visit. The museum contains an eclectic collection of artifacts from around the world and life-size wax figures of amazing people such as the world's tallest man or the lighthouse man, who had a candle holder created in the top of his head. There is also a 5½-inch violin, which can actually be played, and the Fiji Mermaid. By the end of the tour, you will be asking yourself whether you believe it all—or not.

Admission is $8.95 for adults, $6.95 for seniors, and $5.25 for children 4 to 11. Ripley's is open every day of the year from 11 A.M. to 5 P.M. on weekdays and until 6 P.M. on weekends, with shorter hours on holidays. Younger children will not really care for this museum. Older children and adults interested in the bizarre will find it entertaining.

Wild Bill's Wild West Dinner Extravaganza

7600 Beach Boulevard, Buena Park
800-883-1546 or 714-522-6414

This dinner theater takes you back to the Wild West. The two-hour show features Wild Bill and Miss Annie, who sing and dance. A troupe of Native American dancers shares their heritage, and other performances include a magician, a trick rope artist, and much more. While you are watching the show, a four-course dinner is served, which includes salad, stew, biscuits, chicken, ribs, baked potato, corn on the cob, apple pie à la mode, and a beverage. The dinner theater has a saloon-type atmosphere that some families with small children may find uncomfortable.

The cost is $40.95 for adults and $26.95 for kids 3 to 11. Discount coupons are available at most local hotels. Reservations are recommended, especially on the weekends or during the busy season. Call for show times. Try a matinee show, which usually is cheaper than the regular rates.

Long Beach

Long Beach is California's fifth largest city, and its port is one of the busiest shipping centers on the Pacific Coast. It hosts a few attractions that are worth a visit if your vacation offers enough time for them.

Long Beach Aquarium of the Pacific

100 Aquarium Way
562-590-3100
www.aquariumofpacific.org

This aquarium features 17 major habitats as well as 30 smaller exhibits representing three main regions of the Pacific Ocean: Southern California/Baja, the tropical Pacific, and the northern Pacific. Guests will see over 12,000 ocean animals from more than 550 species. These include leopard sharks, giant Japanese spider crabs, sea lions, seals, a giant octopus, sea stars, and much, much more. An exciting exhibit allows guests to observe sea jellies (commonly called jellyfish). New to the aquarium, Shark Lagoon gives guests the opportunity to interact with four types of sharks in shallow pools. There are several other interactive exhibits, making this attraction a lot of fun for children of all ages.

The aquarium is open most every day of the year from 9 A.M. to 6 P.M. Admission to the aquarium is $19 for adults, $15 for seniors, and $10 for children 3 to 11. Parking is $6 if you show your aquarium ticket stub; otherwise, it is $7. This is a popular attraction with the local community, so the best time to come is during the week. Try to get there early in the morning. When it is busy, the aquarium uses timed ticketing so that large groups of people are not crowded into the exhibits. During these periods, you may have to wait until an assigned time to enter the aquarium.

The *Queen Mary*

1126 Queen's Highway at the end of I-710
562-435-3511
www.queenmary.com

Take a tour of this former star of the Cunard Line. It first sailed in 1936 and took its last voyage in 1967, after which it docked in Long Beach. The ship has been converted into a museum and hotel and contains several restaurants as well. Basic admission is $23 for adults, $21 for military and seniors, and $19 for children 3 to 11. This includes a self-guided tour of the ship as well as the new Ghosts and Legends exhibit, which explores supernatural experiences that passengers and crew members have reported. A guided tour is also available and takes you additional places on board the ship that are not accessible with the self-guided tour. This tour is an additional $8 per adult and $5 per child. Parking is $8.

New to the attraction is the Russian Foxtrot submarine *Scorpion*. Admission is $10 for adults and $9 for military, seniors, and children 3 to 11. The self-guided tour of the sub requires children to be at least 48 inches tall, and they cannot be carried. The tour requires guests to climb ladders and walk through narrow and cramped passageways. Wheelchairs and strollers cannot be accommodated, and it is not recommended for expectant mothers or people prone to claustrophobia or motion sickness.

If you plan on spending some time in the Long Beach area, consider staying the night in one of the staterooms. The Hotel Queen Mary's rooms start around $105 per night for an inside stateroom and goes up to $400 a night for a royalty suite. A stay includes a self-guided tour of the ship, and children 17 and under stay free. Several package deals are also offered. Check the Web site or call for more information.

Hollywood

Hollywood can be a lot of fun, especially for families with older children. You can make this a part of your vacation or even a vacation in itself. Just about everything to see in Hollywood has to do with the entertainment industry.

American Cinematheque at the Egyptian Theatre

> 6712 Hollywood Boulevard
> 323-466-3456
> www.americancinematheque.com

The Egyptian Theatre, which opened in 1922, is a Hollywood landmark and was the site of the very first Hollywood premiere (*Robin Hood,* 1922). It now features daily showings of *Forever Hollywood,* a film by the American Cinematheque on the history of Hollywood and filmmaking. This 55-minute movie shows Tuesday through Sunday at 2 and 3:30 P.M. Admission is $7 for adults and $5 for seniors and children under 12. In the evening, the theater shows classic movies, some featuring guest appearances by actors or directors from the film. These run $9 for adults and $8 for seniors and students with a valid ID. Check the Web site or call for a schedule of show times.

The El Capitan Theatre

> 6838 Hollywood Boulevard
> 800-DISNEY6
> www.elcapitantickets.com

First opened in 1926, the El Capitan was one of Hollywood's premier stage theaters. Designed with a Spanish colonial exterior and an East Indian interior, the theater showed a great number of plays until 1936, when it became a movie theater. In 1941 *Citizen Kane* made its world premiere at the El Capitan. Later the theater was remodeled and reopened as the Hollywood Paramount. Then in 1989 Disney purchased and began a restoration of the theater to its original glory. State-of-the-art special effects equipment was also added, and the the-ater now hosts both live performances as well as movies.

The El Capitan now boasts an entirely digital system for showing movies. In addition to showing the latest Disney features, the theater also hosts special productions. In the past they have included sing-alongs of classic musicals such as *Mary Poppins*. During these performances the words to the songs are projected onto the screen and the audience sings along with the characters on screen. Also, for most of the big Disney box office releases, guests are treated to additional entertainment such as a live-action show featuring Disney characters prior to the movie or admission to an interactive exhibit funhouse next to the theater.

Adult tickets are $14, and seniors and children 3 to 11 are $12. All tickets are $5.75 for shows before 5 P.M. VIP seats are $23 per person and include free popcorn and a soft drink, the best seats in the house, early admission, and no waiting in line. Check the theater's Web site for the schedule of show times. If you can fit this into your vacation, it is a fun experience and quite a reasonable way (especially if you see a matinee) to experience the glory of Hollywood while watching a movie.

Guinness World of Records Museum

6764 Hollywood Boulevard
323-463-6433

This museum celebrates the holders of world records through a variety of video and interactive displays. Admission is $11 for adults, $8.50 for seniors, and $7 for children 6 to 12. This can be fun for families if they are interested in the *Guinness Book of World Records*. You can also purchase a combination ticket, which includes admission to the Hollywood

Wax Museum, at $16 for adults, $14 for seniors, and $9 for children 6 to 12.

Hollywood Entertainment Museum

7021 Hollywood Boulevard
323-465-7900
www.hollywoodmuseum.com

This museum is a great deal of fun and features some very interesting video and interactive exhibits and displays. Tour a prop room with actual props from a variety of different movies, learn about the history of filmmaking, see how makeup and special effects are used, and walk onto actual sets from *Star Trek: The Next Generation* and *Cheers.* You can even add sound effects to a movie in the Foley Room.

Admission is $9 for adults, $5.50 for seniors and students with an ID, and $4 for children 5 to 12. Although young children may not appreciate it, older kids will enjoy seeing how movies are made and the host of props and sets the museum contains.

Hollywood Wax Museum

6767 Hollywood Boulevard
323-462-8860

This museum contains around 220 wax replicas of famous people from both television and movies as well as politics. There is even a special section devoted to religious representations, which includes Michelangelo's "Pietà" and Leonardo da Vinci's "The Last Supper." A favorite among teenagers is the Chamber of Horrors, which hosts a number of famous movie monsters, including Dracula, the Wolfman, and many more. Admission is $11 for adults, $8.50 for seniors, and $7 for children 6 to 12.

Money-Saving Tip
You can save money by purchasing a combo ticket good for both the Hollywood Wax Museum and the Guinness World of Records Museum. Prices are $16 for adults, $14 for seniors, and $9 for children ages 6 to 12.

Mann's Chinese Theatre

6925 Hollywood Boulevard

This theater is one of the Hollywood classics from the industry's golden age. Its main claim to fame began in 1927, when actress Norma Talmadge accidentally stepped into wet cement. Since that time, over 200 stars have stepped into immortality by making hand- or footprints in the cement at this theater. There is no charge to browse through the area.

The Walk of Fame

Hollywood Boulevard

The sidewalks along Hollywood Boulevard, between Gower Street and La Brea Avenue, as well as a portion of Vine Street south of Hollywood Boulevard, contain large metal stars with the names of stars from the entertainment industry. This attraction is free and a fun activity while touring Hollywood Boulevard.

Kodak Theatre

6801 Hollywood Boulevard
323-308-6363
www.kodaktheatre.com

This is one of the most televised theaters in America. The site of the Academy Awards Ceremony, this theater offers guided tours every day from 10:30 A.M. to 2:30 P.M. On the tour, you can see an actual Oscar statuette, learn where this year's nominees sat, and see how the entire production is made from a behind-the-scenes view. Admission is $15 for adults and $10 for seniors and children 3 to 12. The theater also features a number of performances throughout the year. Check the Web site for current events.

Sightseeing Tours

One of the ways to see the sights of the Hollywood area, including homes of the stars, is to take one of the bus tours. This can be hard on young children because the buses make few if any stops. However, for families with older children interested in sightseeing, it can be a lot of fun. Starline Tours of Hollywood offers a number of tours, starting at $32 for adults and $28 for children. You can contact this tour company at 800-959-3131 or www.starlinetours.com. Casablanca Sightseeing Tours is another company offering the same service, and you can contact it at 323-461-0156 or www.casablancatours.com.

Helpful Hint

Hollywood Boulevard contains a number of classic and historic buildings. Even if you are only visiting the area for one of its attractions, if you have the time, walk along the boulevard and just look around and see how many famous places you can recognize.

Studio Tours

Many television and movie studios are located in the Los Angeles area. Several offer tours of their facilities, and some allow

Hollywood CityPass

If you plan on spending a day or more in the Hollywood area, consider purchasing a CityPass. This ticket provides admission to a number of attractions for one low price. Currently these include:

- **Universal Studios Hollywood**

- **Hollywood Entertainment Museum**

- **Kodak Theatre Guided Tour**

- **Autry Museum of Western Heritage**

- **Starline Tours of Hollywood**

These passes can be purchased at one of the preceding attractions or in advance from CityPass direct. Order by phone at 707-256-0490 or online at www.citypass.net.

Prices for CityPasses are $69 for adults and $49 for children ages 3 to 11. If you visit Universal Studios and only two other attractions, you will get your money's worth out of this pass— and it is good for 30 days after its first use.

guests to view live tapings of their shows. Before you plan on visiting these places, be sure to check age requirements. Some tours have a minimum age of 10 years or older, and tapings can require 16 years or older.

Note: Since 9/11, some studios have suspended their tours or have limited them to certain days or times. Be sure to call ahead before you leave on your vacation to find out the current status of tours for any studios you plan to visit.

NBC Studio Tours

3000 W. Alameda Avenue, Burbank
818-840-3537

Sony Pictures Studios

10202 W. Washington Boulevard, Culver City
323-520-TOUR

The Warner Bros. Studio VIP Tour

Olive Avenue and Hollywood Way, Burbank
818-972-8687
wbsf.warnerbros.com

Watching a Taping

If you are in the area and have the time, it is fun to watch a show being taped. There are a number of ways to get free tickets for tapings. Tickets for NBC shows are available at the NBC ticket counter at the studios. You can call 818-840-3537 for more information, and you can also request tickets by mail.

Audiences Unlimited offers tickets at its booths at Universal Studios, Universal CityWalk, Mann's Chinese Theatre in Hollywood, and the Los Angeles Convention and Visitors Bureau Information Centers in Hollywood and downtown Los Angeles. The Audiences Unlimited phone number is 818-753-3470. Or check out the Web site at www.audiences unlimited.com.

Several other Web sites offer schedules as well as information on obtaining tickets. Two of the better sites are www.studioaudiences.com and www.tvtix.com. If you would like to see a taping, be sure to get your tickets early. Some popular shows give out all of their tickets a month or more in advance. Also, plan on arriving at least an hour early to wait in line. Just because you have a ticket does not mean you will get in to see the taping.

Most tapings do not allow children under 16, so this is not a good idea for families with young children.

Los Angeles Museums and Parks

Los Angeles has several museums throughout the city, as well as some large and remarkable parks that are attractions in themselves.

Exposition Park

Exposition Boulevard and Figueroa Street

This park contains two museums and is near the L.A. Memorial Coliseum. While visiting these museums, be sure to stop by the seven-acre sunken rose garden. There are 16,000 specimens in 190 different varieties.

California Science Center

700 State Drive, Exposition Park
323-724-3623
www.casciencectr.org

This science-based museum features exhibits covering health, space, physics, and the environment. Many of the exhibits are interactive and let children experience science firsthand. There is a Digital Jam Session, where visitors can play a number of instruments. Body Works features a 50-foot human figure that explains how the various parts of a body function. The Space Docking Simulator uses virtual reality to simulate zero gravity. There is even an IMAX theater showing both 2-D and 3-D movies.

Admission to the museum is free. However, there is a charge for the IMAX movies, ranging between $5 and $8. If you have the time, this is a great educational attraction, and children from elementary to high school will enjoy seeing scientific principles put into action. It is also one of the best bargains in town.

Natural History Museum of Los Angeles County

900 Exposition Boulevard, Exposition Park
213-763-3466
www.nhm.org

This is an impressive museum with several different types of exhibits. Two large halls show African and North American mammals in their natural habitats. The Marine Hall features dioramas of California sea life. The multimedia presentation "Chaparral: A Story of Life from Fire" explores this ecosystem with sights, sounds, and even smells. There is also a hall of birds. The Discovery Center is a great interactive area where children can check out "discovery boxes" filled with educational activities. They can also take fossil rubbings from a rock wall, look at a drop of water under a microscope, and observe live animals, including snakes, lizards, and fish. The Insect Zoo hosts a variety of the creepy and crawly. However, most kids' favorite exhibit is the dinosaurs. Skeletons of a *Tyrannosaurus rex* and a *Triceratops,* ready to do battle, highlight the exhibit, which also includes a cast of a complete skeleton of a *Mamenchisaurus,* the longest-necked dinosaur ever discovered.

Admission to the museum is $8 for adults, $5.50 for seniors, and $2 for children 5 to 12. Everyone can get in free on the first Tuesday of every month. Hours are 10 A.M. to 5 P.M.

daily; the museum is closed on most major holidays. This is a great museum and a great place to spend several hours if you can fit it into your plans.

Griffith Park

Said to be the largest urban municipal park in the United States, Griffith Park covers over 4,000 acres. Bordered by Interstate 5 on the east and the 134 Freeway on the north, this park contains the Los Angeles Zoo and a number of other museums and attractions. There is a miniature railroad, a motion simulator ride, a merry-go-round, hiking trails, and much more. Park admission is free; the rides run from $1 to $2.

Fun Facts

Walt Disney used to take his daughters to the merry-go-round at Griffith Park when they were little. During these visits he came up with the idea of Disneyland as a place for families, with something to do for everyone.

Autry Museum of Western Heritage

4700 Western Heritage Way, Griffith Park

323-667-2000

www.autry-museum.org

This museum was started by and named after one of Hollywood's most popular Western stars, but the museum focuses on the American West as it really was. Children will enjoy the Los Angeles Times Children's Discovery Gallery, where they can learn about history through a number of games and workshops. They will learn how children lived over 100 years ago and get to play some of the same games they played. This gallery is completely hands on, letting kids touch and feel history rather than just look at it through glass. A favorite part of the museum is a horse replica that children can sit on. A video camera captures their image and then projects it into a scene from *The Lone Ranger*. Other exhibits illustrate the real life of a cowboy on the cattle drive. Of course, there are also displays of artifacts from television shows and movies, including one of the Lone Ranger's masks and his silver-inlaid saddle.

Admission is $7.50 for adults, $5 for seniors and teens 13 to 18, and $3 for children 2 to 12. This great museum compares actual history to the myth of the Wild West as portrayed in entertainment and offers something for all ages.

Griffith Observatory and Planetarium

Griffith Park
323-664-1191, 818-997-3624 (Laserium shows)
www.griffithobs.org

Sitting on the southern slope of Mt. Hollywood, the observatory features a 12-inch Zeiss refracting telescope, a planetarium, and a Hall of Science astronomy museum. The telescope is open for public viewing most clear evenings from 7 to 9:45 P.M. Visitors can look through it to get a closer view of the moon, planets, and stars. The Hall of Science—one of the nation's best astronomy museums—features globes of the earth and moon that are six feet in diameter. In addition to many other exhibits, visitors can observe live images of the sun using the observatory's solar telescopes when the sky is clear. Both the telescopes and the Hall of Science are free to the public.

The planetarium reproduces the night sky at any time. For example, it can show what the sky looked like a thousand or more years ago. It also shows natural phenomena that are not visible to the naked eye. The planetarium offers a number of entertaining and educational shows Tuesday through Sunday in the afternoon and evening. Children under 5 are allowed to attend only the 1:30 P.M. show scheduled on certain weekdays and weekends. Admission is $4 for adults, $3 for seniors, and $2 for children 5 to 12. The planetarium also offers Laserium shows that combine music and laser light. Admission to these shows is $8 for adults and $7 for seniors and children 5 to 12. Shows in 3-D are an additional $1 per person. Teens will enjoy these shows, whereas younger children will probably not. Check the Web site listed for dates and show times.

The observatory and planetarium are under construction, which will double the facility's size. It is scheduled to reopen sometime in 2005. This construction period may change or be postponed because of funding, so be sure to check before you go. Until that time, the Griffith Observatory Satellite contains astronomy exhibits, a planetarium, and a telescope for viewing the moon and planets at night. It is in Griffith Park as well, at 4800 Western Heritage Way.

Los Angeles Zoo

5333 Zoo Drive, Griffith Park
323-644-6400
www.lazoo.org

The Los Angeles Zoo contains more than 1,200 animals from around the world. The zoo is divided into a number of different areas by type of animal. Visitors can see a variety of primates, such as monkeys and gorillas, as well as elephants, giraffes, lions, tigers, and bears. For a complete list of animals, check the zoo's Web site. There are several shows throughout the day. The Animal Encounters Program is a favorite among many children because they are allowed to get up close and even touch some of the zoo's residents. They also enjoy Adventure Island, which is a zoo just for young children.

The zoo is spread out, so bring comfortable shoes for walking and a stroller for small children. Although the Safari Shuttle runs about the zoo, it costs adults $3.50 to ride, $1 for seniors, and $1.50 for children 2 to 12 years of age. Admission to the zoo is $8.25 for adults, $5.25 for seniors, and $3.25 for children 2 to 12.

Getty Center

1200 Getty Center Drive, Brentwood
310-440-7300
www.getty.edu

The Getty Center, located in the foothills of the Santa Monica Mountains, consists of the J. Paul Getty Museum, the Central Garden, and the Research Institute Gallery. The collection includes artwork, manuscripts, and much more by many famous artists.

Although this might not seem like a great place to bring children, it is probably one of the best art museums in the country for families. Start off at the Family Room in the East Pavilion. Here you can pick up materials and games to use in the galleries. You can also check out headsets ($3) and use the family audioguide, which will take you on a tour of the galleries, with special stops and activities designed just for families. The Family Room has a number of interactive activities as well as art kits filled with drawing material, which children can use to create their own works of art. You can also pick up Gallery Games, which include such activities as a treasure hunt through the galleries. Many adults who may not be big art fans actually enjoy going through the galleries as part of the family activities. Seeing the center involves a lot of walking, and strollers are welcome.

Admission to the Getty Center is free. However, there is one possible difficulty—getting there. The best way to visit the center is to make reservations for parking and drive yourself. Call the number previously listed a few days in advance to ensure you have a spot to park. You can make reservations at the Web site as well. Also, call or check the site for additional ways of getting to the center, such as public transportation or shuttles.

La Brea Tar Pits (The Page Museum)

5801 Wilshire Boulevard, Los Angeles
323-934-PAGE
www.tarpits.org

This museum features one of the world's most famous finds of fossils from the Ice Age. Mammals, birds, and even plants were caught from 10,000 to 40,000 years ago in the sticky asphalt, commonly called tar, where their bones fossilized. Over a million bones have been uncovered at this site, including the remains of mammoths and saber-toothed cats. Even insects were caught and preserved. Skeletons of these creatures have been assembled for viewing.

Many of the exhibits have been designed with children in mind. Kids can touch bones of long-extinct animals or even test their strength against the pull of asphalt to see if they would have been able to escape from the tar pits. Because the site is still being excavated, visitors can observe fossils being cleaned and prepared for display. Outside the museum are viewing areas and life-size replicas of animals such as mammoths that lived during the Ice Age. In fact, the area is landscaped with plants from species that were around during the

Ice Age; such plants have been found preserved as fossils in the asphalt. During the summer, you can see paleontologists working in Pit 91.

You can visit the park area for free, but admission to the museum is $6 for adults, $3.50 for seniors and students with an ID, and $2 for children 5 to 10 years of age. Children usually enjoy seeing the replicas in the tar pits as well as the fossilized skeletons. This makes a good visit after seeing the Natural History Museum. However, warn your children in advance not to expect any dinosaurs—during the age of the dinosaurs, Los Angeles was under the ocean.

Museum of Television and Radio

465 North Beverly Drive, Beverly Hills
310-786-1000
www.mtr.org

This unique museum houses more than 100,000 television and radio programs and ads from the last 75 years. Visitors can choose a program in the library using computer consoles, then view or listen to them in the console center. There are also special screenings of movies and documentaries on the history of the medium and other related topics throughout the year.

Children 9 to 14 years of age can participate in Re-Creating Radio, a two-hour workshop where they put on an old-time radio drama using scripts, music, and sound effects. The workshop takes them through the many steps of producing a radio show, including casting, training on the equipment, and a practice before putting on the live broadcast. Each broadcast is recorded, and at the end of the workshop each child receives an audiocassette of the show. Tickets are $5 per child, and you must make reservations in advance by calling 310-786-1014. The workshops are offered only on Saturday mornings, and space is limited.

Admission to the museum is free with a suggested contribution of $10 for adults, $8 for seniors and students with an ID, and $5 for children under 13. The museum is open Wednesday through Sunday from noon to 5 P.M. and until 9 P.M. on Thursday evening.

Petersen Automotive Museum

6060 Wilshire Boulevard, Los Angeles
323-930-CARS
www.petersen.org

This museum presents exhibits on the history of the automobile as well as displays featuring over 100 vehicles. There are five galleries with changing exhibits as well as permanent exhibits of cars owned by famous people. The May Family Discovery Center offers a variety of interactive activities that teach children about automobiles as well as the physics that make them work. The Vroom Room lets children play with various sounds and learn how a police radar gun functions. The Activity Area features bottled kits with games and activities. In the Open Road, children put on driving attire and can pose for a picture in a Model T. Other areas teach about how gears work as well as how rotational inertia, momentum, friction, acceleration, and other forces act. You may have a hard time getting the kids away from the Discovery Center so the adults can see the hot rods and other cool cars on display. Teens will like to try the Driver's Education simulator that allows them to experience driving under a variety of situations without actually getting out on the road.

Admission to the museum is $10 for adults, $5 for seniors and students with an ID, and $3 for children 5 to 12. Museum hours are Tuesday through Sunday from 10 A.M. to 6 P.M.

Beaches

Southern California offers some of the most famous beaches in the world, and many families try to visit one of them during their vacation. The Los Angeles area has over a hundred miles of beaches—too many to cover within the scope of this book.

If you are staying in the Anaheim area, there are several great beaches nearby. Driving south on Harbor Boulevard and then the 55 Freeway south will take you to Newport Beach. This city has a nice six-mile-long beach, Newport Beach Municipal Beach, which includes a pier. There is a metered parking lot as well as street parking. For more information, call 714-644-3044.

Driving Beach Boulevard south takes you to Huntington Beach, a city with over eight miles of beaches. The State Beach—714-536-1454—has a $5 entrance fee per vehicle; the Munic-

Insider's Secret

If your family wants to swim or just have fun in the water, it is usually a good idea to do this at your hotel's pool or at a water park. Swimming in the ocean can be dangerous for adults as well as children, especially if they are not accustomed to the waves and currents. The Pacific Ocean can be quite rough at times with dangerous riptides at some places, which can carry a person away from the shore quite rapidly. No matter which beach you choose to visit, be sure to read and heed all warnings. Don't let a tragedy end your family's vacation.

Helpful Hint

If you are interested in hitting the beaches during your vacation, there are some great Web sites that provide helpful information on the various beaches in the area. Check out www.beachcalifornia.com. This site lists beaches by city and includes information on local things to do. Also try www.smart-pages.com; go to Special Features and choose Foghorn Beaches. This shows the locations of various beaches along the coastline and then gives basic information for each.

ipal Beach—714-536-5280—costs $6 per vehicle and includes a pier.

Long Beach also offers several nice beaches if you plan on visiting other attractions in the area. Call 562-594-0951 for more information.

Many of the beaches have playgrounds for children as well as changing facilities, so you do not have to wear beach attire to and from the beach. You can also rent surfboards, Boogie Boards, bikes, jet skis, and even small boats at some beaches. Call ahead or check online to see what is available.

Although most public beaches have lifeguards, they are usually only on duty during the summer and on some weekends. If you are going to the beach with children, don't expect the lifeguards to baby-sit them. They are there for emergencies only. Keep a close eye on your children. Beaches can be quite busy, especially when the weather is warm, and all types of people come to the ocean to cool off. Be aware of beach closings caused by contamination and other problems. When swimming, stay away from piers and storm drains because they can be dangerous.

Catalina Island

Located 22 miles from the mainland, Catalina Island is a unique place to visit for a day or even longer. Native Americans are believed to have lived on the island as far back as 7,000 years ago; Juan Rodriguez Cabrillo claimed it for Spain in 1542. Later, American and English smugglers used the island in their efforts to get goods past the Spanish and later Mexican authorities, to avoid tariffs. Eventually, the island was developed as a resort—first by the Banning family and then by William Wrigley Jr., the chewing gum magnate. The Santa Catalina Island Conservancy was started in 1972, with the mission of preserving and restoring the island's natural flora and fauna. It now owns 88 percent of the island.

Catalina Island offers a variety of different activities and attractions. If your family is considering visiting the island, there are a few things you need to consider. First, how will you get out to the island? Second, how long will you stay? You can see a lot in a single day. However, the island hosts a number of hotels if you choose to stay overnight. Finally, plan ahead what you would like to do.

Money-Saving Tip

If your family is trying to save money during your vacation, don't even think about visiting Catalina Island. It can get quite expensive quickly because the tours and attractions are all quite pricey. It can cost a family of four over $130 just for round-trip passage to the island, then $30 to $100+ for each tour on the island. You can save money by purchasing package deals, which include both passage and tours, but these can still be expensive, especially compared to a day at a theme park, which is not cheap either.

Helpful Hint

For a comprehensive listing of activities, events, shopping, dining, lodging, and even transportation to the island, check out the *Internet Guide to Catalina Island* at www.catalina.com. You can also request a visitors' guide at the Catalina Chamber of Commerce's site at www.visitcatalina.org.

Getting to the Island

There are two main ways to get to Catalina Island: by helicopter or by boat. Helicopter is much faster, but it is also quite a bit more expensive, especially when you have to pay for an entire family.

Helpful Hint

If the waters between the island and the mainland are rough, as during the winter, people prone to motion sickness should consider taking the helicopter rather than the boat.

Island Express Helicopter Service
> 310-510-2525
> www.islandexpress.com

Catalina Express
> 800-418-9159 or 310-519-1212
> www.catalinaexpress.com

Catalina Passenger Service
> 800-830-7744 or 949-673-5245
> www.catalinainfo.com

CHAPTER

14

San Diego
Area
Attractions

ocated about two hours south of Los Angeles and 90 minutes from Anaheim, the city of San Diego hosts a number of interesting places to visit. This was the first European settlement in Alta California (Upper California, as opposed to Baja California, which is down south) and the location of the first of a string of missions founded by Father Junipero Serra. The city of San Diego offers a great deal of history as well as entertainment.

While San Diego is close enough to Anaheim to allow for a day trip, if you plan on spending time at more than one of the attractions in or near San Diego, including LEGOLAND, SeaWorld, and the San Diego Zoo and Wild Animal Park, we suggest staying at least one night or more in the area instead of commuting back and forth. The hotels in San Diego can be less expensive than some of those in the area immediately around the Disneyland Resort. Chapter 2 contains information on a few hotels in the San Diego area to assist in your planning.

Money-Saving Tip

If you are planning to add SeaWorld and the San Diego Zoo to a trip to Disneyland, consider purchasing the Southern California CityPass. It includes a Three-Day Park Hopper ticket for Disneyland and Disney's California Adventure, a one-day ticket to Knott's Berry Farm, and one-day tickets to both SeaWorld and the San Diego Zoo. Adults pay $166 and children 3 to 9 pay $127 for these tickets, for savings of over $70 and over $50, respectively. You can purchase these passes online or at any of the included attractions. For more information, check out the Web site at www.citypass.net and select Southern California.

SeaWorld

1720 South Shores Road, Mission Bay
800-257-4268 or 619-226-3901
www.seaworld.com

SeaWorld is located in Mission Beach, just north of San Diego and about 90 minutes from Anaheim. If traveling from the Los Angeles area, take Interstate 5 southbound, exit west onto SeaWorld Drive, and follow the signs to SeaWorld. Although it began as an animal park for marine life, SeaWorld has grown into a theme park that tries to make each of its attractions educational in some way.

Admission is $44.95 for all adults and $34.95 for children 3 to 11. It is only $4 more per person to purchase two-day tickets. You can purchase tickets at the park or in advance at some hotels or even online.

Money-Saving Tip

You should never have to pay full price for admission. Discounts are available at most hotels. Also, check with your employer or even a credit union for a ClubUSA card, which gives you $5 off tickets as well as other discounts. To take advantage of these discounts, you usually have to purchase your tickets at the park.

Attractions

SeaWorld offers a number of entertaining attractions—many of which are educational as well.

Shipwreck Rapids

This is SeaWorld's version of the popular rafting rides. In addition to running the rapids, guests are trying to get off a deserted island. In the process, the rafts take you past waterfalls and creatures of the sea, through a dark tunnel into the interior of a ship's engine room, and even into a near collision with a ship's propeller. The ride lasts about five minutes, and you can expect to get wet. There is a 42-inch minimum height requirement. The ride can be a bit scary as the rafts bump up and down in the rapids, and the dark parts can also be frightening. Six-year-olds will usually be fine, and younger children who are tall enough and really want to ride will probably enjoy it as well. If you are unsure, there are a few places where you can watch others on the ride. After watching, let the children determine whether they want to go or not.

Wild Arctic

This attraction combines a ride with an exhibit. Guests first board a "jet helicopter" that takes them on a simulated motion ride to an arctic research station. Along the way, the helicopter bumps up and down as well as to the side, avoiding obstacles and dangers during the flight. When you finally arrive at the research station, the attraction is not yet over. Now you walk through an ice tunnel and observe polar bears, beluga whales, and walruses in almost natural environments. This is one of the park's most popular attractions. It has a 42-inch height requirement, and most kids who are tall enough will be fine on this ride.

> **Helpful Hint**
> For younger children and adults prone to motion sickness, nonmoving seats are available during the helicopter flight part of the attraction.

Shark Encounter

In this attraction, guests walk through a 57-foot tube underwater and watch sharks and rays swim overhead and off to both sides. This exhibit makes you feel as if you are in the water with these animals. Children usually like seeing the sharks.

Penguin Encounter

This antarctic habitat houses over 350 penguins at a comfortable 25 degrees. You can watch these birds waddle around and swim within their exhibit. Try to visit this attraction early to midday. Because the habitat is set to antarctic time, the lights are often dimmed by afternoon to represent sunset, making it difficult to observe the penguins. The exhibit also houses puffins, murres, and other arctic birds as well as warm-weather penguins, which are housed outdoors.

Shamu's Happy Harbor

Located near the main entrance, this kids' activity center contains a number of things for children to do, including slides, net climbs, fountains, a water maze, a two-story ship to climb on and in, and much more. This is a good place to hit during the middle of your visit to let the kids burn off some extra energy before seeing more shows and exhibits.

World of the Sea Aquarium

This exhibit features four large habitats housing sea life from local to tropical climes. Because it is just a walkthrough attraction, you can spend as much or as little time as you want here.

Shows

Shows make up a large part of the SeaWorld Experience. You should schedule your day around the show times to ensure you do not miss any of these entertaining and often educational shows.

R. L. Stine's Haunted Lighthouse 4-D

This 3-D movie adds a new dimension to the show by incorporating special effects that make guests feel like they are a part of the show. Featuring an original story by R. L. Stine, author of the popular children's series *Goosebumps,* the show stars Christopher Lloyd and Lea Thompson. You follow children as they take an old fisherman's tale and dare you to explore the haunted lighthouse and the legend surrounding it. Small children may be frightened by some of the special effects, but most of it is visual, so they can avoid it by closing their eyes. If you are unsure how they will react, sit toward the back of the theater, near one of the exits, so you can leave easily if necessary.

Cirque de la Mer

This is a new and exciting show at SeaWorld that features acrobats who perform on land as well as in and on the water. Set in a mythical land of Amphibia, the show is quite impressive and will be enjoyed by guests of all ages.

Fools with Tools

This show is presented like a set for a home-improvement broadcast. The hosts are sea lions Clyde and Seamore and their human partner, Ace. As they show the audience the basics of fixing up a house, nothing seems to go right, and the audience is treated to one humorous problem after another. This is a great show for all ages.

Insider's Secret

For all shows, it is a good idea to get there at least 15 minutes early. This helps ensure that you get not only a seat but also a good one.

The Shamu Adventure

Featuring SeaWorld's most famous mammal, this showcases killer whales and their natural behaviors. This is an entertaining and educational show and a trademark of the park.

Helpful Hint

Note that the first several rows in the stadiums are marked as splash zones. If you sit in them, be prepared to get wet.

Dolphin Discovery

This is another water show—this time, bottlenose dolphins and pilot whales perform.

Time-Saving Tip

Because you want to get to the shows early, use the time you are waiting for a show as well as during the show to have a meal or a snack. Just get the food before you head to the show, or send part of your family for the food while the rest hold the seats.

Wings of the World

This show, billed as the largest bird show in the world, features over 55 birds from all over the world. Young and old will enjoy watching these birds perform.

Interacting with Animals

SeaWorld offers many opportunities for guests to get up close and personal with some of the resident animals. These exhibits are a terrific way for children, as well as adults, to gain a greater understanding of life under the sea.

Forbidden Reef

Guests can reach into the water and touch bat rays as they swim by or even offer them a piece of squid to eat. Then the guests can look through observation windows at moray eels living and hiding in the underwater caverns.

California Tidepool

This exhibit allows guests to pick up live sea stars as well as touch other animals from the intertidal zone, including sea urchins, tube worms, hermit crabs, and much more. Many children consider this one of their favorite parts of SeaWorld.

Seal and Sea Lion Exhibit

At this pool, you can feed the animals. What do seals and sea lions like for a snack? Let's just say that it's fishy. This is another exhibit children enjoy. Be sure to check the schedule for feeding times so as not to miss this.

Helpful Hint

After touching and feeding the various marine life, you may want to clean your hands and especially those of your children. This is when having a few antibiotic wet wipes or towelettes can come in handy. They will usually get the fishy smell off your hands.

Rocky Point Preserve

This exhibit allows you to watch and feed dolphins, as well as to observe sea otters as they dive for their food. There are also several interactive displays for guests to learn more about these fascinating creatures.

Other Programs

SeaWorld also offers a variety of personal programs for interacting with the animals. Dining with Shamu is offered on most weekends and on some weekdays throughout the year. It features a meal with everyone's favorite killer whale. The poolside buffet runs around $30 for adults and $15 for children 3 to 11. You can also choose to have breakfast with Shamu. It is less expensive, at $15 and $12, respectively. Call 619-226-3901 for dates and to make reservations.

The Dolphin Interactive Program and the Trainer for a Day Program offer opportunities for guests to get in the water with dolphins and learn about training them. The costs are $125 and $395, respectively. Call 877-436-5746 for more information and to make reservations if interested.

San Diego Zoo

Zoo Drive, Balboa Park, San Diego
619-234-3153
www.sandiegozoo.org

This is one of the largest zoos in the world, with over 4,000 animals housed in exhibits that simulate their natural habitats. The zoo is also home to a number of endangered and rare animals not normally seen in captivity.

To get to the zoo from the Los Angeles and Anaheim areas, take Interstate 5 south, then State Route 163 north. Take the Zoo/Museums exit at Richmond Street and follow the signs to the zoo. Admission is $19.50 for adults and $11.75 for children 3 to 11. You can usually find discounts at local hotels or through your employer or credit union. These can save you up to $5 per ticket. There are also packages that include rides on the Bus Tour and Skyfari aerial tram for $32 and $19.75, respectively. Or you can also add admission to the San Diego Wild Animal Park for a total of $52.65 and $35.35, respectively. This includes the rides at the zoo. Although the admission may seem high for a zoo, this one is different from most. Plus, parking is free.

The zoo is quite large and spread out, so plan on doing a lot of walking. For families with young children, that translates to "Bring a stroller." Or you can rent a stroller at the zoo for $6.

Transportation

You can walk all over the zoo, but there are a few options to give your feet a rest. The Guided Bus Tour takes you around the zoo on a 40-minute trip while a host tells you about the various animals and habitats within the zoo. This provides a good overview and can help you determine what you want to see. This is included in the Best Value admission package or can be purchased separately for $10 for adults and $5.50 for children. The Express Buses are more like a shuttle, making five stops throughout the zoo, and are included with the Guided Bus Tour packages. Finally, the Skyfari Tram travels from one end of the zoo to the other. Deluxe admission includes this ride, or you can pay $2.50 per person for a one-way trip.

Insider's Secret

If you choose to walk with small children, be sure to either keep them in a stroller or hold on to them tightly. Many of the walkways also serve as roads for the tour buses and are quite narrow. Use caution when walking along these areas, for the safety of your children.

San Diego Wild Animal Park

15500 San Pasqual Valley Road, Escondido
619-234-6541
www.sandiegozoo.org

This 1,800-acre wildlife preserve allows guests to view animals out in the open while the humans are confined within their modes of transportation. The park also includes a number of exhibits and displays that allow guests to view animals in a closer, more zoolike way.

To get to the Wild Animal Park from the Los Angeles and Anaheim areas, take Interstate 5 south, then the State Route 78 east exit at Oceanside. Continue to Interstate 15 and take it south to the Via Rancho Parkway exit. Continue east and follow the signs to the park.

Admission is $26.50 for adults and $19.50 for children ages 3-11. You can also purchase two park tickets, which include admission to the San Diego Zoo, for $52.65 and $35.35 for adults and children, respectively. Strollers and even binoculars are available for rent. Parking is $6.

Plan on doing a lot of walking here. Probably hiking is a more accurate term because you will be taking hikes of over a mile at several of the habitats and exhibits at the park. Wear comfortable shoes, and be sure to either bring or rent a stroller for younger children so you do not end up having to carry them around the park.

Other San Diego Attractions

Balboa Park

The site of the 1915–1916 Panama–California International Exposition, this park contains a number of museums and cultural centers. For $30, you can buy a one-week passport that includes individual tickets to 12 of the museums in the park.

Reuben H. Fleet Science Center

1875 El Prado, Balboa Park, San Diego
619-238-1233
www.rhfleet.org

This museum features an IMAX theater, a motion simulation ride that takes you on a journey through the universe, and five galleries of hands-on science exhibits and demonstrations. The center is open daily. Admission is $6.75 for adults, $6 for seniors, and $5.50 for children 3 to 12. Tickets for the theater and the ride are extra, or you can purchase them as part of a package with admission.

San Diego Aerospace Museum

Ford Building
Pan American Plaza, Balboa Park, San Diego
619-234-8291
www.aerospacemuseum.org

This museum houses over 65 U.S. and foreign aircraft and spacecraft and brings to life the rich heritage of aviation in which Southern California had such a vital and important part. You can see replicas of the Wright Flyer and fighter planes from both world wars as well as the Korean and Vietnam wars. There is even a Blackbird spy plane on display. The people that made aviation history are also featured, as well as exhibits on the physics and principles of flight. Replicas of spacecraft from the Mercury, Gemini, and Apollo missions are also on display, along with a moon rock, space suits, and other related items.

The museum is open daily except on Thanksgiving, Christmas, and New Year's Day. Admission is $8 for adults, $6 for seniors, and $3 for children 6 to 17.

San Diego Natural History Museum

Park Boulevard and Village Place, Balboa Park, San Diego
619-232-3821
www.sdnhm.org

This museum is not as large as the one in Los Angeles but still offers a good variety of exhibits about the flora, fauna, and geology of the area as well as of Baja California. There are also several exhibits that frequently change because they are on loan from other museums. Check the museum's Web site for exhibits during your visit.

The museum is open daily except on Thanksgiving, Christmas, and New Year's Day. Admission is $7 for adults, $6 for seniors, and $5 for children 3 to 17.

Old Town San Diego State Historic Park

Wallace Street and Juan Street, San Diego
619-220-5422

This six-block area contains many of San Diego's original buildings that made up the first European settlement in California. Free guided tours of the area begin at 11 A.M. and 2 P.M. daily except for Thanksgiving and Christmas. You can also purchase a self-guided tour pamphlet for $2. There is no fee for admission to the area and each of its buildings. All of the buildings are minimuseums that feature artifacts and exhibits from various times in San Diego's history.

San Diego Attractions

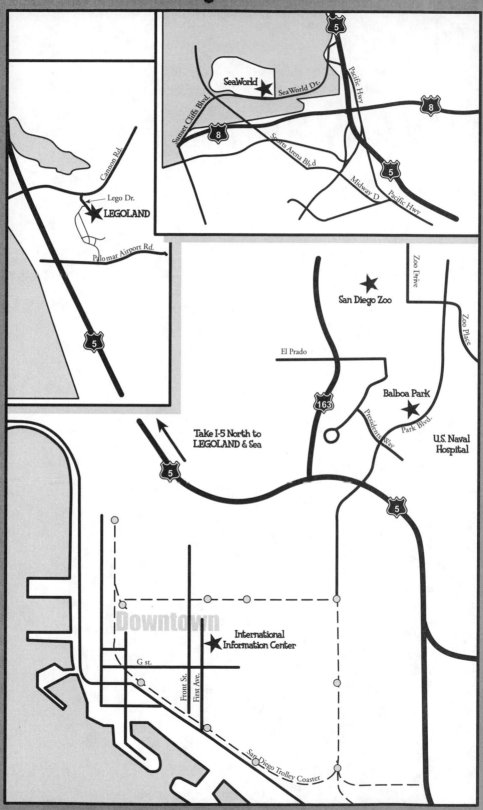

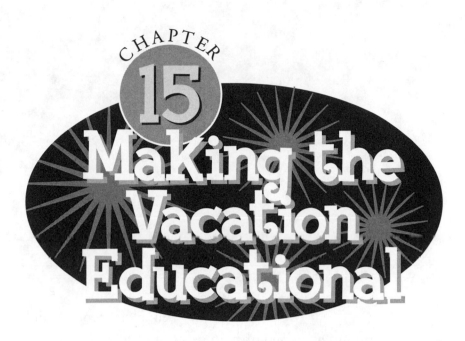

CHAPTER

15

Making the
Vacation
Educational

When most people think of a trip to Disneyland, they think of fun and entertainment. They don't consider how a family vacation to such a place can be educational. However, there are many ways to make your family vacation an educational trip as well as a fun experience for your children.

Taking Kids out of School

If your vacation requires your children to miss school, speak to their teachers at least a week or more in advance. Many schools offer an independent study program in which teachers provide lessons and work for the children to do that covers what they miss. When they return from the vacation, the children are up to speed and ready to continue with the rest of their class.

The earlier you get the schoolwork for your children, the earlier they can begin getting it done. In fact, you should encourage them to get as much of it completed as they can, if not all of it, prior to leaving. The last thing they will want to do immediately after getting home from the vacation is homework.

Let your children's teachers know where you will be going, and ask if there are any special projects or reports your children can do that will incorporate what they learn on vacation with what they are studying in school. Some teachers may be inclined to have the child do such projects instead of some of the schoolwork. The child can then present what he or she learned to the class when you return. If the teacher does not have any ideas in mind, you might suggest some listed in this chapter.

> ### Insider's Secret
>
> Don't hit your children's teachers with the news of your vacation after school the day before you leave. This does not give the teachers enough time to prepare material for your children or to set up an independent study program. Also, teachers appreciate parents letting them know their children will be gone and for how long so modifications to the lesson plans can be made if necessary.

Writing Reports

In lieu of normal schoolwork, some teachers may be interested in having children write reports about their trip. There are a number of different topics from which one could choose. Kids could write about visits to museums and other related places, and there are a number of creative topics as well. If your family is visiting Hollywood, a report on the movie industry or its history or even on how special effects are created would be interesting. Histories of Disneyland or Walt Disney are other good ideas. Children can include pictures they take or pamphlets they pick up during the vacation. Even younger children can do reports. These may consist of nothing more than an album of photos or even postcards with captions written or dictated by the child.

Educational Attractions

Most families try to add some education to their vacations by visiting educational attractions. Museums, zoos, and other related places are specifically designed to be educational. Southern California has a number of these attractions, many of which are designed to be interactive and fun for kids.

Zoos, aquariums, and animal parks teach about the variety of life on our planet as well as how we can help take care of it. Children usually enjoy seeing the different animals and how they live. There are also theme parks designed around animals, such as SeaWorld in San Diego. These places combine rides with animal experiences.

When one thinks of museums, usually art, history, and natural history are the types that come to mind. Although Southern California has several quality museums of these types, there are also unique and specialized museums that showcase automobiles, aircraft, and even the entertainment industry. Take a look at chapters 13 and 14 for some ideas about specialized museums and science centers your family can visit. Find out what your children are interested in as well as what they are studying in school, and then select attractions that will benefit them.

Learning in Other Ways

Whether you decide to include educational attractions in your vacation or not, you can still teach your children while you are away from home. We have assembled a collection of learning activities you can do before you leave, on your way to Southern California, or even while you are there, using the Disneyland Resort as an example.

Preparing for the Vacation

It is important to allow your children, especially as they grow older, to take part in planning the vacation. Ask each child to come up with a list of places he or she would like to visit. Then during a family meeting, each can make a short presentation of why the family should go to these places. Older children should be encouraged to do some research for their presentations, using this book and possibly even the Internet. This exercise will help them with public speaking as well as learning how to research.

Once your family has decided where to go, ask the children to come up with a schedule for each day of the vacation. The older the children, the more detailed the schedules can be. Preschoolers may just list a couple of rides at Disneyland, whereas older children could list times to see shows as well as strategize the best times to hit popular rides.

Older children can even help with travel arrangements. If your family is driving, ask them to plan your route, calculating the distance to travel and how long it will take to get there. They might also find good places to stop along the way for meals or restroom breaks. For families that are flying or making other travel arrangements, let older children call for quotes or check prices on the Internet. An adult should help them as they find the best rates.

In the days leading up to the vacation, children can help get ready by helping pack, checking on the weather in Southern California, and even assisting in getting the car ready if the family is driving. Younger children can make a paper chain (see chapter 3 for details) or use a calendar to count the number of days left until you leave.

While Traveling

Whether you are driving, flying, or taking some other type of transportation to Southern California, there is always something to do on the way. When driving, let an older child navigate. Provide a map, watch, pad of paper, and pen and let them guide you to Disneyland. They can practice their math by determining at various points along the trip how long you have been driving, how far you have traveled, how far you still have to go, and an estimated time of arrival. They can even calculate the miles per gallon of gas your vehicle is using. Although they can use the pen and paper to do the math, encourage them to estimate the answers in their head before doing the calculations on paper.

Younger children can also join in the learning. Have them count cars or keep a running total of the number of cars by color or make. Playing an alphabet game is also fun for kids. This involves searching for letters, starting with A. They can use license plates and road signs to find each letter in the alphabet in order.

While flying or at the airport, children can learn about the various parts of an airplane or look for landmarks on the ground below. You can also have them trace your flight using a map of your own or one in the airline magazines.

At the Resort

Once you are at the Disneyland Resort—or any theme park, for that matter—the learning can still continue. Although younger children may not be able to use the map to help you navigate to Southern California, give them a daily schedule for a theme park, which includes a map, and let them determine where different attractions are located. Then they can lead the family to the attractions. For children learning to read, encourage them to read everything they can, from shop signs to warnings.

There is also a lot of math that children can do at a theme park. They can count how many Dumbos are on the ride, add up what a meal for the family would cost, or even estimate how many people could ride an attraction within an hour's time. While you are in line for an attraction, keep them thinking.

Disneyland has a few attractions that are specifically educational. Innoventions contains several exhibits that teach about topics ranging from the human body to computer animation. The sailing ship *Columbia* has a small museum below deck. In fact, a report on the actual ship and its voyage around the world could be accompanied by ship photos taken at Disneyland.

California Adventure has several attractions that are designed to be educational while at the same time entertaining. They are all located in the Golden State and include the tours of the bakery and tortilla factory, the Bountiful Valley Farm, and the Golden Dreams movie.

Index